Global Issues

Series Editors
Paolo D. Farah, West Virginia University
John D. Rockefeller IV School of Policy and Politics West Virginia University
Morgantown, USA
Jim Whitman, Wakefield, UK

The rapid pace of globalizing dynamics has brought in its wake a proliferation of crises, governance challenges and large-scale stresses, unprecedented in their range, seriousness and urgency. These emerging conditions and relations are variously global is their range, inclusiveness and impacts; and many of them are outpacing our legal, political and ethical systems of deliberation and control. Climate change, the ravages of contagious diseases and financial turmoil are all cases in point. Similarly, the transformative implications of new scientific and technological developments, from Big Data to gene editing, are already upon us. This book series is dedicated to providing insights into the complex interaction of human and natural systems; modes of cooperation and conflict; and the ways and degrees to which human values can be reconciled and more effectively enacted. The concentration throughout is on an integration of existing disciplines toward the clarification of political possibility as well as impending crises.

The series is published in cooperation with gLAWcal - Global Law Initiatives for Sustainable Development.

Ondřej Svaček • Martin Faix
Editors

Prosecution of War Crimes before the ICC

Achievements and Challenges

palgrave
macmillan

Editors
Ondřej Svaček
Centre for International Humanitarian and Operational Law
Faculty of Law
Palacký University
Olomouc, Czech Republic

Martin Faix
Centre for International Humanitarian and Operational Law
Faculty of Law
Palacký University
Olomouc, Czech Republic

ISSN 2947-8863 ISSN 2947-8871 (electronic)
Global Issues
ISBN 978-3-031-84218-4 ISBN 978-3-031-84216-0 (eBook)
https://doi.org/10.1007/978-3-031-84216-0

Cover credit: Bernt Ove Moss / EyeEm / Getty Images

This Palgrave Macmillan imprint is published by the registered company Springer Nature Switzerland AG
The registered company address is: Gewerbestrasse 11, 6330 Cham, Switzerland

Acknowledgments

The editors would like to thank all the authors for their contributions and patience in process of finalization of this book. Ema Šromová and Charles Bird deserve gratitude for their accurate unification of contributions format and language proofreading. Last but not least, this book would not have been published without the kind support of prof. Paolo D. Farah, the editor of the series "Global Issues".

Contents

Notes on Contributors

Emma Brandon is an international criminal lawyer working as a Project Officer at the International Nuremberg Principles Academy. Prior to joining the Nuremberg Academy, she has held internship positions at the ICC (including in the Prosecution Division of the Office of the Prosecutor) and worked as a (Senior) Research Associate at the Public International Law and Policy Group, among other work in international legal research and practice. She holds a PhD in International Law from the University of Oslo, a Juris Doctor (JD) degree from the American University Washington College of Law, and a Bachelor of Arts (BA) degree in International Relations and Political Science from Boston University. She is licensed to practice law in Virginia and the District of Columbia.

Martin Faix is Senior Lecturer in International Law at the Faculty of Law, Palacký University Olomouc, where he also serves as the Head of the Centre of International Humanitarian and Operational Law. He obtained his law degree from the Justus Liebig University Giessen, Germany. In 2011, he completed his PhD on international law aspects of the EU's military operations at Charles University, Prague. Between 2015 and 2020, Martin served as an alternate member of the Management Board of the EU Agency for Fundamental Rights. Martin's research interests include general international law, international institutional law, international law on the use of force, international humanitarian law, and human rights.

Alejandro Sánchez Frías is Associate (tenured) Professor of Public International Law and International Relations and Legal Advisor to the Vice-president of Teaching and Research Personnel at the University of Málaga. He holds a PhD in Law with Extraordinary Prize from the University of Malaga, as well as a Law degree and a Master's degree in Law from the same university. He also has a Master's degree in European Union Studies from the University of Salamanca (Spain) and a Master's degree in European Law from the College of Europe (Bruges, Belgium). He has been a visiting researcher at the Max Planck Institute for Comparative Public Law and International Law (Heidelberg), the Max Planck Institute Luxembourg for International, European and Procedural Law (Luxembourg), the Institute for European Integration (University of Hamburg), the Centre of Excellence for International Courts (University of Copenhagen), the Center for European Law (Université Libre de Bruxelles), and the Center for Studies and research of the Hague Academy of International Law. Thanks to his research, he has received awards such as the European research and mobility grants of the Carlos V Award organized by the European and Ibero-American Academy of Yuste, the European Federation of Pharmaceutical Industries and Associations prize for the best work on public health policies, and one of the mentions of the Blattmann, Odio Benito, and Steiner.

Khrystyna Gavrysh is a Senior Research Fellow in International Law at the Department of Law, University of Ferrara (Italy), where she lectures on International Human Rights Law (in English) since 2022 and International Human Rights and Humanitarian Law in Armed Conflicts (in Italian; the course is also offered to military personnel) since 2024. She also serves as a member of the Editorial Committee of the *Rivista di Diritto Internazionale*. Dr. Gavrysh has authored numerous scholarly articles in the fields of international human rights, international judicial cooperation, and international criminal law.

Milan Lipovský is a lecturer and researcher at the Department of International Law, Faculty of Law, Charles University (Prague). He graduated from the Charles University in 2010 (Master's degree) and 2015 (PhD). His PhD thesis focused on the crime of aggression. His academic focus includes international criminal law and the law of international peace and security.

Laurie Morgan is an Attorney Advisor with the Commercial Law Development Program (CLDP) in the Office of the General Counsel of the U.S. Department of Commerce. Her overseas work focuses on legal reform issues related to economic security. Prior to joining CLDP, Ms. Morgan worked as an attorney in the Dispute Resolution and Public International Law practices at Freshfields Bruckhaus Deringer LLP in New York. Ms. Morgan received her Juris Doctor (JD) from Georgetown University Law Center in Washington, D.C., where she was a Global Law Scholar. She received her Bachelor of Arts (BA) in International Justice from Leiden University College in The Hague, The Netherlands. She is admitted to practice law in New Jersey.

Yael Naggan is SJD Candidate, Georgetown University Law Center, and holds LL.M, Columbia Law School (2015); LL.B and B.A. International Relations, the Hebrew University of Jerusalem (2013). The author is currently on academic leave from her position as legal advisor at the Israel Ministry of Justice, Office of the Deputy Attorney General (International Law). This chapter was written strictly in the author's academic capacity.

Ondřej Svaček is an associate professor at the Department of International and European Law, Faculty of Law, Palacký University Olomouc and the same department of Faculty of Law, Masaryk University, Brno. He also serves as an assistant to Justices of the Czech Constitutional Court, Lucie Dolanská Bányaiová and Jiří Přibáň. He regularly lectures abroad and completed long-term research stays at the T. M. C. Asser Instituut in The Hague and the Max Planck Institute in Heidelberg. He specializes in international criminal law, international human rights law, and general issues of public international law (e.g., law of state responsibility, jurisdictional immunities, and creation of states).

CHAPTER 1

Introduction

Ondřej Svaček and Martin Faix

That international criminal law (ICL) is almost intimately connected to international humanitarian law (IHL), because IHL forms part of ICL and the ICL of war crimes in turn forms part of IHL,[1] and that substantive international criminal law and its effectivity is made conditional on its procedural continuation, because their isolated existence would be in the fact meaningless, are two presumptions that are hardly disputed. These axioms are largely followed even in this book.

This book is a continuation of the previous co-editors' outcome published in Palgrave Macmillan series Global Issues,[2] which explored contribution of the International Criminal Court (ICC) to the development of

[1] M. Sassòli, "Humanitarian Law and International Criminal Law," in A. Cassese (ed.), *The Oxford Companion to International Criminal Justice* (Oxford: Oxford University Press, 2009), at 111.

[2] M. Faix, O. Svaček (eds.), *ICC Jurisprudence and the Development of International Humanitarian Law* (Cham: Palgrave Macmillan, 2024), 273 p.

O. Svaček (✉) • M. Faix
Centre for International Humanitarian and Operational Law, Faculty of Law, Palacký University, Olomouc, Czech Republic
e-mail: ondrej.svacek@upol.cz

O. Svaček, M. Faix (eds.), *Prosecution of War Crimes before the ICC*, Global Issues, https://doi.org/10.1007/978-3-031-84216-0_1

IHL and focused both on methodological issues of law finding and identification before the ICC (especially relationship between customary IHL and the Rome Statute) and issue of substantive ICL related to responsibility for war crimes. Given the interconnectedness between substance and procedure, the purpose of this book is to add a procedural limb to the ICC's contribution to the prosecution and punishment of war crimes.

In their contributions, authors assess procedural mechanisms enshrined in the Rome Statute of the ICC that are employed by this Court for prosecution of crimes under international law forming part of its subject-matter jurisdiction, including war crimes. The default question to be answered here is quite straightforward: do the respective components of the ICC's procedural design facilitate prosecution of war crimes, or do they challenge or eventually even hinder their prosecution? The aforesaid concatenation between substance and procedure is obvious, because if this question is answered in the positive and therefore the procedural mechanisms are appraised as facilitators of the prosecution of war crimes, it is to be expected that the ICC's contribution to the development of IHL through application and interpretation of substantive ICL on war crimes will be—simply put—bigger and vice versa.

It should be stressed that the terms *process* or *procedure* are perceived here as autonomous concepts, or more precisely, they are interpreted extensively. The co-editors are, for example, aware that issue of cooperation is not strictly speaking a part of a set of rules regulating international proceedings before the ICC,[3] but is rather a component of so-called horizontal ICL.[4] Nevertheless, the obligation of states to cooperate with the ICC, stemming from the ICC or from any other source of international law (e.g. the Geneva Conventions—see *infra*), might be rightly qualified as substantive obligations of a procedural character given its ultimate purpose what is a subjecting the accused to the ICC's enforcement mechanism. Then, concerning the issue of cumulative charges, there is no doubt that through this institute of ICL both its substantive and procedural limb overlap what nevertheless does not disqualify it to be assessed in this volume, which focuses on procedure before the ICC.[5]

[3] A. Cassese, P. Gaeta et al. *Cassese's International Criminal Law* (3rd edn., Oxford: Oxford University Press, 2013), at 3.

[4] C. Kress, "International Criminal Law," in R. Wolfrum (ed.) *The Max Planck Encyclopedia of Public International Law*. Vol. V (Oxford: Oxford University Press, 2012), at 720.

[5] The selection of this topic is well substantiated by the fact that it concerns charge as a pivotal procedural decision that predetermines the subject-matter of proceedings in trial

Given the extent of this book, hardly all contentious aspects of procedural ICL relevant for the prosecution of war crimes could have been included. The co-editors had to be selective. They followed the same idea like in the previous publication concerning methodology of law-finding and substantive ICL, namely that the book should at least touch upon all main areas of procedural ICL. Despite the selectivity, we tried to encompass the whole system of procedural ICL, starting with jurisdiction, and continuing with immunity, complementarity (admissibility), charging, trial (law of evidence), reparation for victims, and cooperation.

In the opening chapter, *Alejandro Sánchez Frías* devotes to jurisdictional issues of the ICC related to the prosecution of war crimes. He focuses on a historical decision adopted by the ICC's Appeal Chamber in the context of the situation of Afghanistan on 5 March 2020 regarding the scope of application of IHL and the Rome Statute: contrary to the decision of the Pre-trial Chamber, it accepted the possibility of investigating alleged crimes committed outside the territory of the state where hostilities are occurring, when there is a nexus to such non-international armed conflict. This chapter analyses the two main theories about the territorial applicability of Common Article 3, how they have influenced the reasoning of both the Pre-Trial Chamber and the Appeals Chamber, and, finally, why the decision of the latter should not be read in the context of the "global battlefield" debate, pointing out that the arguments in favour of the extraterritorial applicability of the *jus in bello* for the purpose of criminal prosecution should not be extrapolated to legitimize a relaxation of the rules of the *jus ad bellum*.

The second contribution by *Ondřej Svaček* concerns an exception from the jurisdictional framework of the ICC or rather the extent of jurisdiction *ratione personae*. The chapter analyses available case law of the ICC concerning the applicability of personal immunities in proceedings before it and assesses possible prospect of its usage in recent or eventual future cases before the ICC. The author presents critical stance against the conclusion of the Appeals Chamber adopted in the *Al-Bashir* that personal immunities disappear in the proceedings before the ICC due to existence of the respective rule of customary international law, which is allegedly codified in Article 27(2) of the Rome Statute. The author is aware that the conclusion (whether positive or negative) on the applicability of personal

stage. See Art 74(2) of the Rome Statute dictating that the decision shall not exceed the facts and circumstances described in the charges and any amendments to the charges.

immunities before the ICC has a direct impact on prosecution of crimes under international law, including war crimes, committed by members of the troika before the ICC itself, but also before any other international criminal tribunals, including those that will eventually be created (e.g. the special ad hoc tribunal for the crime of aggression committed against Ukraine). Ondřej Svaček explores the possible paths to disregard personal immunity of troika members coming from the third states (non-state parties to the Rome Statute) and admits that the removal of immunity might stem from a Security Council resolution, once it is expressly provided in such a resolution. Otherwise, he aims at the customary international law path—not yet established under his opinion—which might be nevertheless brought about by dynamic (i.e. not merely deductive) creation of customary international law and assesses also a possibility to remove the personal immunity through application of circumstances precluding wrongfulness, namely the self-defence.

In the following chapter, *Milan Lipovský* analyses existing practice concerning the backbone of the Rome Statute, part of an admissibility test to be assessed once the jurisdiction of the ICC is established: the principle of complementarity. Its basic premise is that states are primarily responsible for the investigation and prosecution of crimes under international law, including war crimes. Thus, in ideal situation, should states carry their obligations perfectly, the principle would render the ICC superfluous. In a real world, however, the principle counts with states being "unwilling or unable" genuinely to carry out these obligations, and under those conditions, the ICC steps in. As such, the principle is a tool to solve vertical conflict of jurisdictions (domestic and international). As the ICC has exercised its jurisdiction for more than 22 years, it has already had an opportunity to elaborate upon the principle, yet certain unclarity remains. This chapter critically points out some problematic interpretations and deals with both theoretical, yet not addressed topics, as well as those already addressed by the ICC case law.

The chapter by *Yael Naggan* focuses on a prominent feature in ICL practice—cumulative charges and convictions, which best confirms the presumption of this book concerning the close inter-relationship between substantive and procedural ICL. This chapter addresses issues that arise when considering this practice, with respect to instances where both war crimes and crimes against humanity charges are based on the same underlying conduct, from the perspective of the promotion of adherence to IHL, as one of the goals of the war crimes regime in ICL. The chapter argues that the adoption of a strict policy for cumulative charges and convictions, based on a rigid, technical jurisprudential test, is not conducive to ensuring results that are sufficiently attuned to the circumstances of each case. It surveys the recent proceedings in the *Ongwen* case before the ICC and discusses the Court's failure to provide more comprehensive doctrinal guidance in this regard. The author proposes the adoption of a more nuanced approach when contemplating cumulative charges for these two categories of crimes that involve an in-depth examination of the "nexus to an armed conflict" requirement of war crimes.

The next chapter concentrates on very heart of proving international crimes in international criminal proceedings. Within the purview of the law of evidence, *Khrystyna Gavrysh* turns her attention to digital evidence, such as satellite imagery or videos shared on social media, which may play a crucial role in prosecuting individuals for war crimes. Indeed, social media platforms have become de facto repositories for storing evidence of the most heinous crimes committed during recent international and non-international armed conflicts. Given that the ICC enjoys a certain degree of autonomy in admitting and evaluating evidence, this type of evidence can contribute to enhancing the Court's activity. However, it must meet the admissibility criteria set forth by Article 69(4) of the ICC Statute, as well as the standards for evaluating documentary evidence—which also includes digital evidence—as developed in the Court's case law. For this reason, digital evidence has so far been recognized as having limited probative value before the ICC in the prosecution of war crimes. This, however, might change in proceedings concerning the international armed conflict between Russia and Ukraine, considering the high involvement of civil society in recording and sharing evidence of events mainly perpetrated by the Russian armed forces.

In her chapter, *Laurie Morgan* focuses on the innovative position of victims in the proceedings before the ICC, quite unprecedented in whole history of ICL. While adopting provisions concerning the participation of victims, the drafters of the Rome Statute endorsed the idea that the object and purpose of procedure before the ICC is not only the eventual punishment of perpetrators of crimes under international law but also securing of justice for those who *vis-à-vis* these crimes suffered physically, mentally, or materially. Therefore, the Rome Statute endeavours to achieve not only retributive justice but also its restorative counterpart. Laurie Morgan identifies two major flaws of the ICC Trust Fund for Victims (TFV) reparation mandate, which is linked to accountability, arising from individual criminal responsibility of a convicted person. She argues that reparations are often given only to a select group of victims (issues of narrowness) and are not given in a timely manner (issue of timeliness). Therefore, she proposes that the assistance mandate that unlike its reparation counterpart is not dependent on the conviction of the accused and establishment of their individual criminal responsibility, be strengthened to provide reparations to victims before the end of a trial, weakening the tie between the reparations and the perpetrator. She discusses this recommendation in the context of an analysis of reparations in general, the ICC TFV system at large, and four TFV reparations case studies: *Lubanga*, *Katanga*, *Al Mahdi*, and *Bemba*.

The last chapter concerns an issue of vital importance for every international criminal tribunal, obviously including the ICC.[6] In this part, *Emma Brandon* notices that without its own police force, the ICC relies on cooperation from states to perform their mandates which is—nevertheless—not always forthcoming. In many circumstances, the ICC requires cooperation from states who are not parties to the Rome Statute that created it. Obtaining cooperation from these non-state parties is complicated by the fact that they do not have the relatively clear and binding cooperation obligations under those treaties that state parties have. One underexplored aspect of this much-discussed quandary is the potential for non-state parties to have cooperation obligations under other international human rights and humanitarian law treaties to which they are parties. Given the key role that the ICC plays in the enforcement of international humanitarian law and particularly the Geneva Conventions, this chapter explores this potential by investigating possible obligations to cooperate with these tribunals under all four Geneva Conventions and their Additional Protocols. It examines potential cooperation obligations under both the specific prosecution obligation in the grave breaches provisions and the more general Common Article 1 obligation to ensure respect for the conventions. The chapter also highlights the role that such an

[6] As famously described by A. Cassese, international criminal tribunals, dependent on cooperation from states, are like giants without arms and legs. Cf. A. Cassese, "On the Current Trends towards Criminal Prosecution and Punishment of Breaches of International Humanitarian Law" 9 *European Journal of International Law* (1998), at 13.

obligation could play in current geopolitical crises such as the Russian invasion of Ukraine.

It is the humble wish of the co-editors that this book will contribute to the wider ongoing debate over complex issues of mutual relationship between IHL and ICL, including its benefits, limits, and pitfalls.

CHAPTER 2

The 'Nexus' Between International Humanitarian Law and International Criminal Law in the Decision of the Appeals Chamber of the ICC in the Situation of Afghanistan: Toward a Global Battlefield?

Alejandro Sánchez Frías

1 Introduction and Contextualization of the Procedure in Afghanistan

In 2006, the Office of the Prosecutor of the International Criminal Court (ICC) started a preliminary examination of the situation of Afghanistan. After ten years of gathering and verifying information on alleged crimes, the Prosecutor requested the Pre-Trial Chamber (PTC) the authorization for opening a *proprio motu* investigation pursuant to Article 15 of the

A. Sánchez Frías (✉)
Public International Law and EU Law, University of Málaga, Málaga, Spain
e-mail: asanchezfrias@uma.es

O. Svaček, M. Faix (eds.), *Prosecution of War Crimes before the ICC*, Global Issues, https://doi.org/10.1007/978-3-031-84216-0_2

Statute.[1] Based on the information available, the Prosecutor identified a wide list of alleged crimes against humanity and crimes against humanity.[2] Regarding the places of alleged commission of the crimes, it included not only the territory of Afghanistan but also the territories of Poland, Romania, and Lithuania.[3] Finally, it is also important to note that the persons or groups involved included the Taliban and affiliated armed groups, as well as the Afghan National Security Forces, US armed forces, and members of the Central Intelligence Agency.[4]

The PTC made its decision available on 12 April 2019.[5] Regarding the admissibility test, it accepted that the requisites of complementarity—no domestic criminal proceedings had been started against those identified by the prosecution—and gravity—considering the responsibility of potential offenders, the high number of victims, the nature of the crimes, the modalities of the conducts, and their impact on the victims—had been fulfilled.[6] In relation to the jurisdiction, the PTC declared that the jurisdiction *ratione materiae* was satisfied as "there is a reasonable basis to believe that the incidents underlying the Request occurred and that they may constitute crimes within the jurisdiction of the Court".[7] However, it declared to have jurisdiction *ratione loci* only over the acts committed in Afghanistan, thus excluding an investigation over alleged crimes in Poland, Romania, and Lithuania.[8]

Finally, the PTC decided, for the first time in the not very long history of the ICC, to enter in the analysis of the requisite of the 'interests of justice' for the purpose of Article 53(1) of the Statute. Furthermore, it considered that the opening of an investigation in the situation of Afghanistan would not be 'in the interests of justice' for three main reasons: the significant time elapsed between the alleged crimes and the Request (1)[9]; the

[1] Request for authorisation of an investigation pursuant to article 15, *Situation in the Islamic Republic of Afghanistan* (ICC-02/17-7-Conf-Exp), Office of the Prosecutor, 20 November 2017.

[2] Ibid., § 42.

[3] Ibid., §§ 43–49.

[4] Ibid., §§ 53–71.

[5] Decision Pursuant to Article 15 of the Rome Statute on the Authorisation of an Investigation into the Situation in the Islamic Republic of Afghanistan, *Situation in the Islamic Republic of Afghanistan* (ICC-02/17-33), Pre-Trial Chamber II, 12 April 2019.

[6] Ibid., §§ 70–86.

[7] Ibid., § 60.

[8] Ibid., §§ 49–59.

[9] Ibid., § 93.

lack of cooperation of the relevant states (2)[10]; and the necessity to devote the limited resources of the ICC to other scenarios which appear to have more realistic prospects to lead to trial (3).[11]

The decision of the PTC was strongly criticized by the scholarship, which considered it "the anti-climax of more than a decade-long preliminary examination by the Office of the Prosecutor and one-and-a-half years of judicial deliberations".[12] The criticism focused mainly on the ultra vires examination of the 'interests of justice' by the PTC and the extra-statutory elements valued within this concept.[13] Aware of this criticism, the Appeals Chamber (AC) decided in its decision of 5 March 2020 that the PTC had no competence to examine the 'interests of justice' in requests for *proprio motu* investigations and, in an *obiter dictum*, that the substantive analysis did not properly assess the interests of justice.[14]

The 'interests of justice', however, is not the only relevant clash between the PTC and the AC. It is also interesting to note that the AC completely overturned the decision of the AC regarding the jurisdiction *ratione loci*, including within the scope of the investigation crimes allegedly committed beyond the territory of Afghanistan. This study will not focus on the debate of whether the ICC has territorial jurisdiction over US personnel in Afghanistan explicitly,[15] but on the two different approaches to the interpretation of Common Article 3 for the purpose of establishing a

[10] Ibid., § 94.

[11] Ibid., § 95.

[12] S. Vasilev, 'Not just another 'crisis': Could the blocking of the Afghanistan investigation spell the end of the ICC? (Part I)', EJIL! Talk, 19 April 2019, available at https://www.ejiltalk.org/not-just-another-crisis-could-the-blocking-of-the-afghanistan-investigation-spell-the-end-of-the-icc-part-i/ (last visited 19 May 2021).

[13] For studies on the 'interests of justice' in this context see, among others, T. De Souza Dias, "Interests of justice': Defining the scope of Prosecutorial discretion in Article 53(1)(c) and (2)(c) of the Rome Statute of the International Criminal Court', 30 *Leiden Journal of International Law* (2017) 731; E. O. Calatayud, 'La autorización para investigar los crímenes cometidos en Afganistán. Luces y sombras de la sentencia, de 5 de marzo de 2020, de la Sala de Apelaciones de la Corte Penal Internacional', 39 *Revista electrónica de estudios internacionales* (2020) 1; L. Poltronieri Rossetti, 'The Pre-Trial Chamber's Afghanistan Decision: A Step Too Far in the Judicial Review of Prosecutorial Discretion?', 17 *Journal of International Criminal Justice* (2019) 585.

[14] Judgment on the appeal against the decision on the authorisation of an investigation situation in the Islamic Republic of Afghanistan, *Situation in the Islamic Republic of Afghanistan* (ICC-02/17 OA4), Appeals Chamber, 5 March 2020, § 49.

[15] See, for this purpose, M. Cormier, 'Testing the boundaries of the ICC's territorial jurisdiction in the Afghanistan situation', 78 *Question of International Law* (2021) 43.

'nexus' between the alleged crime and the armed conflict. First, I will address the scholarship and case law in favor and against a wide understanding of the geographical borders of Common Article 3, and how these positions have influenced, respectively, the decisions of the PTC and of the AC. Second, I will present the 'global battlefield' debate and how this issue should not be included in the framework of the decision of the AC. Finally, I will conclude with some assessments on the decisions of both chambers and their potential impact in future cases.

2 The 'Nexus Requirement' and the Legal Geography of Non-international Armed Conflicts

To distinguish war crimes from ordinary crimes—for the purpose of establishing the jurisdiction of international criminal tribunals, among other reasons—it has been common to introduce a link between International Humanitarian Law (IHL) and International Criminal Law (ICL) in the statutes of these judicial organs.[16] This link, commonly known as 'nexus', requires, according to the elements of the crime, that "the conduct took place in the context of and was associated with an armed conflict not of an international character".[17] In this sense, regarding the situation of Afghanistan, the Prosecutor considered in her request that the alleged crimes committed by members of the US armed forces and the Central Intelligence Agency (CIA) both on the territory of Afghanistan as well as on the territory of other States Parties to the Statute "took place in the context of or was associated with an armed conflict not of an international character".[18]

The decisions of both the PTC and the AC about the opening of an authorization are extremely relevant on this point because it was the first time that the ICC decided about the 'nexus requirement' beyond the territory of the state in conflict. Though it is true that other international criminal tribunals have analyzed this issue, as we will see in the next part of this study, the jurisdiction of the International Criminal Tribunal for

[16] G. Mettraux, *International Crimes and the* ad hoc *Tribunals* (Oxford: Oxford University Press, 2005), at 39.

[17] Rome Statute of the International Criminal Court (adopted 17 July 1998, entered into force 1 July 2002), 2187 UNTS 90 (hereafter Rome Statute), Art. 8(2)(c)(i) – 4, Elements of Crimes.

[18] Request for authorisation of an investigation pursuant to Article 15, *supra* note 1, § 190.

the former Yugoslavia (ICTY) was limited to the territory of the former Yugoslavia,[19] and that of the International Criminal Tribunal for Rwanda (ICTR) only to Rwanda and neighboring states were the conflict spilled over.[20] The next two sections are devoted to analyzing the two contending approaches to the application of Common Article 3, being each one of them the basis of the legal reasoning in the decisions of the PTC and the AC in the situation of Afghanistan.

2.1 The Restrictive Approach to Common Article 3

According to the restrictive approach to Common Article 3, the application of the rules for a non-international armed conflict (NIAC) is geographically confined to the hostilities taking place within the national borders of a state. Dinstein, for instance, considers that the first constitutive element in the definition of a NIAC is the fact that it "must take place within the borders of a High Contracting Party, that is to say, a single state".[21] Moir also considers that this is the less 'problematic' element of the definition of NIAC, being "a positive requirement" as regards the geographical location of the conflict, which must take place "in the territory of one of the High Contracting Parties (in the sense of being limited to the territory of a High Contracting Party)".[22] The San Remo Manual on NIACs emphasizes this narrow conception of the geographical limits: "non-international armed conflicts are armed confrontations occurring within the territory of a single state".[23] Bartels concludes that these definitions "using the terms 'within a state', 'in the territory of one of the High Contracting Parties', 'in the territory of a High Contracting Party' and

[19] Statute of the International Criminal Tribunal for Former Yugoslavia (adopted 25 May 1993, entered into force 14 March 1994), UN Dos. S/INF 49(1993) (hereafter 1 ICTYSt), Art. 1.

[20] Statute of the International Tribunal for Rwanda (adopted 8 November 1994, entered in force 29 June 1995) UN Doc.S/RES/955 (1994) (hereafter ICTRSt), Art. 1.

[21] Y. Dinstein, 'Concluding Remarks on Non-International Armed Conflicts', in K. Watkin and A.J. Norris (eds), *Non-International Armed Conflict in the Twenty-first Century* (United States: Naval War College, 2012) 399–421, at 400.

[22] L. Moir, *The Law of Internal Armed Conflict* (Cambridge: Cambridge University Press, 2002), at 31.

[23] International Institute of Humanitarian Law, *The Manual on the Law of Non-International Armed Conflict* (San Remo, 2006), at 2.

'within the territory of a single state', all create a restriction; some seem more restrictive (e.g., 'a single state') than others ('a state')".[24]

This approach is supported in the reading of two different provisions. First, on a literal interpretation of Common Article 3, according to which the Geneva Conventions apply "in the case of armed conflict not of an international character occurring *in the territory of one of the High Contracting Parties*". Pejic highlights that the plain meaning of this provision seems to suggest that IHL only governs the acts committed in the territory of one of the High Contracting Party where the conflict is taking place exclusively.[25] Second, on Article 1 of Additional Protocol II because, as Schmitt points out, "[t]he phrase can plausibly be understood as referring to the territory of the state that is involved in the conflict, much as Additional Protocol II appears to make such a limitation explicit during conflicts to which it applies".[26] The most cited source backing this approach is probably the 1958's Commentary to the Fourth Geneva Convention:

> Speaking generally, it must be recognized that the conflicts referred to in Article 3 are armed conflicts, with armed forces on either side engaged in hostilities -- conflicts, in short, which are in many respects similar to an international war, but take place *within the confines of a single country*. In many cases, each of the Parties is in possession of a portion of the national territory, and there is often some sort of front.[27]

In addition, it could be argued that the drafters of Common Article 3 deliberately confined its field of application to the territory of a single state. Indeed, the original version of this provision, adopted at the XVII International Red Cross Conference in Stockholm, explicitly referred to "all cases of armed conflict not of an international character which may

[24] R. Bartels, 'Timelines, borderlines and conflicts: The historical evolution of the legal divide between international and non-international armed conflicts', 91 *International Review of the Red Cross* (2009) 35, at 39.

[25] J. Pejic, 'The protective scope of Common Article 3: more than meets the eye', 93 *International Review of the Red Cross* (2011) 1, at 11.

[26] M. N. Schmitt, 'Charting the Legal Geography of Non-International Armed Conflict', 90 *International Law Studies* (2014) 1, at 9.

[27] J. Pictet, 'Article 3: Conflicts not of an international character', in J. Pictet (ed.), *Commentary to the IV Geneva Convention Relative to the Protection of Civilian Persons in Time of War* (Geneva: International Committee of the Red Cross, 1958).

occur *in the territory of one or more* of the High Contracting Parties".[28] However, as explained in the next section, nothing in the *travaux préparatories* suggests that the article was changed for to exclude non-international armed conflicts involving the territory of more than one single state.[29]

As I mentioned above, the geographical scope of application of IHL in NIAC is a crucial point for the determination of the jurisdiction *ratione loci* of the ICC. A restrictive approach to Common Article 3 constitutes a limitation of the principle of territoriality, on which the ICC may base its jurisdiction. In its decision about the opening of an investigation in Afghanistan, the PTC started its reasoning on this point by distinguishing two kind of situations over which the ICC may exercise its territorial jurisdiction: conducts that have occurred in full in the territory of Afghanistan or of other State Party to the Statute (a), and conducts that were initiated in the territory of a state party and continued in the territory of a non-State Party to the Statute (b).[30] Regarding the alleged acts of torture committed in the framework of the detention program carried out by the CIA, which does not initially fall within the two previous categories, Prosecutor Bensouda requested acts against victims associated to the conflict in Afghanistan but captured outside its territory to be included in the investigation.[31] Contrary to her view, the PTC borrowed the theory on the restrictive approach and hold that:

> [T]he *relevant nexus* between the conflict and the alleged criminal conducts required by the Statute *is only satisfied when the victims were captured within the borders of Afghanistan*. Both the *wording and the spirit of common article 3* to the Geneva Conventions are univocal in confining its *territorial scope within the borders of the State where the hostilities are actually occurring*: In the case of armed conflict not of an international character occurring in the

[28] Joint Committee, *Seventh Report drawn up by the Special Committee of the Joint Committee* (1949), Final Record of the Diplomatic Conference of Geneva, Vol. II, Section B., at 120, available at
https://www.legal-tools.org/doc/488639/pdf/ (last visited 19 May 2021).

[29] N. Melzer, *Targeted Killing in International Law* (Oxford: Oxford University Press, 2008), at 258.

[30] Decision Pursuant to Article 15 of the Rome Statute on the Authorisation of an Investigation, *supra* note 5, § 50.

[31] Request for authorisation of an investigation pursuant to Article 15, *supra* note 1, § 249.

territory of one of the High Contracting Parties, each Party to the conflict shall be bound to apply, as a minimum, the following provisions.[32]

The PTC did not make a great effort in arguing why the literal and teleological interpretations of Common Article 3 justify a restrictive approach, though we can imagine that it was greatly influenced by the ideas described above. I will come back later to this point when describing the arguments in favor of an expansive approach to Common Article 3. In any case, the minimalist understating of what is the 'relevant nexus' in that brief paragraph helped the PTC, along with the assessment of the 'interest of justice', to dodge the request for this politically sensitive investigation:

> [T]he Chamber finds that *the extension of the scope of international humanitarian law beyond the territory of Afghanistan*, where a non-international armed conflict was occurring at the time of the relevant conducts, as advocated by the Prosecutor, *does not find adequate support in the relevant texts.* The Chamber considers that the alleged war crimes whose victims were captured outside Afghanistan fall out of the Court's jurisdiction due to the lack of the nexus with an internal armed conflict which is required to trigger the application of international humanitarian law as well as the Court's jurisdiction.[33]

It is also interesting to note that even if the concerned person were captured in the territory of Afghanistan, this would not be sufficient to establish its jurisdiction over crimes of torture. According to the PTC,

> *[I]f the conducts* of inflicting 'severe physical or mental pain or suffering' *were to occur entirely on the territory of a non-State Party, the fact that the concerned person has been captured in Afghanistan* within the context of the there ongoing non-international armed conflict - and is therefore entitled to the protection of international humanitarian law and international criminal law alike - *would not constitute an adequate jurisdictional link for the purposes of establishing territorial jurisdiction.* Otherwise stated, for the Court to have jurisdiction on the crime of torture, it is necessary that the alleged conduct of 'inflicting severe physical or mental pain' - not its mere antecedents (i.e., the fact of having been captured and abducted) - takes place at

[32] Decision Pursuant to Article 15 of the Rome Statute on the Authorisation of an Investigation, *supra* note 5, § 53.

[33] Ibid., § 55.

least in part in the territory of a State Party; provided that the victims were captured in Afghanistan.[34]

In short, the PTC required not only that the person was captured in the territory of Afghanistan to comply with the 'nexus requirement' but also that the acts of ill-treatment took place in the territory of a State Party to the Statute. However, even under this extremely restrictive approach, I consider that the PTC should have assessed positively its jurisdiction considering the facts of the situation in Afghanistan as presented by the Prosecutor. The centers where the torture allegedly took place were in the territories of Poland, Lithuania, and Romania, all of which are parties to the Rome Statute. As Pothelet correctly points out, "[t]he three countries were indeed parties to the NIAC(s) against the Taliban (and other armed groups) at the time of the alleged crimes, as they were contributing troops to Operation Enduring Freedom and ISAF since early 2002".[35] This situation would enter within the fourth category of 'internationalized' internal armed conflicts described by Schindler—between non-state groups and the forces of a state that supports the established government—and, therefore, within the scope of Common Article 3.[36] As already observed by Schmitt in 2014, this perspective on the applicability of IHL has "enormous implications in light of, for instance, international support of Afghanistan in its NIAC with the Taliban and associated armed groups".[37]

2.2 *The Expansive Approach to Common Article 3*

The expansive approach to Common Article 3 implies that the application of the rules for NIAC is not geographically confined to the hostilities taking place within the national borders of a state. There are various reasons to support this approach. The first one would be a historical interpretation of Common Article 3. After an in-depth analysis of the records of the Geneva Conference and the statements of the Mexican and Russian

[34] Ibid., § 54.

[35] E. Pothelet, 'War crimes in Afghanistan and Beyond: Will the ICC Weigh in on the "Global Battlefield" Debate?', EJIL! Talk, 9 November 2017, available at https://www.ejiltalk.org/war-crimes-in-afghanistan-and-beyond-will-the-icc-weigh-in-on-the-global-battlefield-debate/ (last visited 19 May 2021).

[36] D. Schindler, 'International Humanitarian Law and Internationalized Internal Armed Conflicts', 22 *International Review of the Red Cross* (1982) 255, at 261.

[37] Schmitt, *supra* note 26, at 11.

delegates, Melzer concludes that the sentence "in the territory of one of the High Contracting Parties" had its reason on the fact that, at that time, not all states had ratified the Geneva Conventions:

> [A]s the applicability of Article 3 GC I to IV, contrary to Article 2 GC I to IV, does not require the involvement of a contracting State as a party to the conflict, it is only logical that this criterion was replaced by the prerequisite of a territorial link to a contracting State. The legislative novelty of Article 3 GC I to IV was that each contracting State established binding rules not only for its own conduct, but also for that of the involved non-State parties. The authority to do so derives from the contracting State's domestic legislative sovereignty, wherefore a territorial requirement was incorporated in Article 3 GC I to IV. This is not say, however, that a conflict governed by Article 3 GC I to IV cannot take place on the territory of more than one contracting State. From the perspective of a newly drafted treaty text, it appears more appropriate to interpret the phrase in question simply as emphasizing that Article 3 GC I to IV could apply only to conflicts taking place on the territory of States which had already become party to the new Conventions.[38]

After studying the drafting history of this provision, Sivakumaran also arrives to the same conclusion:

> [T]he delimitation that was sought was between states parties and non-states parties and the modified wording resulted from the usual workings of diplomatic conferences. Importantly, the treaty rules do not refer to armed conflicts fought within a *single* High Contracting Party or within the territory of one High Contracting Party *alone*, both of which would suggest territorial limits.[39]

In this very same line, the International Committee of the Red Cross (ICRC) holds that because of the universal ratification of the Geneva Convention,[40] this requirement 'has lost its importance in practice'.

[38] Melzer, *supra* note 29, at 258.

[39] S. Sivakumaran, *The Law of Non-International Armed Conflict* (Oxford: Oxford University Press, 2012), at 230.

[40] We could also add to the conventional obligations derived from the ratification the recognized status of customary law of the Geneva Conventions. See, among others, Advisory Opinion, *Legality of the Use by a State of Nuclear Weapons in Armed Conflict* (I.C.J. Reports 1996), 8 July 1996, at §§ 79–82.

Indeed, any armed conflict between governmental armed forces and armed groups or between such groups cannot but take place on the territory of one of the Parties to the Convention.[41]

As I mentioned above, the PTC decided that the 'spirit' of Common Article 3 leads to the conclusion that it should be geographically limited. However, the PTC did not develop any argument to support its decision. By contrast, the opposite view has been argued in depth by other judicial organs as well as most of the scholarship. In *Hamdan v. Rumsfeld*, the US Supreme Court established the applicability of Common Article 3 to the conflict between the US and Al Qaeda because of the nature of the parties involved and regardless of the geographical scope of the conflict. This was possible because the US Supreme Court considered that the object and purpose of Common Article 3—or the 'spirit', if we may—was to furnish minimum protection to all individuals involved, in comparison to Common Article 2:

> Common Article 3, by contrast, affords some minimal protection, falling short of full protection under the Conventions, to individuals associated with neither a signatory nor even a nonsignatory Power who are involved in a conflict in the territory of a signatory. The latter kind of conflict is distinguishable from the conflict described in Common Article 2 chiefly because it does not involve a clash between nations (whether signatories or not). In context, then, the phrase 'not of an international character' bears its literal meaning.[42]

The US Supreme Court clearly established that the distinguished feature of a NIAC is not the fact that the conflict takes place in the territory of a single state but the very nature of the parties, which just excludes a clash between states.[43] In a reasoning like that in *Hamdan*, the ICTY ruled in the famous *Tadic* case that:

> The geographical and temporal frame of reference for internal armed conflicts is […] broad. This conception is reflected in the fact that beneficiaries

[41] International Committee of the Red Cross, *How is the Term "Armed Conflict" Defined in International Humanitarian Law?* (2008), available at https://www.icrc.org/en/doc/assets/files/other/opinion-paper-armed-conflict.pdf (last visited 19 May 2021).

[42] Judgment, *Salim Ahmed Hamdan v. Donald H. Rumsfeld* et al. [548 U.S. 557 (2006)], 29 June 2006, at 67.

[43] See also L. Zegveld, *The Accountability of Armed Opposition Groups in International Law* (Cambridge: Cambridge University Press, 2002), at 136.

of Common Article 3 of the Geneva Conventions are those taking no active part (or no longer taking active part) in the hostilities. This indicates that the rules contained in Article 3 *also apply outside the narrow geographical context of the actual theatre of combat operations.*[44]

This expansive approach to Common Article 3 was later confirmed in the *Kunarac* case, in which the ICTY noted that:

> There is no necessary correlation between the area where the actual fighting takes place and the geographical reach of the laws of war [...]. The requirement that the acts of the accused must be closely related to the armed conflict would not be negated if the crimes were temporally and geographically remote from the actual fighting.[45]

The ICTY went even further and developed the factors that, inter alia, could be assessed in the nexus requirement:

> The fact that the perpetrator is a combatant; the fact that the victim is a non-combatant; the fact that the victim is a member of the opposing party; the fact that the act may be said to serve the ultimate goal of a military campaign; and the fact that the crime is committed as part of or in the context of the perpetrator's official duties.[46]

Most of the scholarship supports geographically unfocused interpretations of the wording Article 3, including within its field of application the so-called spillover conflicts[47] and scenarios of foreign intervention.[48] Bradley critically describes how the 'gap theory' has increasingly gained support among scholars and how it has also contributed to the develop-

[44] Decision in the defence motion for interlocutory appeal on jurisdiction, *Prosecutor v. Dusko Tadic* (IT-94-1-I), Trial Chamber, 2 October 1995, at § 69.

[45] Judgment, *Prosecutor v. Dragoljub Kunarac* et al. (IT-96-23 & IT-96-23/1-A), Appeals Chamber, 12 June 2002, at § 57.

[46] Ibid., at § 59.

[47] See, among others, C. Kreß, 'Some Reflections on the International Legal Framework Governing Transnational Armed Conflicts', 15 *Journal of Conflict and Security Law* (2010) 245, at 265–266.

[48] For many authors, the intervention of the US in Afghanistan by invitation of its governments means that it is involved in a cross-border NIAC against Al-Qaeda and the Taliban. See, among others, S. Vité, 'Typology of armed conflicts in international humanitarian law: legal concepts and actual situations', 91 *International Review of the Red Cross* (2009) 69, at 93.

ment of this 'contemporary interpretation' of Common Article 3.[49] Sassòli, for instance, analyzes the purpose of this provision and concluded that "if such wording meant that conflicts opposing states and organized armed groups and spreading over the territory of several states were not 'non-international armed conflicts', there would be *a gap in protection*, which could not be explained by states' concerns about their sovereignty".[50] Milanovic and Hadzi-Vidanovic illustrate this perspective: "[w]hile domestic law could to an extent *fill the regulatory gap*, in some cases at least such a result would morally be completely arbitrary; a rape by a rebel soldier on one side of the border would constitute a war crime, but not on the other".[51] Therefore, one of the consequences of this interpretation of Common Article 3 is "an emphasis on the parties to the conflict, reducing the importance of territory".[52]

Contrary to the restrictive approach chosen by the PTC in its decision about the opening of an investigation in Afghanistan, the AC unanimously opted for this expansive approach:

> While it is true that the chapeau of Common Article 3 refers to an 'armed conflict not of an international character occurring in the territory of one of the High Contracting Parties', this phrase does not have the function ascribed to it by the Pre-Trial Chamber, namely to limit the applicability of the provision to the State on the territory of which the armed conflict occurs. Rather, in the view of the Appeals Chamber, it simply describes the circumstances under which Common Article 3 applies: there must be an armed conflict not of an international character in one of the States Parties to the Geneva Convention.[53]

[49] M. M. Bradley, 'Expanding the Borders of Common Article 3 in Non-International Armed Conflicts: Amending Its Geographical Application Through Subsequent Practice?', 64 *Netherlands International Law Review* (2017) 375, at 386–391.

[50] M. Sassòli, 'Transnational Armed Groups and International Humanitarian Law', 6 *HPCR Occasional Paper Series* (2006) 1, at 9.

[51] M. Milanovic and V. Hadzi-Vidanovic, 'A taxonomy of armed conflict', in N. D. White and C. Henderson (eds), *Research Handbook on International Conflict and Security Law: Jus ad Bellum, Jus in Bello and Jus Post Bellum* (Cheltenham: Edward Elgar Publishing, 2013) 256, at 290–291.

[52] S. Radin, 'Global Armed Conflict? The Threshold of Extraterritorial Non-International Armed Conflicts', 89 *International Law Studies* (2013), 696, at 718.

[53] Judgment on the appeal against the decision on the authorisation of an investigation, *supra* note 14, § 73.

The judgment of the AC reproduces, almost literally, the arguments exposed above in favor of a broad understanding of the geographical application of Common Article 3. After mentioning the *amicus curiae* submission of Professor Rona, which makes a succinct explanation of the issue,[54] the AC bases its position almost completely in the 2016 commentaries of the ICRC and the judgment of the US Supreme Court in *Hamdan v. Rumsfeld*.[55]

The assumption of the expansive approach leads the AC to conclude that:

> it is incorrect to assume that, merely because the alleged capture of the victim did not take place in Afghanistan and the alleged criminal act also occurred outside Afghanistan, the conduct cannot possibly have taken place in the context of, and have been associated with, the armed conflict in that state[56]

and, therefore, authorized the opening of an investigation "in relation to [...] alleged crimes that have a nexus to the armed conflict in Afghanistan and are sufficiently linked to the situation and were committed on the territory of other States Parties in the period since 1 July 2002".[57] This change of mind at the ICC was considered by the Trump administration as an attack against the sovereignty of the US, which imposed sanctions on ICC staff[58] that were not lifted until the arrival of the Biden administration.[59]

[54] Observations of Professor Gabor Rona on the Pre-Trial Chamber's Conclusion that Events Beyond the Territory of Afghanistan Lack Sufficient Nexus to the Armed Conflict There for Purposes of Application of Rome Statute War Crimes, *Situation in the Islamic Republic of Afghanistan* (ICC-02/17-111), 14 November 2019.

[55] Judgment on the appeal against the decision on the authorisation of an investigation, *supra* note 14, at 73–75.

[56] Ibid., at 76.

[57] Ibid., at 79.

[58] B. Van Schaack, 'Executive Order 13928 On Blocking Property Of Certain Persons Associated With The International Criminal Court', 60 *International Legal Materials* (2020) 18.

[59] J. Biden, 'Executive Order on the Termination of Emergency With Respect to the International Criminal Court', The White House, 1 April 2021, available at https://www.whitehouse.gov/briefing-room/presidential-actions/2021/04/01/executive-order-on-the-termination-of-emergency-with-respect-to-the-international-criminal-court/ (last visited 19 May 2021).

3 The 'Global Battlefield' Debate

The expansive approach adopted by the AC to authorize investigations for acts allegedly committed beyond the territory of Afghanistan, including those involving US personnel, has been widely applauded by the civil society[60] and the scholarship.[61] However, we should not ignore the dangers raised by those who criticize that the expansive approach could lead to a 'global battlefield'. Indeed, the PTC pointed out at the end of its decision, in a reference to the judgment in *Ntaganda*,[62] that "it is also worth recalling that the Appeals Chamber has rightly interpreted the nexus requirement with rigour, warning against any undue expansion of the reach of the law of war crimes".[63]

This 'warning against any undue expansion of the reach of the law of war crimes' is the basis of the 'global battlefield' debate. This debate revolves around the "the line of practice on the relationship between IHL and IHRL, in which the former has been invoked by states in a permissive sense so as to broaden the powers available to them under the latter".[64] From the perspective of state rights, the debate focuses on the idea that an expansion of the field of application of IHL beyond the territory of the actual hostilities also means the possibility of targeting individuals outside the actual 'battlefield'.

The concept of a 'global battlefield' finds its clear foundation in the doctrine of the Bush administration on a 'global war on terrorism', in which the entire world is considered a war zone, entitling US personnel to kill enemies wherever and whenever they are found.[65] This debate has

[60] Amnesty International, 'Afghanistan: ICC authorizes historic investigation', 5 March 2020, available at https://www.amnesty.org/en/latest/news/2020/03/afghanistan-icc-authorizes-historic-investigation/ (last visited 15 October 2024).

[61] See, among others, J. Trahan, 'The Significance of the ICC Appeals Chamber's Ruling in the Afghanistan Situation', Opinio Juris, 10 March 2020, available at http://opiniojuris.org/2020/03/10/the-significance-of-the-icc-appeals-chambers-ruling-in-the-afghanistan-situation/ (last visited 19 May 2021).

[62] Judgment, *The Prosecutor v. Bosco Ntaganda* (ICC-01/04-02/06-1962), Appeals Chamber, 15 June 2017.

[63] Decision Pursuant to Article 15 of the Rome Statute on the Authorisation of an Investigation, *supra* note 5, at 53.

[64] L. Hill-Cawthorne, 'Rights under International Humanitarian Law', 28 *European Journal of International Law* (2018) 1187, at 1212.

[65] L. R. Blank, 'Defining the Battlefield in Contemporary Conflict and Counterterrorism: Understanding the Parameters of the Zone of Combat', 39 *Georgia Journal of International and Comparative Law* (2010) 1, at 21.

been fostered even more after the first reported armed done strike outside the scope of a traditional armed conflict in 2002 in Yemen.[66] The last report of the UN Special Rapporteur on extrajudicial executions, focused on the killing of Iranian General Soleimani, describes the growing use of armed drones against targets within and outside NIACs.[67] In the words of Quintin, here the risk is:

> To reverse the logic of reasoning: instead of looking first at *jus ad bellum* in order to decide whether a use of force would be lawful [...] to determine how such force should be used, the tendency now is to first look at whether a specific target would, in the context of an armed conflict, be a lawful target, and in case of a positive answer, to justify the resort to force on the basis of the lawfulness of the target. In the end, *jus ad bellum* is ignored, render useless, replaced by an automatic application on the basis of the object of targeting.[68]

In this scenario, it is not strange that some authors are contrary to a geographically unfocused application of IHL, considering that the "implications of allowing the use of armed force to capture or kill enemies outside a country's own territory, and outside a theater of traditional armed conflict, may include spiraling violence, the erosion of territorial sovereignty, and a weakening of international cooperation".[69] In this context, could we say that the decision of the AC in the situation of Afghanistan supports such a dangerous expansion of IHL?

Going back to the case of the drone strikes, it has been proposed by some authors that the arguments developed in the field of international criminal law for the 'nexus requirement' could be extended, under certain conditions, to determine the geographical scope of IHL during NIACs beyond the immediate territory of the hostilities. In particular,

> First, it is clear that the nexus requirement does not demand a strict geographical or temporal proximity to the immediate sphere of hostilities.

[66] C. Heyns, *Report of the Special Rapporteur on extrajudicial, summary or arbitrary executions*, UN Doc. A/HRC/26/36, 1 April 2014, at 21.

[67] A. Callamard, *Report of the Special Rapporteur on extrajudicial, summary or arbitrary executions*, UN Doc. A/HRC/44/38, 15 August 2020, at 4.

[68] A. Quintin, *The Nature of International Humanitarian Law: a Permissive or Restrictive Regime?* (Cheltenham: Edward Elgar Publishing, 2020) at 18.

[69] G. Blum and P. Heymann, 'Law and Policy of Targeted Killing', 1 *Harvard National Security Journal* (2010) 145, at 163.

> Second, the existence of a sufficient nexus is not everlasting but dependent upon the actions of an individual and the relation of those actions to the existing armed conflict, and a range of factors exist that may dissolve the nexus between the acts or omissions of the accused and the armed conflict. The advantage of the 'nexus approach' is that it is not territorially bound, but rather focuses on the link between an individual or conduct and an existing armed conflict. Such an approach to the scope of applicability of IHL is supported by the scope of conventional IHL applicable during NIAC. [...] The 'nexus approach' provides a legally tenable avenue to determine the extent to which IHL is applicable outside the immediate geographical spheres of hostilities. Invariably, this approach will require a case-by-case determination and in practice will be dictated by the specific provision or principle of IHL being applied.[70]

In the previous section, I mentioned that the expansive approach to Common Article 3 puts an emphasis on the parties to the conflict and reduces the importance of the territory. However, we should read this approach in line with the teleological interpretation in which it is founded, meaning that the objective and purpose of Common Article 3 is to guarantee certain minimum protections in the context of the *jus in bello*, and that the 'nexus requirement' is required to distinguish ordinary crimes from war crimes in international criminal proceedings whose final purpose is to avoid criminal impunity in armed conflicts. The jurisprudence and scholarship examined above in favor of the expansive approach focus on the fact that the person, in some way, carries the protections of Common Article 3. But, as the ICRC correctly points out, this does not mean that the person carries a NIAC with them for the purpose of the *jus ad bellum*, as such approach:

> [W]ould have the effect of potentially expanding the application of rules on the conduct of hostilities to multiple states according to a person's movements around the world as long as he is directly participating in hostilities in relation to a specific NIAC. In addition to possible *ius ad bellum* issues that this scenario would raise there are others, such as the consequences that would be borne by civilians or civilian objects in the non-belligerent state(s). The proposition that harm or damage could lawfully be inflicted on them in operation of the IHL principle of proportionality because an individual

[70] N. Lubell and N. Derejko, 'A Global Battlefield? Drones and the Geographical Scope of Armed Conflict', 11 *Journal of International Criminal Justice* (2013) 65, at 75–76.

> sought by another state is in their midst (the result of a "nexus" approach), would in effect mean recognition of the concept of a "global battlefield.[71]

Of course, we could argue that if the effect of expanding the application of Common Article 3 consists only in the expansion of the protections of the *ius in bello*, it would be better to avoid any discussions on this matter and just stick to the more protective norms of human rights law. However, as Pothelet correctly points out, the applicability of IHL here "opens the possibility of war crime prosecutions and, as the ICC announcement just demonstrated, such prospect may be less hypothetical than it seems".[72]

We should read the decision of the AC in Afghanistan in its own context, which is the criminal prosecution of activities prohibited by Common Article 3 (cruel treatment and torture) which took place in the territory of a State Party to the Statute, but not in the territory where the hostilities are taking place. In order to distinguish these war crimes from ordinary crimes, the AC still requires a 'nexus', but this has not to be exclusively territorial, as the PTC erroneously held.[73]

The decision of the AC in Afghanistan upholds the prohibitions of Common Article 3 happening in the territory of the hostilities and beyond, by criminalizing conducts with a sufficient nexus with the armed conflict, but in any way authorizes the expansion of the use of force beyond the territory in conflict. In the same way that, according to Additional Protocol I, IHL does not give this kind of authorization: "nothing in this Protocol or in the Geneva Conventions of 12 August 1949 *can be constructed as legitimizing or authorizing* any act of aggression or any use of force inconsistent with the Charter of the United Nations". In his study, Quintin

[71] ICRC, *Official working document of the 31st International Conference of the Red Cross and Red Crescent 28 November to 1 December 2011 International Humanitarian Law and challenges of contemporary armed conflicts* (2011), 31IC/11/5.1.2, at 22, available at https://www.icrc.org/en/doc/assets/files/red-cross-crescent-movement/31st-international-conference/31-int-conference-ihl-challenges-report-11-5-1-2-en.pdf (last visited 19 May 2021).

[72] Pothelet, *supra* note 35.

[73] In this sense, the SC recognized that "this is not to say that the Appeals Chamber has determined that any or all of the incidents listed in Annex 2C to the Request would necessarily have the requisite nexus to qualify as war crimes. When the relevant circumstances have been established in the course of an investigation into the situation as whole, the Prosecutor will be in a position to evaluate the applicable law, the significance of the fact that capture is alleged to have taken place outside Afghanistan and whether one or more individual cases fall within the Court's jurisdiction". See Appeals Chamber, *supra* note 14, § 78.

eloquently highlights that "[t]his is precisely what the preamble of AP I aimed to avoid. The principle that *jus in bello* cannot legitimize any illegal use of force under *jus ad bellum* precisely implies that whatever the nature of the rules under IHL, they cannot be used to circumvent the rules of *jus ad bellum*".[74]

4 Conclusions

With 124 States Parties, the preamble of the Rome Statute announces an ambitious and, at the same time, necessary goal: "that the most serious crimes of concern to the international community as a whole must not go unpunished". Externally, the fulfillment of this objective usually crashes with the particular interests of both States Parties and non-State Parties to the Statute alike. Internally, the action of the ICC is constrained by the rules of the Statute. The requirements of jurisdiction establish that a *proprio motu* investigation can only be opened when the alleged crime has taken place in the territory of a State Party or when the person accused is a national of a State Party to the Statute. In addition, in order to distinguish ordinary crimes from war crimes, it requires that the alleged conduct has a 'nexus' with an armed conflict, thus creating a link between IHL and ICL.

The opening of an investigation in Afghanistan proved particularly difficult for the ICC. Apart from the lack of cooperation of States Parties and the sanctions imposed on ICC officials by the US government, the PTC decided that internal constraints impeded the opening of an investigation in the terms requested by the Prosecutor. One of them related to the jurisdiction *ratione loci*, an original issue as it was the first time that an investigation was going to be opened in the territory of a State Party to the Statute where the armed conflict is not taking place. The scholarship defending a restrictive approach to Common Article 3 was used by the PTC to establish that the alleged war crimes whose victims were captured outside Afghanistan are outside its jurisdiction due to the lack of the nexus with the armed conflict, which is required to trigger the application of IHL law as well as the jurisdiction of the ICC.

By contrast, the AC decided to remove the internal obstacle created by the PTC and establish that the 'nexus requirement' has not to be strictly territorial, making use of the previous doctrine and case law in favor of an

[74] Quintin, *supra* note 68, at 19.

expansive interpretation of Common Article 3. Indeed, a contemporary interpretation of this provision shows that a geographically limited interpretation would create a gap in the minimum level of protection offered by this article. This first decision about the geographical scope of the AC will undoubtedly have an enormous impact in future situations, as many of the alleged international crimes are not confined to the borders of a single state. The reports mentioned on the growing use of drones by both state and non-state actors, for instance, show how crimes in the context of armed conflicts are less territorialized every day.

Finally, I have addressed the more than justified concerns about the creation of a 'global battlefield' due to the expansive approach to Common Article 3. While the expansion of the geographical reach of IHL has in fact been used by some states to justify the use of force beyond the territory of the hostilities, the last part of this study shows that the decision of the AC regarding Afghanistan should not be read in this context. As the preamble of AP I clearly establishes, the application of the rules of the *jus in bello* cannot legitimize any illegal use of force under *jus ad bellum*. This conclusion, present in scenarios of violations of IHL committed by states, is even more applicable to cases in which the rules of the *jus ad bellum* are interpreted to determine the ICC's jurisdiction to prosecute war crimes.

CHAPTER 3

Putin on Trial: Personal Immunities Before the International Criminal Court

Ondřej Svaček

1 Introduction

There are not many issues that attract more attention in theory and practice of international law than the issue of personal immunities and their application in proceedings before the International Criminal Court (ICC or Court). This issue became a nightmare for the ICC which had considered it extensively in the *Al-Bashir* case. Even if the saga of a former president of Sudan had already come to its conclusion by the authoritative finding of the Appeals Chamber (ACH),[1] it is hardly possible to say that

[1] Judgment in the Jordan Referral re Al-Bashir Appeal, *The Prosecutor v. Omar Hassan Ahmad Al Bashir*, ICC-02/05-01/09-397, ACH, 6 May 2019 (Judgment).

O. Svaček (✉)
Centre for International Humanitarian and Operational Law, Faculty of Law, Palacký University, Olomouc, Czechia

Faculty of Law, Masaryk University, Brno, Czechia
e-mail: ondrej.svacek@upol.cz

O. Svaček, M. Faix (eds.), *Prosecution of War Crimes before the ICC*, Global Issues, https://doi.org/10.1007/978-3-031-84216-0_3

the question of the applicability of personal immunity in proceedings before the ICC is definitively settled. Quite the contrary, the recent agenda of the Court proves that the issue remains to be "in the line of fire." Enough is to mention the arrest warrant issued against sitting president of the Russian Federation, Vladimir Putin, by the Pre-Trial Chamber (PTCH) II for the war crime of unlawful deportation of population (children) and that of unlawful transfer of population (children) from occupied areas of Ukraine to the Russian Federation under Articles 8(2)(a)(vii) and 8(2)(b)(viii) of the Rome Statute on 17th March 2023. Another test case might be proceedings against the Prime-Minister of Israel, Benjamin Netanyahu.

The aim of this contribution is to analyse available case law of the ICC concerning the applicability of personal immunities in proceedings before it and assess the possible prospect of its usage in recent or eventual future cases before the ICC. The author of this contribution presents critical stance against the conclusion of the ACH adopted in the *Al-Bashir* that personal immunities disappear in the proceedings before the ICC due to the existence of the respective rule of customary international law, which is allegedly codified in Article 27(2) of the Rome Statute. Obviously, the conclusion (whether positive or negative) on the applicability of personal immunities before the ICC has a direct impact on the prosecution of crimes under international law, including war crimes, committed by members of the troika before the ICC itself, but also before any other international criminal tribunals, including those that will eventually be created (e.g. the special ad hoc tribunal for the crime of aggression committed against Ukraine).

1.1 Setting the Stage: Introductory Remarks and Development of the ICC's Position

This contribution builds on the traditional dichotomy between functional and personal immunity. It follows generally acknowledged conclusions that personal immunity represents a procedural obstacle for the prosecution of troika members during their term of office, which encompasses both public and private acts.[2] Personal immunity is absolute in its nature

[2] The contribution considers recent discussion concerning the crime under international law exception from functional immunity, which casts doubt—in the opinion of this author rather artificially—on a character of functional immunity and very definition of crime under international law. *Cf.* O. Svaček, 'Crime of Aggression before Domestic Courts: Some

and therefore is fully applicable in relation to domestic prosecution of crimes under international law what is confirmed, among others, by the referential *Yerodia* case rendered by the International Court of Justice (ICJ).[3] The absolute character is firmly rooted in state practice concerning prosecution at a domestic level, where it represents a bar for any criminal legal action.[4]

The all-embracing character of personal immunity was called into question only in relation to prosecution before international criminal tribunals. The author of this contribution agrees with assessment of R. O'Keefe who differentiates between various international criminal tribunals based on the legal character of their founding international instruments. Accordingly, the denial of such immunities is lawful once a tribunal is established and empowered by the decision of the United Nations Security Council (UN SC), or by the international treaty if—in the latter case—the prosecution concerns state officials of state party to that international treaty.[5]

The crucial question remains how to justify a denial of personal immunities in relation to the third states (i.e. states who are not bound by the respective international treaty) and their officials. Before an assessment of this question, it is firstly suitable to summarize existing case law of the ICC on personal immunities and its development, as provided in the seminal *Al-Bashir* case. Definitively, this case and especially the conclusions of the ACH will be a starting point of any discussion on availability of personal immunities before the ICC, even if—formally speaking—decisions adopted in this case are not binding for any other chamber deciding other cases [see Article 21(2) of the Rome Statute]. Although the PTCH II chose to keep the content of the arrest warrant against Putin secret, it is evident that this decision follows the authority of the ACH's Judgment of 2019.

Contemporary Challenges', 2, *International and Comparative Law Review* (2023), at 111–128.

[3] Judgment, *Arrest Warrant of 11 April 2000 (Democratic Republic of the Congo v. Belgium), I.C.J. Reports 2002. Cf.* also International Law Commission (ILC), Draft Articles on Immunity of State Officials from Foreign Criminal Jurisdiction with commentaries, 2022.

[4] This position remained unchanged even in the light of the ongoing French attempts to prosecute Bashar Al-Assad for crimes against humanity committed in Syria—*cf.* the arrest warrant issued in November 2023 by the Paris Judicial Court (*Tribunal Judiciaire de Paris*), which charged Assad with using prohibited chemical weapons against civilians in the city of Douma and the Eastern Ghouta region in 2013, resulting in the deaths of over 1000 people. This conclusion was upheld also by the Paris Court of Appeal in June 2024.

[5] R. O'Keefe, *International Criminal Law* (Oxford: Oxford University Press, 2015), at 111.

In *Al-Bashir*, the ICC identified four sources or lines of argumentation stripping the former (that time serving) head of state personal immunity: (a) Article 27(2) of the Rome Statute; (b) customary international law [codified in Article 27(2) of the Rome Statute]; (c) the SC resolution 1593 (2005) and the implicit waiver theory; and (d) the SC resolution 1593 (2005) and the analogous position theory.

The first line of reasoning was introduced to case law of the ICC as early as in decisions concerning arrest warrants against Al-Bashir issued in 2009 and 2010.[6] According to this argument, a sitting head of state cannot rely on personal immunity before the ICC, because its applicability before the ICC was excluded by the Rome Statute itself. Article 27(2) of the Statute operates as an *in abstracto* withdrawal of personal immunities. The ICC Statute derogates from the customary international regulation on personal immunities, which is inapplicable once the Statute entered into force.

The argument of customary international law entered the floor one year later. In 2011, the PTCH I responded to Al-Bashir's visits to Malawi and Chad and their failure to comply with cooperation requests to arrest and surrender the Sudanese president to The Hague.[7] Accordingly, the shield of immunity is denied through customary international law that applies not only in proceedings before domestic courts (see *supra*) but also in proceedings before international criminal tribunals, namely the ICC.

In 2014, the ICC's referred to the SC resolution 1593. The PTCH II ruled that "by *issuing Resolution 1593* (2005) [...] *the SC implicitly waived the immunities granted to Omar Al Bashir under international law and attached to his position as a Head of State*."[8] It explained its conclusion with a reference to the obligation of the full cooperation of Sudan with the ICC provided in the SC resolution, whose obligation would be entirely meaningless if personal immunities sustain.

Then, in 2017, in its decision concerning failure of South Africa to cooperate with the ICC, the PTCH II adopted arguments advocated by

[6] Decision, *The Prosecutor v. Omar Hassan Ahmad Al Bashir*, ICC-02/05-01/09-3, PTCH I, 4 March 2009, at 41.

[7] Decision, *The Prosecutor v. Omar Hassan Ahmad Al Bashir*, ICC-02/05-01/09-139, PTCH I, 12 December 2011, and Decision, *The Prosecutor v. Omar Hassan Ahmad Al Bashir*, ICC-02/05-01/09-140, PTCH I, 13 December 2011.

[8] Decision, *The Prosecutor v. Omar Hassan Ahmad Al Bashir*, ICC-02/05-01/09-195, PTCH II, 9 April 2014, at 29.

D. Akande[9] and concluded that the necessary effect of the SC resolution triggering the Court's jurisdiction in the situation in Darfur and imposing on Sudan the obligation to cooperate fully with the Court is that, for the limited purpose of the situation in Darfur, Sudan has rights and duties analogous to those of states parties to the Statute.[10] According to this theory of analogous position, all immunities based on official capacity which could bar the ICC from exercising its jurisdiction have been made inapplicable as a result of the effects of Article 27(2) of the Rome Statute and the SC resolution 1593 (2005).

The Al-Bashir saga was authoritatively solved by the judgement of the ACH rendered in 2019.[11] The ACH confirmed the PTCH II finding that Jordan had failed to comply with its obligation to cooperate with the ICC, but contrary to the PTCH II it did not follow the SC path, but got back to the customary international law argument and ruled that "*there is neither State practice nor opinio juris that would support the existence of Head of State immunity under customary international law vis-à-vis an international court. To the contrary, such immunity has never been recognized in international law as a bar to the jurisdiction of an international court.*"[12] According to the ACH, "*international courts act on behalf of the international community as a whole. Accordingly, the principle par in parem non habet imperium, which is based on the sovereign equality of States, finds no application in relation to an international court such as the International Criminal Court.*"[13]

1.2 Critical Analysis of the ICC's Stance on Personal Immunity

The short summarization of the ICC's case law concerning personal immunities of the third states reveals that it has dramatically evolved. The author of this contribution opines that the ICC's practice is controversial and problematic.

Starting with the Rome Statute and its Article 27(2) as the legal basis for denial of personal immunities, it is evident that this line of reasoning

[9] D. Akande, 'The Legal Nature of Security Council Referrals to the ICC and its Impact on Al Bashir's Immunities', 2 *Journal of International Criminal Justice* (2009), at 342.

[10] Decision, *The Prosecutor v. Omar Hassan Ahmad Al Bashir*, ICC-02/05-01/09-302, 6 July 2017, at 88, 96.

[11] *Cf. supra*, note 1.

[12] *Ibid.*, at 113, 119.

[13] *Ibid.*, at 115.

originally neglected one of the leading principles of the international law of treaties, namely a relative effect of international treaties. According to Article 34 of the Vienna Convention on the Law of Treaties, a treaty does not create obligations or rights for a third state without its consent. Article 27(2) of the Rome Statute operates as an *in abstracto* withdrawal of personal immunities. The ICC Statute derogates from the customary international regulation on personal immunities which is inapplicable once the Statute entered into force. Nevertheless, this derogation concerns state parties to the Rome Statute and states that accepted jurisdiction of the ICC based on Article 12(3) of the Rome Statute (e.g. formerly Ukraine), and without explicit consent it is incapable to produce legal effects towards any third state. This conclusion is now part of the ICC's practice.[14] The treaty-based character of Article 27(2) has also already been employed in proceedings before the ICC given the prosecution of the former (and at the time of prosecution still serving) president of Kenya as state party to the Rome Statute.

Also, the second line of reasoning, based on the UN SC referral, is far from being unproblematic what is evident in relation to the implicit waiver theory. The PTCH II misinterprets the concept of waiver of immunities. Clearly, the SC has no authority to rule on the waiver of immunities held by a different legal person, in that case Sudan, because a waiver of immunities constitutes a unilateral act which is reserved only to an entity possessing these immunities. This position is confirmed also in the work of the International Law Commission (ILC) on unilateral acts of states.[15] Then, even if one accepts that the SC possesses this authority, probably based on Article 103 of the UN Charter, it is necessary to remember the conclusion of the ICJ in the *Nuclear Tests* that a unilateral declaration may have the effect of creating legal obligations only if it is stated in clear and specific terms.[16] This requirement is hardly satisfied by the expansive interpretation

[14] Decision, *The Prosecutor v. Omar Hassan Ahmad Al Bashir*, ICC-02/05-01/09-195, PTCH II, 9 April 2014, at 26. The PTCH II confirmed that the Statute is a multilateral treaty governed by the rules set out in the Vienna Convention on the Law of Treaties, the Statute cannot impose obligations on third states without their consent. Thus, the exception to the exercise of the Court's jurisdiction provided in Article 27(2) of the Statute should, in principle, be confined to those states parties who have accepted it.

[15] ILC, Report of the Commission to the General Assembly on the Work of its 58th Session, A/CN.LASER.AJzoo6/Add.1 (Part 2), at 163, 165.

[16] Judgments, *Nuclear Tests (Australia v. France; New Zealand v. France), I.C.J. Reports 1974*, at 267, § 43, 269, § 51, and 472, § 46, and 474, § 53.

of the obligation of full cooperation as the grounds for the implicit waiver of immunity. Moreover, the ICC has already admitted that its previous argumentation operating with the concept of waiver is not persuasive from the legal perspective, even though it justified its conclusion with a reference to related theory of analogous position.[17]

This latter theory might be evaluated both from internal perspective (with the Rome Statute as a referential framework) and external perspective (with the UN Charter).

From the perspective of the Rome Statute, the mutual relationship between the ICC and the SC is defined explicitly and exhaustively through Article 13 (referral of situation) and Article 16 (deferral of situation). There is no other provision in the Rome Statute describing the position of the SC in proceedings before the ICC, which made a part of scholars to conclude that the SC cannot extend jurisdiction of the ICC.[18] Since disregarding of personal immunity connotes extension of personal jurisdiction, it must be refused. This conclusion can be inferred also from the preparatory work of the Rome Statute, which confirms that any possibilities to subject the ICC to the UN, potentially opening doors for intervention of this body to the work of the ICC, were unequivocally rejected during the Rome negotiations. Therefore, from the perspective of the Rome Statute, any SC resolution referring a situation to the ICC and triggering its mechanism is thus nothing more than exercise of power provided in Article 13 that must respect jurisdictional framework of the ICC, which does not encompass sitting head of the third states.[19]

Another reason to dismiss the denial of personal immunity through the SC resolution presents W. Schabas, who opines that if accepted, this

[17] Decision, *The Prosecutor v. Omar Hassan Ahmad Al Bashir*, ICC-02/05-01/09-302, PTCH II, 6 July 2017, at 96. The PTCH II clarified that, indeed, it sees no such waiver in a Security Council resolution and that, in any case, no such waiver—whether explicit or implicit—would be necessary. A waiver can be conceived of only where immunity applies. However, as explained above, all immunities based on official capacity which could bar the Court from exercising its jurisdiction have been made inapplicable as a result of the effects of Article 27(2) of the Statute and Security Council Resolution 1593 (2005).

[18] L. Condorelli, S. Villalpando, 'Can the Security Council Extend the ICC's Jurisdiction?', in A. Cassese *et al.* (eds.), *The Rome Statute of the International Criminal Court: A Commentary* (Oxford: Oxford University Press, 2002), at 573.

[19] O. Svaček, 'Al-Bashir and the ICC—Tag, Hide-and-Seek ... or Rather Blind Man's Bluff?', in P. Šturma (ed.), *The Rome Statute of the ICC at its Twentieth Anniversary (Achievements and Perspectives)* (Leiden: Brill, 2019), at 182.

approach bifurcates the jurisdictional régime of the ICC.[20] He continues that under no circumstances can a state party referral or the Prosecutor acting *proprio motu* remove personal immunities and stresses out the same regime must be observed when the situation is referred by the SC. Schabas concludes that

> *There is a little dispute that under the Statute the Security Council is without authority to add new crimes, or alter the temporal jurisdiction of the Court, or lower the age of criminal responsibility* [...] [w]*hy then should it have the power to make article 27(2) applicable when it is otherwise inapplicable?*[21]

All these considerations substantiate the conclusion that under the Rome Statute, the theory of the analogous position induced by the SC referral is not an available option.

The external evaluation may potentially produce different results. The idea of the analogous position theory—as already mentioned—presupposes the power of the SC to displace personal immunity and other rules of treaty or customary international law based on Article 25 and Article 103 of the UN Charter. Once the situation is referred to the ICC by the SC, the third State gets into the analogous position with the State Party what makes Article 27(2) of the Rome Statute applicable. Accordingly, any state and the ICC have a right to disregard personal immunity of that third state's troika members they are otherwise obliged to accord under customary international law.

The crucial issue how clear the wording of the SC resolution must be to induce the removal of immunity. Similarly to the previous implicit waiver theory, even the analogous position theory accepts that the SC can remove personal immunity by implication, nevertheless this outcome would not be result of the unilateral act of waiver (see *supra*), but rather a product of conflict between international obligations that would be solved through the supremacy clause (Article 103 of the UN Charter) in favour of disregarding of personal immunity.

This issue was much contested during the proceedings before the ACH in the *Al-Bashir*.[22] According to T. de Sousa Diaz, "*the requirement that*

[20] W. Schabas, *The International Criminal Court: A Commentary on the Rome Statute* (Oxford: Oxford University Press, 2016), at 604.

[21] *Ibid*.

[22] For positions of participants *cf*. T. de Sousa Diaz, 'The 'Security Council Route' to the Derogation from Personal Head of State Immunity in the Al-Bashir Case: How Explicit must

the SC adopt explicit language when derogating from existing treaty or customary obligations only seems to arise in the context of human rights."[23] This conclusion is derived from *Al-Jedda v. the UK*, where the European Court of Human Rights (ECHR) famously ruled that in interpreting its resolutions, there must be a presumption that the SC does not intend to impose any obligation on member states to breach fundamental principles of human rights. In the event of any ambiguity in the terms of a SC resolution, the ECHR must therefore choose the interpretation which is most in harmony with the requirements of the European Convention on Human Rights (European Convention) and which avoids any conflict of obligations.[24] Given the existence of Article 21(3) of the Rome Statute, this interpretation must be cautiously considered also in the proceedings before the ICC.

Diaz then mentions that explicit or express wording is not required for derogations by the SC from pre-existing international law, but only a clear enough intention to do so. He refers to a remark of C. Kress in the context of the use of force, where the authorization by the SC to use all necessary means has been clearly understood to refer to the use of military force. Therefore, he accepts that removal of immunity might be implicit and derived from the obligation of full cooperation (in that case) of Sudan with the ICC given the constant use of constructive ambiguity in the practice of the SC.[25]

In the opinion of this author, there is nevertheless one point in this discussion that militates in favour of the requirement of explicit wording as a basis for denial of personal immunity through a SC resolution. All these doubts and disagreements (and a clash between arguments in support or against) have significant legal consequences: according to the principle in *dubio pro reo*, arising from the principle *nullum crimen sine lege stricta* contained in Article 22 of the Statute, and among others in Article 7 of the European Convention, in case of doubt an interpretation favouring a perpetrator must be adopted. An objection might be raised that this

Security Council Resolutions be?' in *EJIL: Talk!*, 19 September 2018, available at: https://www.ejiltalk.org/the-discussion-of-the-security-council-roots-to-the-derogation-from-personal-immunities-in-the-al-bashir-case-how-explicit-must-security-council-resolutions-be/ (last visited 13 October 2024).

[23] *Ibid.*

[24] Judgment, ECHR, *Al-Jedda v. the United Kingdom*, appl. no. 27021/08, Grand Chamber, 7 July 2011, at 102.

[25] T. de Sousa Diaz, *supra* note.

principle can be employed only with respect to the interpretation of elements of crimes under international law; nevertheless, its range has the potential to also cover the jurisdictional ambit of the ICC.[26] Once a SC resolution is used as a source of law in international criminal proceedings, its application must conform to rules of interpretation standardly required in relation to any other source of international criminal law. The author of this text believes that to come up with these requirements, the explicit language must be used in the text of a SC resolution.

The last source to be discussed here for the removal of personal immunity is customary international law. Here, the crucial question is whether any such a rule disregarding personal immunity in proceedings before international tribunals exists?

The first problematic issue in the ACH's Judgment concerns the reversal of the burden of proof in its methodology of identification of customary international law. The ACH concluded that there is neither state practice nor *opinio juris* that would support the existence of head of state immunity under customary law *vis-à-vis* an international court. According to the ACH, the starting position in this discussion is zero immunity, what is far from evident. Quite the contrary, if this ruling is accepted, the question remains what is the function of Article 27(2) of the Rome Statute? This chapter already explained that this provision serves the purpose of *in abstracto* and *ex ante* waiver of personal immunities that would be otherwise applicable even in the proceedings before the ICC. If there is no personal immunity at all, as the ACH contends, this provision is simply meaningless what is not compatible with the principle of effective interpretation of international treaties.

The more proper methodological approach would therefore presuppose identification of an exception to personal immunity before international courts in the practice of states. This practice is very scarce now. Although the majority did not find it necessary to prove the existence of state practice showing an exception to personal immunity, the separate opinion gave some examples that are unfortunately not very persuasive.[27] In their analysis of the development of the international norm rejecting immunity before international tribunals, concurring judges refer among

[26] *Situation in Kenya*, Dissenting Opinion of Judge Hans-Peter Kaul, ICC-01/09-19, 31 March 2010, at 30.

[27] Joint Concurring Opinion of Judge Eboe-Osuji, Morrison, Hofmański and Bossa, *The Prosecutor v. Omar Hassan Ahmad Al Bashir*, ICC-02/05-01/09-397-Anx1.

else to example of Kaiser Willem II of Hohenzolern, trial of Karl Dönitz, Hideki Tojo, Slobodan Milosević, Jean Kambanda, and Charles Taylor.[28] All these examples are nevertheless problematic as they refer to functional immunity (Willem II, Dönitz, Tojo, Kambanda) or originate from different international legal background where the inapplicability of personal immunity was widely accepted (Milosević and his prosecution before the International Criminal Tribunal for the Former Yugoslavia as a tribunal established by the SC resolution).[29] The only case capable to be perceived as a precedent is the *Taylor* case. A closer look at the reasoning of the ACH of the Special Court for Sierra Leone (SCSL) reveals that the conclusion on denial of personal immunity is substantiated by the mere assertion that the SCSL is an international court.[30] Nevertheless, the SCSL ignored the fact that the legal basis for its creation rests in the bilateral international treaty between Sierra Leone and the UN and therefore cannot produce effect towards any third state (Liberia).[31]

Another problematic aspect concerns the ACH's conclusion that international courts act on behalf of the international community what makes—simply put—immunity inapplicable before the ICC. This contention opens floodgate and brings about plenty of controversial issues. Firstly, strictly speaking, from the legal perspective, there is nothing like *ius puniendi* of international community.[32] It is hardly something else than a wishful thinking of academics or a theoretical construction that is often employed for theoretical explanation of exercise of domestic jurisdiction over crimes under international law based on the principle of universality. It is difficult to sustain that states can do collectively (as an international community) what none of them could do singly (*nemo plus iuris ad alium transfere potest quam ipse habet*). There is hardly any debate that, e.g., the Czech Republic cannot prosecute Putin while he is in office. The same holds true if it initiates the adoption of a special international treaty establishing *ad hoc* tribunal. Why should the ICC, as a potentially universal international criminal body, established by the international treaty, the Rome Statute, benefit from more favourable treatment? And who then

[28] *Ibid*., At 77, 128, 158, 162, 166

[29] See *supra*, note 5.

[30] Decision, *Charles Ghankay Taylor*, SCSL-2003-01-I, ACH, 31 May 2004, at 52.

[31] The decision was criticized by scholars—*cf.* K. Novotná, *Head of state Immunity in International Law: The Charles Taylor Case before the Special Court for Sierra Leone* (Brno: Masaryk University 2013).

[32] *Cf.* position of O'Keefe before the ACH in *re Al-Bashir*—Judgment, at 84.

defines the moment which has norm-generating effect? Or to put it differently: who decides what numbers are sufficient to establish an international tribunal of a different quality which can transgress limits (relative effect) inherent in its founding document, an international treaty as a primary source of particular international law? All these questions are difficult to respond to in a satisfactory manner in legal terms and therefore should not be admitted in any criminal proceedings at all, since they potentially leave too much leeway for arbitrariness.

The conclusion of the ACH can be thus accepted only if one accepts a deductive (value-based) approach to the formation of customary international law, which is prospective and based on emerging values and interests which were considered only insufficiently in the pre-existing legal balance. The deductive approach does not look back and does not necessarily require a consistent pattern of previous practice. Quite the contrary, inductive or traditional method for identification of customary international law is based on the assumption that to determine the existence and content of a rule of customary international law, it is necessary to ascertain whether there is a general practice (*usus*) that is accepted as law (*opinio iuris*).[33] The latter approach is accepted both in the practice of the ICJ[34] and the ILC.[35] It is therefore the preferable option also for this author who subscribes under the ICJ's opinion that that presence of customary rules "*can be tested by induction based on the analysis of a sufficiently extensive and convincing practice, and not by deduction from preconceived ideas.*"[36]

1.3 Possible Prospects: Immunity of Third-Party State Officials

Under existing circumstances, any discussion concerning the possibility of denial of personal immunity of V. Putin in the proceedings before the ICC must focus on the customary international law argument. The

[33] Both approaches are well described here: E. Cannizzaro, 'Customary International Law on the Use of Force: Inductive Approach v. Value-Oriented Approach', in: E. Cannizzaro, P. Palchetti, *Customary International Law on the Use of Force: Methodological Approach* (Brill: Leiden, 2005), at. 248.

[34] Judgment, *Military and Paramilitary Activities in and against Nicaragua (Nicaragua v. United States of America), I.C.J. Reports 1986*, at 109, § 207.

[35] ILC, Report of the ILC, 68th session, A/71/10, at 84.

[36] Judgment, *Delimitation of the Maritime Boundary in the Gulf of Maine Area*, I.C.J. Reports 1984, at 299, § 111.

treaty-based avenue for disregarding the immunity has already been relinquished by the ICC itself. The possibility of the ICC to refer the situation of Russia to the ICC is unrealistic. If only Russia stop blocking any such initiative, it means that Putin is removed from power and therefore is no more a beneficiary of personal immunity.

The author of this contribution argues that as for now, the rule of customary international law that would preclude the application of personal immunity in proceedings before the ICC simply does not yet exist. The development of such exception to personal immunity before international courts is nevertheless possible, but—in accordance with the preferred inductive approach to formation of customary international law—must be firmly rooted in the existing practice of states. For sure, the content of international law may shift. As pointed out by the Dutch Advisory Committee on Public International Law, "*States' thirst for international accountability, possibly triggered by Russia's blatant violation of international law, may well translate into explicit support for a norm on the irrelevance of personal immunity before international criminal tribunals.*"[37]

The development of this rule—under an idealistic scenario—might be induced no less than by one single "brave" state that would arrest Putin (e.g. South Africa during a rumoured Putin's attendance of the BRICS summit in 2023). If other states, in the next step, express their opinion in sufficient and representative numbers that the Russian president, as the most responsible Russian official, must be put on trial even if he holds office, the rule of customary international law might be dynamically established. Such scenario, though idealistic, would be compatible with rules on creation of customary international law. Enough is to mention that even verbatim acts can be counted as practice,[38] a passage of even a short period of time would not in itself be bar for creation of the respective rule on denial of personal immunity either.[39] This ICJ's dictum is reflected also in the Draft Conclusions on Identification of Customary International Law (2018), which confirms that once the practice is general, no particular duration is required.

[37] R. van Alebeek *et al.*, 'Prosecuting Russian Officials for the Crime of Aggression: What About Immunities?' 4, *European Convention on Human Rights Law Review* (2022), at 128.

[38] *Cf.* ILC, Draft Conclusions on Identification of Customary International Law with commentaries, 2018, Conclusion 6 (1).

[39] Judgment, *North Sea Continental Shelf, I.C.J. Reports 1969*, at 43, § 74.

Then, the denial of personal immunity might be eventually justified by an application of circumstances precluding wrongfulness.[40] The ICC can eventually assert that exercise of jurisdiction in relation to the serving head of the third state is illegal but justified by self-defence.[41] It means that an aggressor state (Russia) cannot require the full respect of its sovereign rights *vis-à-vis* its act of aggression and must stand in interference into these rights, among else through exercise of jurisdiction over its head of state. The argument would follow that the disregarding of personal immunity in proceedings before the ICC might be said to be related to breach of customary international law on the prohibition of the use of force.

The inherent problem of this approach nevertheless lies in the fact that all conditions for the lawful exercise of self-defence must have been satisfied. Especially troubling would be the fulfilment of *ratione temporis* elements which broadly speaking dictate that once the armed attack is over, any defensive response must also be stopped.[42] According to J. A. Green, "*when the measures taken either by the Security Council, the victim state, or both have suitably resolved the situation, then any individual self-defence action must end.*"[43] It would be possible to argue that the post-conflict situation has not been suitably resolved—and therefore it would be possible to continue with a prosecution based on removal of immunity (once they are still available)—until settlement of territorial claims.[44] The mandate to exercise self-defence might therefore continue even after cessation of the armed attack by the aggressor state. The requirements of the victim state might be even broader and include reparations for war damages or repatriation of population transferred to territory of the aggressor state. If, for example, the victim state would seek to restore *status quo ante bellum*, any prosecution of the sitting head of the third state would remain intact.

[40] O. Svaček, *supra*, note 2, at 124–125. The author used this argument for possible justification of exercise of universal jurisdiction for prosecution of the crime of aggression before domestic courts.

[41] ILC, Draft Articles on the Responsibility of States for Internationally Wrongful Acts with commentaries, 2001, at 74, § 2. According to the ILC, self-defence may justify non-performance of certain obligations other than that under Article 2(4) of the Charter of the United Nations, provided that such non-performance is related to the breach of that provision. *Cf.* O. Corten, Olivier, V. Koutroulis, *Tribunal for the crime of aggression against Ukraine—a legal assessment* (Brussels, EU, 2022), at 29.

[42] J. A. Green, 'The ratione temporis elements of self-defense' 1, *Journal on the Use of Force and International Law* (2015), at 111.

[43] *Ibid.*, at 113.

[44] *Ibid.*

This mandate would nevertheless cease at the moment, when the victim state reaches settlement of territorial claims that satisfies its requirements. Consequently, any ongoing prosecution justified by self-defence must have been stopped at that moment.

Finally, there are also related conceptual issues to be solved. The applicability of this line of argumentations presupposes that concept of self-defence, firmly rooted in inter-state practice, is transferred to relations as between state and international organization, here the ICC.[45] The ILC accepted this position already in 2011 in the project concerning responsibility of international organizations. According to Article 21 of Draft Articles on the Responsibility of International Organizations for Internationally Wrongful Acts (DARIO), the wrongfulness of an act of an international organization is precluded if and to the extent that the act constitutes a lawful measure of self-defence under international law. The ILC stressed that "*for reasons of coherency, the concept of self- defence which has thus been elaborated with regard to States should be used also with regard to international organizations, although it is likely to be relevant for precluding wrongfulness only of acts of a small number of organizations.*"[46] The commentary of DARIO reveals that the ILC approached the act of self-defence to be primarily a military measure, what would limit its applicability only towards international organizations with mandate in the area of the use of force (e.g. the UN or regional organizations like NATO, the European Union, or the African Union). Nevertheless, if non-military measures justified by the self-defence are considered, the potential range of international organizations that would employ collective self-defence as the circumstance precluding wrongfulness of their conduct might increase, encompassing also the ICC.

The overlap between self-defence as an instrument stemming from the law of state or international organizations responsibility and prosecution of crimes under international law would be also an important point of contact as between state/international organization responsibility and responsibility of individual in international law.[47] It would be then difficult to sustain an argument that state/international organization responsibility

[45] The ICC is considered here as an international organization. *Cf.* S. R. Lüder, 'The legal nature of the International Criminal Court and the emergence of supranational elements in international criminal justice' 845, *International Review of the Red Cross* (2002), at 91.

[46] ILC, DARIO with commentaries, 2011, at 71, § 2.

[47] Judgment, *Application of the Convention on the Prevention and Punishmentof the Crime of Genocide (Bosnia and Herzegovina* v. *Serbia and Montenegro), Judgment, I.C.J. Reports*

on the one hand and responsibility of individual on the other are completely separated concepts.[48]

2 Conclusion

This contribution analysed available case law of the ICC on personal immunities in proceedings before it and assessed the possible prospect of its usage in recent or eventual future cases before the ICC, and eventually also before other international criminal body potentially to be established in future (especially the ad hoc tribunal for the crime of aggression against Ukraine). The author of this contribution presented critical stance against the conclusion of the ACH adopted in *Al-Bashir* that personal immunities disappear in the proceedings before the ICC due to existence of the respective rule of customary international law, which is allegedly codified in Article 27(2) of the Rome Statute. This contribution stressed out lack of practice, as a legal ingredient for creation of any rule of customary international law. It rejected the possible subsidiary argument that rules of customary international law concerning the disregarding of personal immunity before the ICC can be tested through deduction. Concerning the Rome Statute itself [Article 27(2)], the author emphasized its relative effect which precludes its applicability towards the third states. Last but not least, the text assessed possible SC avenue for denial of personal immunity, which is clearly unavailable in the Russian situation at the moment, and recommended that stripping personal immunities in a SC resolution should be made expressly, and not implicitly; otherwise the proceedings takes the chance that it will not be compatible with internationally recognized standards of human rights, incorporated into proceedings before the ICC through Article 21(3) of the Rome Statute. With respect to prospects, the argument was submitted that removal of personal immunity of the sitting head of the third states may be derived from dynamic (but still inductive) creation of customary international law or eventually in relation to Russia—with all its flaws and drawbacks—from the use of non-military measures of self-defence adopted in response to the act of aggression against Ukraine.

2007, at 116, § 173. The ICJ observed that that duality of responsibility continues to be a constant feature of international law

[48] *Cf.* B. Bonafé, *The Relationship between State and Individual Responsibility for International Crimes* (Leiden: Brill, 2009), at 63.

In conclusion, the final contemplation might be presented: any cathedral must be built on stable structures; otherwise, it risks its own collapse. The ICC is not an exception. Too eager stance may undermine its own legitimacy and credibility, which would be an unwanted outcome for anybody who is rooting for international criminal justice.

CHAPTER 4

The Principle of Complementarity

Milan Lipovský

1 Introduction

The principle of complementarity is often mentioned as one of the cornerstones or underlying principles of the system of the International Criminal Court (ICC or the Court).[1] Its purpose is not only to decrease the possible overburdening of the ICC (because the Court was never intended to investigate and prosecute all crimes under international law occurring in the world), but it is also an embodiment of the obligation of states to investigate and prosecute crimes under international law themselves and a

[1] For example, W. Schabas and M. El Zeidy, 'Art. 17. Issues of admissibility,' in K. Ambos (ed.), *Rome Statute of the International Criminal Court. Article-by-Article Commentary* (Munich/Oxford/Baden-Baden: Beck/Hart/Nomos, 2022) at 949; P. Wrange, 'The crime of aggression, domestic prosecutions and complementarity,' in C. Kreß and S. Barriga (eds), *The Crime of aggression: A commentary Vol. 1* (Cambridge: Cambridge University Press, 2017) at 730.

M. Lipovský (✉)
Department of International Law, Faculty of Law, Charles University, Prague, Czech Republic
e-mail: lipovsky@prf.cuni.cz

O. Svaček, M. Faix (eds.), *Prosecution of War Crimes before the ICC*, Global Issues, https://doi.org/10.1007/978-3-031-84216-0_4

reflection of primacy of domestic proceedings[2]; only if states are not genuine in their activities (unwilling or unable to do so), will the ICC step in as a complementary procedural mechanism.[3] Unlike in the previous international criminal tribunals (especially the ICTY and ICTR) where the relationship between the domestic and international levels was solved to the advantage of the international level and based on primacy of the tribunals over domestic courts, the principle of complementarity of the ICC theoretically favours domestic procedural mechanisms. Theoretically, it should be highlighted, though, as some of the interpretations and ways of application of the applicable law under the Rome Statute (RS or the Statute)[4] may be doubted to entirely respect this primacy of domestic jurisdictions.

Assessing complementarity is not an easy task because it 'is not static, it must necessarily remain dynamic, attuned to the changing landscape at the national level and the possibility that the factor underpinning an

[2] Rome Statute's preamble mentions 'duty of every state to exercise its criminal jurisdiction over those responsible for international crimes.' The Court also pointed out that '[t]he Chamber must [...] stress that the complementarity principle, as enshrined in the Statute, strikes a balance between safeguarding the primacy of domestic proceedings vis-à-vis the International Criminal Court on the one hand, and the goal of the Rome Statute to "put an end to impunity" [footnote omitted] on the other hand.' Judgment on the Appeal of Mr. Germain Katanga against the Oral Decision of Trial Chamber II of 12 June 2009 on the Admissibility of the Case, *Prosecutor v. German Katanga and Mathieu Ngudjolo Chui* (ICC-01/04-01/07-1497), Appeals Chamber, 25 September 2009, § 85. Similarly, Judgment on the appeal of the Republic of Kenya against the decision of Pre-Trial Chamber II of 30 May 2011 entitled "Decision on the Application by the Government of Kenya Challenging the Admissibility of the Case Pursuant to Article 19(2)(b) of the Statute," *Prosecutor v. William Samoei Ruto, Henry Kiprono Kosgey and Joshua Arap Sang* (ICC-01/09-01/11-307), Appeals Chamber, 30 August 2011, § 37. Doctrine also addressed the issue and even challenged the terminology. For example, '[R]ather than being truly "complementary" to national criminal jurisdiction, the Court's jurisdiction can be trumped by it.' R. O'Keefe, *International Criminal Law* (Oxford: Oxford University Press, 2015) at 554.

[3] In fact, in ideal world, if states always fulfilled their obligations, the ICC would not have any cases admissible before it. 'Thus, if States fulfil their obligations under international law by exercising effective jurisdiction over the crimes set out in the Rome Statute, then the Court, recognizing the primacy of national jurisdictions explicitly provided for in the Statute, will not be seized of any cases. [footnote omitted]' J. T. Holmes, 'Complementarity: National Courts versus the ICC,' in A. Cassese, P. Gaeta and J.R.W.D. Jones (eds), *The Rome Statute of the International Criminal Court: A Commentary Vol. I* (Oxford: Oxford University Press, 2002) at 667.

[4] Rome Statute of the International Criminal Court (adopted 17 July 1998, entered into force 1 July 2002), 2187 UNTS 90 (hereafter RS, or the Rome Statute).

admissibility assessment may change over time.'[5] Thus, the following pages are dedicated to commenting upon the principle as it stands now, but it may evolve further soon.[6]

When the Rome Statute was negotiated, embedding the principle of complementarity into the ICC applicable law[7] was in fact considered so important that without it, the negotiated treaty might now have been adopted.[8] Exercising judicial powers is indeed one of the sovereign rights of states and it is unfortunately sometimes highly political because crimes under international law draw a lot of attention. Thus, the importance of the principle of complementarity for the functioning of the ICC can hardly be overstated.

Considering the importance, it is interesting how rarely the RS mentions complementarity. Following its brief reference in the preamble[9] and Art. 1,[10] the Rome Statute describes the basic framework of the principle of complementarity in Art. 17 (and the procedural issues in Arts. 18 and 19, together with the *ne bis in idem* in Art. 20) within the regulation of issues of admissibility where complementarity clearly dominates but is not called so.

Admissibility is a procedural mechanism that may prevent a judicial mechanism from exercising its otherwise existing jurisdiction. Art. 17(1)(a)–(d) RS states that there are four reasons for the ICC to determine that a case is inadmissible:

(a) The case is being investigated or prosecuted by a state which has jurisdiction over it, unless the state is unwilling or unable genuinely to carry out the investigation or prosecution;

[5] The Office of the Prosecutor of the ICC, *Draft: Policy on Complementarity and Cooperation* (2023), para. 148, available at https://www.icc-cpi.int/sites/default/files/2023-10/DRAFT-Complementarity-and-Cooperation-Policy-Paper_September-2023%20%281%29.pdf (last visited 11 October 2024).

[6] As evidenced, e.g., by claims about "return of positive complementarity." See K. Ambos, 'The return of "positive complementarity",' EJIL:Talk!, 3 November 2021, available at https://www.ejiltalk.org/the-return-of-positive-complementarity/ (last visited 11 October 2024).

[7] Rome Statute, *supra* note 4, Art. 21.

[8] W. Schabas, *The International Criminal Court: A Commentary on the Rome Statute* (1st edn., Oxford: Oxford University Press, 2010) at 336.

[9] 'Emphasizing that the International Criminal Court established under this Statute shall be complementary to national criminal jurisdictions.'

[10] '[ICC] shall be complementary to national criminal jurisdictions.'

(b) The case has been investigated by a state which has jurisdiction over it and the state has decided not to prosecute the person concerned, unless the decision resulted from the unwillingness or inability of the state genuinely to prosecute;
(c) The person concerned has already been tried for conduct which is the subject of the complaint, and a trial by the Court is not permitted under article 20, paragraph 3;
(d) The case is not of sufficient gravity to justify further action by the Court.

Except for the preamble and Art. 1, the RS does not mention the word complementary/-ity, nor in Arts. 17–20.[11] As a result, it was left for doctrine and case law to clarify the issue. The fourth reason stipulated in Art. 17(1)(d) RS concerns the threshold of sufficient gravity and is thus of no concern for the principle of complementarity. The first two reasons are without doubt the core of complementarity. Regarding the third reason regulated in letter (c) and dealing with the matter of *ne bis in idem*, there are varying opinions. Some authors distinguish it from the complementarity principle[12] and classify it as a reason for inadmissibility on its own, while others place it among the complementarity regime.[13] While it must be admitted that there are differences between the first two and the third reasons, it should also be kept in mind that they are all basically focusing at a conflict of jurisdiction. For this very reason, the author of this chapter deals with *ne bis in idem* as one of the reasons for inadmissibility related to the principle of complementarity.

Consequently, as can be seen, the principle of complementarity basically aims to solve possible conflicts of jurisdictions. Thus, its purpose is to regulate the preference of the competent body to deal with a case where there are more than one judicial body available. The conflict of jurisdictions may occur both on the horizontal (e.g., between two or more domestic bodies) as well as on vertical levels (e.g., where there is an

[11] It may be explained also by the fact that the term complementarity 'was adopted informally by the negotiators of the ICC Statute – and then by scholars writing about the ICC in commentaries.' M. Bergsmo and P. Webb, 'International Criminal Courts and Tribunals, Complementarity and Jurisdiction,' in R. Wolfrum (ed.), *The Max Planck Encyclopedia of Public International Law. Vol. V* (Oxford: Oxford University Press, 2012) para. 12.

[12] O. Svaček, *Mezinárodní trestní soud (2005–2017)* [International Criminal Court (2005–2017)] (Prague: C. H. Beck, 2017) at 48.

[13] Wrange, *supra* note 1, at 731; Schabas and El Zeidy, *supra* note 1, at 957.

international as well as domestic body entitled to exercise jurisdiction). The complementarity-related admissibility issues of Art. 17 belong among the solutions of vertical-level conflicts of jurisdictions as, for example, the preamble of the RS confirms by stating the complementary nature of the ICC towards the national criminal jurisdictions.

It should be stressed however that none of the three inadmissibility grounds based on the principle of complementarity limit the conflict of jurisdictions of the ICC with RS state parties only. Letters (a) and (b) mention 'a state which has jurisdiction' and letter (c) (and Art. 20(3) RS) talk about the person already having been tried by another court. Thus, the principle of complementarity is applicable to a conflict of jurisdictions with respect to state parties of the Rome Statute as well as to non-state parties. When it comes to the crimes under international law, states are entitled to exercise universal jurisdiction. Thus, even a state different from "territory of the crime" as well as state not related to the suspects by link of nationality may claim to investigate and prosecute the crimes.[14] Hence, the formulation that is also a logical consequence of the fact that even the United Nations Security Council can refer to the ICC a situation otherwise outside of its jurisdictional limits *ratione loci* and *ratione personae*[15] and that a non-state party can also accept jurisdiction of the ICC.[16]

2 In-built Contradiction

Before continuing, it should be stressed that while the principle of complementarity is considered as one of the cornerstones of the system of the ICC, it may under certain circumstances also present a significant (political) problem for the Court.

The principle is built among others upon the notion of unwillingness or inability of a state to genuinely carry out proceedings[17] for crimes under international law.[18] On the one hand, the Court is supposed to decide that

[14] For the universal jurisdiction and the crime of genocide, see, e.g., M. Lipovský, 'Universal Jurisdiction and the Crime of Genocide,' in P. Šturma and M. Lipovský (eds), *The Crime of Genocide: Then and Now. Evolution of a Crime* (Leiden/Boston: Martinus Nijhoff, 2022).

[15] Rome Statute, *supra* note 4, Art. 13(b) and Art. 12(2) *a contrario*.

[16] Rome Statute, *supra* note 4, Art. 12(3).

[17] For the purposes of this chapter, term proceedings are understood as encompassing every stage of criminal proceedings, i.e. including investigation and prosecution.

[18] See Rome Statute, *supra* note 4, Arts. 17(1)(a)–(b) and 20(3) that repeat the elements of unwillingness in Art. 17(2)(a) and (c).

a state did not sufficiently fulfil its obligations under international law to investigate and prosecute crimes under international law. On the other, due to the fact that the Court is a giant without arms and legs—meaning that it does not have its own forces to enforce decisions—it relies on cooperation with the states,[19] including the one whose unwillingness and/or inability the Court decided upon. The contradiction between the need to embarrass a state and at the same time rely on its cooperation in areas such as providing evidence, may cause significant troubles.

On the other hand, as will be seen bellow, fulfilling the complementarity conditions is not always related to the unwillingness to investigate or prosecute by the domestic authorities and even when it is, the cooperation of states is an obligation under the Statute, regardless of the negative perception of the decision regarding complementarity.

3 The Stages of Deciding Upon Inadmissibility

When deciding upon inadmissibility on complementarity grounds, the Court first addresses whether any proceedings are actually taking place or have taken place, or whether the person has already been tried (see the text of Art. 17(1)(a)–(c) RS). The first step is called the action/inaction analysis.[20] And only if the Court finds that the proceedings are ongoing, took place followed by a decision not to prosecute, or that the person has been tried, then it continues to the second stage (genuineness analysis) where it assesses whether the decision or proceedings are/were compliant with a genuine willingness and ability to investigate and/or prosecute.[21]

This kind of division of decision-making upon admissibility into various stages has been already repeatedly referred to by the ICC in several cases

[19] Entire Part 9 of the RS is called International Cooperation and Judicial Assistance.

[20] *Draft: Policy on Complementarity and Cooperation*, *supra* note 5, para. 129.

[21] *Katanga and Ngudjolo Chui* (Judgment on the Appeal of Mr. Germain Katanga against the Oral Decision of Trial Chamber II of 12 June 2009 on the Admissibility of the Case), *supra* note 2, § 78; as well as, e.g., *Ruto, Kosgey and Sang* (Judgment on the appeal of the Republic of Kenya against the decision of Pre-Trial Chamber II of 30 May 2011 entitled "Decision on the Application by the Government of Kenya Challenging the Admissibility of the Case Pursuant to Article 19(2)(b) of the Statute," *supra* note 2, § 41; Judgment on the appeal of Mr. Jean-Pierre Bemba Gombo against the decision of Trial Chamber III of 24 June 2010 entitled "Decision on the Admissibility and Abuse of Process Challenges," *Prosecutor v. Jean-Pierre Bemba Gombo* (ICC-01/05-01/08-962), Appeals Chamber, 19 October 2010, §§ 107–108. It is confirmed by the Prosecutor in *Draft: Policy on Complementarity and Cooperation*, *supra* note 5, para. 129.

and can thus be considered as a persuasively established interpretation of the law.[22] Although it is not supported by the explicit textual interpretation of the Statute, it also in fact allows the ICC to avoid several otherwise possible interpretations of the Rome Statute that would lead to absurd results.

The first one concerns inaction of the state having jurisdiction and is based upon the idea that without division of the stages of decision-making upon inadmissibility, if unwillingness and inability (second stage) had to be taken into account during the first stage in case of complete inaction[23]/inactivity[24] of a state, i.e., in situation of lack of any investigation or prosecution, the claimed theoretical willingness and ability of the state having jurisdiction would be a ground for inadmissibility of the case in front of the ICC. Such interpretation would possibly allow states to reach impunity for perpetrators of crimes under international law.[25] This problem is

[22] K. Urbanová, 'The International Criminal Court Principle of Complementarity in Practice and the Situation in Colombia,' in O. de Frouville and P. Šturma (eds), *Vers la Pénalisation du Droit International des Droits de l'Homme?* (Paris: Editions A. Pedone, 2022) at 34.

[23] It was called inaction e.g., in Judgment on the appeal of Côte d'Ivoire against the decision of Pre-Trial Chamber I of 11 December 2014 entitled "Decision on Côte d'Ivoire's challenge to the admissibility of the case against Simone Gbagbo," *Prosecutor v. Simone Gbagbo* (ICC-02/11-01/12-75-Red), Appeals Chamber, 27 May 2015, § 30.

[24] It was called inactivity e.g., in Judgment on Mr. Yekatom's appeal against Trial Chamber V's "Decision on the Yekatom Defence's Admissibility Challenge," *Prosecutor v. Alfred Yekatom and Patrice-Edouard Ngaïssona* (ICC-01/14-01/18-678-Red), Appeals Chamber, 11 February 2021, § 47.

[25] Appeals Chamber elaborated that 'the Court would be unable to exercise its jurisdiction over a case as long as the State is theoretically willing and able to investigate and to prosecute the case, even though that State has no intention of doing so.' *Katanga and Ngudjolo Chui* (Judgment on the Appeal of Mr. Germain Katanga against the Oral Decision of Trial Chamber II of 12 June 2009 on the Admissibility of the Case, *supra* note 2, § 79). The effects of theoretical willingness (and ability) could however be to certain extent limited by unjustified delays grounds of unwillingness under Art. 17(2)(b) RS that would result from it. Since the burden of proof for inadmissibility rests with the challenging party (Decision on the 'Admissibility Challenge by Dr. Saif Al-Islam Gadafi pursuant to Articles 17(1)(c), 19, and 20(3) of the Rome Statute,' *Prosecutor v. Saif Al-Islam Gaddafi* (ICC-01/11-01/11-662), Pre-Trial Chamber I, 5 April 2019, § 32); Decision on the Admissibility and Abuse of Process Challenges, *Prosecutor v. Jean-Pierre Bemba Gombo* (ICC-01/05-01/08-802), Trial Chamber III, 24 June 2010, § 201), should the theoretically willing and able state wish to challenge admissibility of a case in front of the ICC, it would have to 'provide the Court with evidence of a sufficient degree of specificity and probative value that demonstrates that [the state] is indeed investigating the case. It is not sufficient merely to assert that investigations

however avoided by interpretation of the Rome Statute in the lines where inaction is considered in the first stage, while unwillingness and inability are not considered yet. Thus, in case of domestic inaction, the case is directly admissible before the ICC[26] because already in the first stage, it is clear that the case is admissible and there is no need to continue to the second one. As it was stated above, the second stage is only approached if the answer to the first question (whether any proceedings/decision took place) is in the affirmative. Should the answer be negative, inaction of state is implied, and case is admissible before the ICC. Such an interpretation allows the Court to disregard the complicated process of assessing unwillingness or inability. It is no surprise that it was adopted. What should be completely avoided then is to start mixing unwillingness/inability considerations to the first stage though because that makes the ICC case law unpredictable and even complicates situation for the Chambers themselves.

A second possible absurdity in interpretation of the RS avoided by division of decision-making upon admissibility concerns surrendering the suspects to the ICC. For whichever (including primarily political) reasons, the state of jurisdiction may be motivated to surrender a suspect in a particular case to the ICC. After all, several states have in fact already referred situations within their territories to the ICC and thus indicated that at least in some cases, they were motivated to have the perpetrators prosecuted, nonetheless rather by the ICC than themselves.[27] In such situations, the division of stages of deciding upon inadmissibility under letters

are ongoing.' Judgment on the appeal of the Republic of Kenya against the decision of Pre-Trial Chamber II of 30 May 2011 entitled "Decision on the Application by the Government of Kenya Challenging the Admissibility of the Case Pursuant to Article 19(2)(b) of the Statute," *Prosecutor v. Francis Kirimi Muthaura, Uhuru Muigai Kenyatta and Mohammed Hussein Ali* (ICC-01/09-02/11-274), Appeals Chamber, 30 August 2011, § 61.

[26] '[I]n case of inaction, the question of unwillingness or inability does not arise; inaction on the part of a State having jurisdiction [...] renders a case admissible before the Court, subject to article 17 (1) (d) of the Statute.' *Katanga and Ngudjolo Chui* (Judgment on the appeal of Mr. Germain Katanga against the Oral Decision of Trial Chamber II of 12 June 2009 on the Admissibility of the Case), *supra* note 2, § 78.

[27] This statement should not be seen as conflating self-referrals and admissibility as the same topics though. They are of course not. Self-referral triggers jurisdiction of the Court; admissibility limits the exercise of jurisdiction by it. They might however have similar reasons. William Schabas criticized the claim that self-referral indicates willingness or ability of state to investigate and/or prosecute, but he was doing so at the early stages of functioning of the ICC while he was criticizing the very concept of self-referrals as not being accounted for in the *travaux préparatoires*. In fact, he accepted that in cases of both "self-referral' and [waiver of] admissibility [...] the State agrees to cooperate with international justice, rather

(a) and (b) allows for the avoidance of an otherwise significant problem. Under letter (b), a case is inadmissible in front of the ICC if domestic investigation took place, but the state decided not to prosecute (provided it was not motivated by unwillingness or inability genuinely to prosecute). Thus, if a state is willing to prosecute but rather by the ICC and thus decides not to prosecute domestically, it could lead to an absurd conclusion where the domestic proceedings would be halted (due to surrendering the suspect to ICC), and at the same time, the ICC would be forced to decide the case was inadmissible before it due to the state's willingness.

This absurdity is again avoided by the stages of deciding upon inadmissibility. First, there is a consideration whether any proceedings/decision took place/are taking place. And only then (having decided positively in the first stage) comes unwillingness and or inability into question.

For these reasons, both the Trial Chamber and the Appeals Chamber refused to understand a domestic decision of the Central African Republic to seize the ICC instead of domestic proceedings, as a decision not to prosecute.[28]

Thus, a state's decision to close investigation (i.e., not to prosecute domestically) is not to be understood as a decision not to prosecute within the meaning of Art. 17(1)(b) RS when it is preceded by surrendering the suspect to The Hague. Otherwise,

> [i]f the decision of a State to close investigation because of the suspect's surrender to the Court were considered to be a 'decision not to prosecute', the peculiar, if not absurd, result would be that *because* of the surrender of a suspect to the Court, the case would become inadmissible. [...] Thus, a 'decision not to prosecute' in terms of article 17 (1) (b) of the Statute does

than to resist it.' W. Schabas, 'Complementarity in Practice: Some Uncomplimentary Thoughts,' 19 *Criminal Law Forum* (2008) 5, at 15–16.

[28] See *Bemba Gombo* (Judgment on the appeal of Mr. Jean-Pierre Bemba Gombo against the decision of Trial Chamber III of 24 June 2010 entitled "Decision on the Admissibility and Abuse of Process Challenges"), *supra* note 21, §§ 67, 74. While it is true that in this case, the CAR bodies did not in fact halt the domestic proceedings because the domestic charges were upheld (para. 67 of the Appeals Chamber's Judgment), the reasoning of the Court did not rely on that and equated it to a situation where there is a decision to close domestic proceedings (see para. 74 of the Appeals Chamber's Judgment) and consider the effects of it upon admissibility.

not cover decisions of a State to close judicial proceedings against a suspect because of his or her surrender to the ICC.[29]

In other words, Art. 17(1)(b) RS is focused at guaranteeing inadmissibility of cases before the ICC where there was an illegitimate decision not to prosecute taken, not at domestic decisions to halt prosecution accompanied by surrendering the accused to the ICC. Consequently, the reasoning is in line with the fact that exercise of jurisdiction is a sovereign right of every state combined with the obligation to prosecute crimes under international law.[30]

4 A Case Being Investigated or the Person Prosecuted

If there is any activity at the domestic level, the question is whether there is indeed a conflict of jurisdiction with the ICC. Consequently, Article 17 allows for a determination of inadmissibility of *a case* to make sure of it. Letters (a) and (b) of first paragraph also refer to a case however without clarifying details and elements of it, and so the ICC had to define the meaning of the term.

How exactly is a case understood however depends on the phase of proceedings (in front of the ICC). Admissibility is not only considered at the beginning of investigation (or later) under Art. 19, where the contours of a case must already be established, but also under Art. 18 that regulates preliminary rulings on admissibility, i.e., in time when "only" situation is dealt with by the Court. While assessing the conflict of jurisdiction under Art. 18 RS, it may be that the particular individuals are not yet perfectly clear nor is their conduct more than vaguely known,[31] and so due to early stages of the proceedings even the contours of the potential case

[29] *Bemba Gombo* (Judgment on the appeal of Mr. Jean-Pierre Bemba Gombo against the decision of Trial Chamber III of 24 June 2010 entitled "Decision on the Admissibility and Abuse of Process Challenges"), *supra* note 21, § 74.

[30] This line of reasoning is confirmed in *Katanga and Ngudjolo Chui* (Judgment on the appeal of Mr. Germain Katanga against the Oral Decision of Trial Chamber II of 12 June 2009 on the Admissibility of the Case), *supra* note 2, § 83.

[31] *Ruto, Kosgey and Sang* (Judgment on the appeal of the Republic of Kenya against the decision of Pre-Trial Chamber II of 30 May 2011 entitled "Decision on the Application by the Government of Kenya Challenging the Admissibility of the Case Pursuant to Article 19(2)(b) of the Statute"), *supra* note 2, § 39.

as such will be relatively vague.[32] As a consequence, what is relied upon to identify *potential cases* is 'information about the acts that may constitute crimes referred to in article 5, relevant for the purposes of article 18, paragraph 2.'[33] Logically, the more details the state can provide, the likelier it is that the Court will defer to it under Art. 18(2) RS.

If there is investigation initiated under Art. 53 RS, however, the elements of a *concrete case*[34] must be much more precise. The ICC case law defined those elements as the following: (a) the same person and (b) substantially the same conduct[35] as they are also defined for example in the summons to appear.[36]

This notion of the "same case" finds its reflection even in the text of the Rome Statute in Article 90(1)[37] and also with a hint in paragraph 7. However, the Court's case law added the term "substantially" and by doing so established a certain space for creativity.

Article 17(1)(a) and (b) RS refer to the case being investigated, that means that it is required for the state to be taking 'steps directed at ascertaining whether those suspects are responsible for [substantially the same][38] conduct, for instance by interviewing witnesses or suspects,

[32] *Muthaura, Kenyatta and Ali* (Judgment on the appeal of the Republic of Kenya against the decision of Pre-Trial Chamber II of 30 May 2011 entitled "Decision on the Application by the Government of Kenya Challenging the Admissibility of the Case Pursuant to Article 19(2)(b) of the Statute"), *supra* note 25, § 38.

[33] Rules of Procedure and Evidence of the ICC, Rome Statute, *supra* note 4, rule 52(1).

[34] Term used by *Ruto, Kosgey, and Sang* (Judgment on the appeal of the Republic of Kenya against the decision of Pre-Trial Chamber II of 30 May 2011 entitled "Decision on the Application by the Government of Kenya Challenging the Admissibility of the Case Pursuant to Article 19(2)(b) of the Statute"), *supra* note 2, § 40.

[35] 'It follows that for such a case to be inadmissible under article 17 (1) (a) of the Statute, the national investigation must cover the same individual and substantially the same conduct as alleged in the proceedings before the Court.' *Ruto, Kosgey, and Sang* (Judgment on the appeal of the Republic of Kenya against the decision of Pre-Trial Chamber II of 30 May 2011 entitled "Decision on the Application by the Government of Kenya Challenging the Admissibility of the Case Pursuant to Article 19(2)(b) of the Statute"), *supra* note 2, § 40.

[36] Ibid., § 41.

[37] 'A State Party which receives a request from the Court for the surrender of a person under article 89 shall, if it also receives a request from any other State for the extradition of *the same person for the same conduct* which forms the basis of the crime for which the Court seeks the person's surrender, notify the Court and the requesting State of that fact' [highlighting added].

[38] Added in *Ruto, Kosgey, and Sang* (Judgment on the appeal of the Republic of Kenya against the decision of Pre-Trial Chamber II of 30 May 2011 entitled "Decision on the

collecting documentary evidence, or carrying out forensic analyses [footnote omitted].'[39] Thus, in order for the state to prove (with evidence of a sufficient degree of specificity and probative value)[40] that it is investigating, it needs to submit material proving it is conducting 'concrete progressive investigative steps'[41] and do so in a way that is convincing. Purely informing that charges have been raised is not sufficient, neither is a pure claim that investigation is ongoing,[42] or suggesting the test of substantially the same conduct to be satisfied if the challenging party claims that discrete aspects of the case before the ICC are investigated domestically.[43]

In any case, the facts to be considered by the ICC in assessing the complementarity test may vary in time. Thus, an originally inadmissible case may become admissible and the other way around. If the facts however change later than during the first assessment by a pre-trial chamber or a chamber[44] under Art. 19, the new facts cannot be taken into account during appeal because the test assesses the facts as they are at the time of the proceedings before pre-trial or trial chamber.[45]

4.1 The Same Person

Depending on the stage of the proceedings in front of the ICC, the same person test may vary.

Application by the Government of Kenya Challenging the Admissibility of the Case Pursuant to Article 19(2)(b) of the Statute"), *supra* note 2, § 62.

[39] Ibid., para. 41.

[40] *Muthaura, Kenyatta, and Ali* (Judgment on the appeal of the Republic of Kenya against the decision of Pre-Trial Chamber II of 30 May 2011 entitled "Decision on the Application by the Government of Kenya Challenging the Admissibility of the Case Pursuant to Article 19(2)(b) of the Statute"), *supra* note 25, § 61.

[41] *Draft: Policy on Complementarity and Cooperation*, *supra* note 5, para. 136.

[42] *Ruto, Kosgey, and Sang* (Judgment on the appeal of the Republic of Kenya against the decision of Pre-Trial Chamber II of 30 May 2011 entitled "Decision on the Application by the Government of Kenya Challenging the Admissibility of the Case Pursuant to Article 19(2)(b) of the Statute"), *supra* note 2, § 62.

[43] Judgment on the appeal of Libya against the decision of Pre-Trial Chamber I of 31 May 2013 entitled "Decision on the admissibility of the case against Saif Al-Islam Gaddafi," *Prosecutor v. Saif Al-Islam Gaddafi and Abdullah Al-Senussi* (ICC-01/11-01/11-547-Red), Appeals Chamber, 21 May 2014, § 77.

[44] Rome Statute, *supra* note 4, Art. 19(6).

[45] *Gbagbo* (Judgment on the appeal of Côte d'Ivoire against the decision of Pre-Trial Chamber I of 11 December 2014 entitled "Decision on Côte d'Ivoire's challenge to the admissibility of the case against Simone Gbagbo") *supra* note 23, § 32.

During a preliminary examination (before investigation is initiated), the focus is on a potential case. Thus, while it is possible that domestically the exact same person is not subject to criminal proceedings, the ICC indicated that at this stage, the focus of investigation should be directed at the suspects at the same hierarchical level.[46] The Prosecutor stated that they 'will examine whether there are any domestic proceedings that correspond to the "potential cases" the Office has identified, namely the category of conduct and persons/groups of persons that the Office has provisionally identified as warranting investigation [footnote omitted].'[47]

After an investigation is initiated by the ICC though, the individual needs to be identified clearly and unequivocally. Knowing the person's identity, the same person test is a simple request by the systematics of the RS in order to decide upon admissibility. What if however the ICC is faster and initiates investigation against individual(s) when the domestic proceedings are yet at preliminary stages? Under such circumstances, there is either no conflict of jurisdictions identifiable (if the domestic criminal proceedings have not identified any individual suspects yet) or the case might be admissible before the ICC due to the third ground for inadmissibility, i.e., undue delays.

In any way, however, the state's interests are guaranteed until the proceedings in front of the ICC do not yet make it to trial,[48] because the state is up until then still entitled to challenge admissibility of a concrete case as long as it does so 'at the earliest opportunity,'[49] i.e., among others, as soon as its investigation reaches a concrete individual suspect identification.

4.2 Substantially the Same Conduct

In the *Gaddafi* case, the Appeals Chamber defined the conduct element as being 'both that of the suspect, Mr. Gaddafi, *and* that described in the incidents under investigation which is imputed to the suspect.'[50] The rea-

[46] *Ruto, Kosgey, and Sang* (Judgment on the appeal of the Republic of Kenya against the decision of Pre-Trial Chamber II of 30 May 2011 entitled "Decision on the Application by the Government of Kenya Challenging the Admissibility of the Case Pursuant to Article 19(2)(b) of the Statute"), *supra* note 2, § 42.

[47] *Draft: Policy on Complementarity and Cooperation*, *supra* note 5, para. 133.

[48] Rome Statute, *supra* note 4, Art. 19 (4).

[49] Rome Statute, *supra* note 4, Art. 19 (5).

[50] *Gaddafi and Al-Senussi* (Judgment on the appeal of Libya against the decision of Pre-Trial Chamber I of 31 May 2013 entitled "Decision on the admissibility of the case against

son for this formulation lays in the mode of liability he was accused of having committed the crimes through, that being an indirect co-perpetrator. He was accused of using the security forces to commit the crimes rather than perpetrating them himself. An incident is then defined as 'a historical event, defined in time and place, in the course of which crimes within the jurisdiction of the Court were allegedly committed by one or more direct perpetrators.'[51] Consequently, the Court requires all circumstances, context of the crimes, and the overall allegations against the suspect to be taken into account in assessment of the same conduct.

Because in order to decide on admissibility, the conduct must be substantially the same in front of the ICC as well in front of domestic courts, the admissibility challenging party must submit evidence about the same conduct being investigated/prosecuted domestically as well as by the ICC. This fact however poses several question marks: e.g., whether the definition of conduct presented above is only specific to cases where the suspect is investigated or prosecuted as indirect (co-)perpetrator or whether it applies to any mode of liability; why and how exactly does the ICC case law require the conduct to be substantially the same; whether the substantially same conduct means that the suspect must be domestically investigated or prosecuted for the same legal qualification of an offence, in other words, do they have to be charged with crimes under international law; etc.

Applicability to All Modes of Liability

The Appeals Chamber's concept of substantially the same conduct in the *Gaddafi* case mentioned above (as including both the one of the suspect as well as in the incidents imputed to them) might be read as requiring the domestic proceedings to be investigating the suspect under the same mode of liability in order to satisfy the substantially same conduct test. If however the domestic proceedings were required to apply the same mode of liability as the ICC, that would certainly be too strict,[52] especially considering that many state parties' legal systems do not utilize the same modes of liability like the Rome Statute. But it is not really a problem because such reading of the judgement would be too rigid. It should be kept in mind that the Appeals Chamber repeatedly referred to its

Saif Al-Islam Gaddafi"), *supra* note 43, § 62.

[51] Ibid., § 62.

[52] Schabas and El Zeidy, *supra* note 1, at 967.

considerations as being *within the context of the case at hand*, i.e., where the suspect was accused of acting via others.[53] Thus, it did not generally require the mode of liability to be considered domestically exactly in the same way like in front of the ICC. The fact is also supported by the words it used: not only the conduct of the suspect but also that in the incidents *imputed to him*. If the Appeals Chamber intended the incidents to play exact role in same conduct test regardless of the mode of liability, it would not necessarily need to add the "imputed to him."

Legal Qualification as Crimes Under International Law or Ordinary Domestic Crimes

One of the questions that relate to the nature of the evaluated conduct that comes into mind, is whether for deciding on inadmissibility of a case before the ICC, the Court may rely on domestic proceedings that do not legally qualify the conduct as a crime under international law but rather charge the individual for "ordinary" crimes.

From purely theoretical view, doctrine also dealt with the issue, and it has been suggested that rather than focusing on the legal qualification of the crimes as either crimes under international law or ordinary domestic crimes, what should be taken into account is the sentence and its extent instead. Juxtaposing the hard mirror thesis (that domestic proceedings must legally qualify the activities as crimes under international law in order to be willing and able to investigate and prosecute) and the soft mirror thesis (indicating that it is not absolutely necessary to qualify the activities as crimes under international law in domestic proceedings, but nonetheless it is advantageous because not doing so may be an indication of unwillingness and/or inability), under this third theory, basically '*any* national prosecution of an ordinary crime satisfies the principle of complementarity as long as it results in a sentence equal to, or longer than, the sentence the perpetrator would receive from the ICC.'[54]

While the ICC does not rely on the legal qualification and keeps the focus on the conduct,[55] it has not yet taken upon that idea though.

[53] Roger O'Keefe also points out the distinction between cases where the perpetrators acted themselves (with own hands) and through others. O'Keefe, *supra* note 2, at 558.

[54] K. J. Heller, 'A Sentence-Based Theory of Complementarity,' 53 *Harvard International Law Journal* (2012) 85, at 87.

[55] Decision on admissibility of the case against Saif Al-Islam Gaddafi, *Prosecutor v. Saif Al-Islam Gaddafi and Abdullah Al-Senussi* (ICC-01/11-01/11-344-Red), Pre-Trial Chamber I, 31 May 2013, § 85.

Substantially the Same Conduct

When it comes to substantially the same conduct, the overlap between the scope of incidents investigated domestically and by the ICC plays a significant role. The Court stated that when the incidents completely overlap, assuming willingness and ability existing, the case will be inadmissible before the ICC. At the same time, if the incidents does not overlap at all, there is no same case[56] (and substantiality of the overlap does not matter). While the Court did not pronounce it, it would be a situation of inaction as it was discussed above.

The possibilities ranging between those two scenarios present a grey area though and the scope of overlap is not clear at first sight there. The Court claimed that '[w]hat is required is a judicial assessment of whether the case that the State is investigating sufficiently mirrors the one that the Prosecutor is investigating.'[57] And so, when the overlap is not complete but the domestic investigation focuses at the core of what the ICC Prosecutor investigates, the substantially same conduct is fulfilled.

While this kind of flexibility of approach (reflecting the use of the word substantially) is understandable and certainly reflects respect to state sovereignty, it in fact creates problems. Had the Court case law not added "substantially" to the same conduct test, the above-stated would be moot because there would simply have to be full overlap between the incidents investigated domestically and in front of the ICC. It is surprising that the ICC was rather strict when it hinted at possibly demanding the domestic investigations to focus on the same mode of liability, as elaborated above, while in case of overlap of the incidents, it is flexible. The correct approach seems to be exactly the other way around—to be flexible when it comes to the modes of liability and strict when it comes to the incidents overlapping. That way, guaranteeing justice for perpetrators of all events and their victims is likelier safeguarded.

[56] *Gaddafi and Al-Senussi* (Judgment on the appeal of Libya against the decision of Pre-Trial Chamber I of 31 May 2013 entitled "Decision on the admissibility of the case against Saif Al-Islam Gaddafi"), *supra* note 43, § 72.

[57] Ibid., § 73.

5 Genuine Efforts

When the first stage of decision-making upon admissibility turns affirmative answers, i.e., the Court is convinced that the national proceedings are/were ongoing, and it also finds out that they concerned the same case regarding substantially the same conduct, the second stage turns to genuineness of the domestic activities. Thus, the case may be admissible before the ICC if the domestic proceedings were not genuine enough.

The lack of genuineness can be found either in the domestic investigation, prosecution, halting of the prosecution, or also (due to the conditions partially overlapping) in the fact that despite the domestic courts already decided upon guilt (and possibly sentence) of the accused, the decision was in fact not genuine.

The focus thus turns to unwillingness and inability of the state to genuinely carry out proceedings. The reason is in Art. 17(1)(a) and (b) RS, where the Court is told to assess whether the state is willing and able to genuinely carry out the investigation or prosecution in question.[58] And similarly in Art. 17(1)(c) RS, where the Court is obliged to focus on the question whether existence of domestic trial of the accused created the *ne bis in idem* obstacle.

Unwillingness is then defined in Art. 17(2) RS, inability in Art. 17(3) RS, and the conditions of admissibility of the case in front of the ICC despite previous trial in Art. 20(3) RS.

It can be said that the consequence of the ICC Prosecutor bringing a case to the ICC in fact is the claim 'that none of the States that would have jurisdiction over a particular suspect or accused are actually making genuine efforts to bring that person to justice [footnote omitted].'[59]

The term "genuinely" was chosen during negotiation of the Rome Statute in order to determine activities of states as objectively as it was possible and avoid discussions on varying level of development of states and

[58] '[T]he question of unwillingness or inability of a State having jurisdiction over the case becomes relevant only where, due to ongoing or past investigations or prosecutions in that State, the case appears to be inadmissible.' *Katanga and Ngudjolo Chui* (Judgment on the appeal of Mr. Germain Katanga against the Oral Decision of Trial Chamber II of 12 June 2009 on the Admissibility of the Case), *supra* note 2, § 75.

[59] *Yekatom and Ngaissona* (Judgment on Mr. Yekatom's appeal against Trial Chamber V's "Decision on the Yekatom Defence's Admissibility Challenge"), *supra* note 24, § 42.

their judiciaries.[60] And the genuine effort is connected to investigation or prosecution by the domestic bodies.

5.1 Unwillingness

The Rome Statute defines unwillingness in Art. 17(2) as follows:

> In order to determine unwillingness in a particular case, the Court shall consider, having regard to the principles of due process recognized by international law, whether one or more of the following exist, as applicable:
>
> (a) The proceedings were or are being undertaken or the national decision was made for the purpose of shielding the person concerned from criminal responsibility for crimes within the jurisdiction of the Court referred to in article 5;
> (b) There has been an unjustified delay in the proceedings which in the circumstances is inconsistent with an intent to bring the person concerned to justice;
> (c) The proceedings were not or are not being conducted independently or impartially, and they were or are being conducted in a manner which, in the circumstances, is inconsistent with an intent to bring the person concerned to justice.

Thus, there are three ways how unwillingness may be proven, either based on shielding from criminal responsibility, or in relation to unjustified delays, or in relation to lack of impartiality and/or independence of the domestic proceedings. Any of those three forms of unwillingness must be however linked to some of the grounds for inadmissibility under paragraph 1. Thus, unwillingness must either be materialized in the investigation or prosecution (Art. 17(1)(a) RS) or in the decision not to prosecute (Art. 17(1)(b) RS). Some authors have claimed that the investigation preceding the decision not to prosecute (under Art. 17(1)(b) RS) must also fulfil the criteria set for investigation in Art. 17(1)(a) RS.[61] The authors support the claim based on interpretation of the text of *Katanga* Appeals Chamber's judgement.[62] On the other hand, it could be that this require-

[60] Holmes, *supra* note 3, at 674.

[61] Schabas and El Zeidy, *supra* note 1, at 973.

[62] *Katanga and Ngudjolo Chui* (Judgment on the Appeal of Mr. Germain Katanga against the Oral Decision of Trial Chamber II of 12 June 2009 on the Admissibility of the Case), *supra* note 2, § 76.

ment does not stem from the text of the judgement (that only links unwillingness and inability to the decision not to prosecute, not to the preceding investigation) but rather from the fact that it would be illogical to demand an investigation to be genuine when it is ongoing (letter a) and refuse to demand it to already closed investigation (letter b).

As stated above, the text of Art. 17(2) RS allows for considerations of unwillingness based on three scenarios: (a) shielding the person from responsibility, (b) unjustified delay, and (c) lack of independence or impartiality. The two latter options must also be based on an inconsistency with intent to bring the person to justice.

At first sight, the third option concerning a lack of independence or impartiality and manner of the proceedings incompliant with intent to bring the accused to justice, seems to be the most general provision that to large extent covers the prior two. If there was a decision taken to shield a perpetrator from criminal responsibility (letter a) and the domestic criminal proceedings were influenced in that regard, the proceedings were not independent and impartial. And similarly, if the criminal mechanisms allow for unjustified delays (letter b) motivated by lack of intent to bring the perpetrator to justice, the proceedings are similarly suffering from lack of independence and/or impartiality. Consequently, the elements of unwillingness may be overlapping.

The list of options to conclude upon unwillingness is exhaustive,[63] and when deciding upon any of them, the ICC needs to keep principles of due process in mind because of the wording of chapeau of Art. 17(2) RS. That further confirms the value of human rights protection within the system of the ICC as confirmed already in Art. 21(3) RS. On the other hand, the Court stressed that 'in the context of admissibility proceedings, the Court is not primarily called upon to decide whether in domestic proceedings certain requirements of human rights law or domestic law are being violated. Rather, what is at issue is whether the State is willing [to]

[63] While the Appeals Chamber refused to answer the question about demonstrativeness or exhaustiveness of the list (*Katanga and Ngudjolo Chui* (Judgment on the Appeal of Mr. Germain Katanga against the Oral Decision of Trial Chamber II of 12 June 2009 on the Admissibility of the Case), *supra* note 2, § 73), it would be illogical to find it demonstrative given the textual interpretation of the provision and given the fact that the Rome Statute is built upon primacy of domestic jurisdiction. Other authors also stated that the *travaux préparatoires* do not support the list's demonstrative nature—Holmes, *supra* note 3, at 675.

genuinely investigate or prosecute.'[64] Thus, the Court is there to assess the due process from the perspective of admissibility, not to demand completely equal protection of fair trial all over the state parties as will be seen below.

Shielding the Person from Justice
The underlying nature of this option is to prevent domestic "sham trials." Thus, if the domestic investigation and/or prosecution leads to sham trial, the purpose of which is to theatrically conduct proceedings that were never intended to fairly assess the guilt and potential sentence of the accused, this option of unwillingness will be fulfilled. One of the most typical examples could be utilizing special judicial or procedural bodies that would stand sideways from the regular judicial system and would be related to the accused.[65]

Unjustified Delays
The unjustified delays option may utilize the extensive human rights bodies jurisprudence on the right to fair trial, particularly related to the length of proceedings. Since the right to fair trial is often the most complained to be violated and also found to be violated, the sources are indeed vast.

The delays must however be inconsistent with the intent to bring the person to justice. Thus, if there are delays but justified by procedurally legitimate reasons, the element will likely not be fulfilled.

Lack of Independence or Impartiality
As it was stated above, the role of the Court is not to review the human rights standard of protection by the domestic judicial bodies but to see whether in the context of the admissibility considerations, the state wished to genuinely investigate or prosecute. Thus, while the Court agreed that lack of access to own lawyer could have a role in independence/impartiality option,[66] it denied it as sole grounds for fulfilling unwillingness of a

[64] Judgment on the appeal of Mr. Abdullah Al-Senussi against the decision of Pre-Trial Chamber I of 11 October 2013 entitled "Decision on the admissibility of the case against Abdullah Al-Senussi," *Prosecutor v. Saif Al-Islam Gaddafi and Abdullah Al-Senussi* (ICC-01/11-01/11-565), Appeals Chamber, 24 July 2014, § 190.

[65] Holmes, *supra* note 3, at 675.

[66] *Gaddafi and Al-Senussi* (Judgment on the appeal of Mr. Abdullah Al-Senussi against the decision of Pre-Trial Chamber I of 11 October 2013 entitled "Decision on the admissibility of the case against Abdullah Al-Senussi"), *supra* note 64, § 190.

state under Art. 17(2)(c) RS. In order for the unwillingness to be fulfilled (on the grounds of lack of independence and impartiality and the conducting of proceedings inconsistently with intent to bring the person to justice), the 'violation of [the accused's] rights [would have to be] so egregious that the proceedings can no longer be regarded as being capable of providing any genuine form of justice to the accused.'[67]

The interplay between human rights protection and admissibility is thus quite limited. The Court will however take human rights into account and for the purposes of admissibility, their violations in domestic investigation or prosecution could lead to conclusion that the case is admissible before the ICC if the domestic proceedings were 'little more than a predetermined prelude to an execution, and which are therefore contrary to even the most basic understanding of justice.'[68] Similarly, the case could be admissible before the ICC if 'the violations of the rights of the suspect [domestically] are so egregious that it is clear that the international community would not accept that the accused was being brought to any genuine form of justice.'[69]

5.2 *Inability*

Inability is defined in Art. 17(3) RS as follows:

> In order to determine inability in a particular case, the Court shall consider whether, due to a total or substantial collapse or unavailability of its national judicial system, the State is unable to obtain the accused or the necessary evidence and testimony or otherwise unable to carry out its proceedings.

There are three scenarios to trigger inability: a total collapse of domestic judicial system, a substantial collapse of domestic judicial system, and the unavailability of the domestic judicial system.[70] Finding any of those

[67] Ibid., § 190.

[68] Ibid., § 230.

[69] *Gaddafi and Al-Senussi* (Judgment on the appeal of Mr. Abdullah Al-Senussi against the decision of Pre-Trial Chamber I of 11 October 2013 entitled "Decision on the admissibility of the case against Abdullah Al-Senussi"), *supra* note 64, § 230.

[70] As some authors noted (e.g., K. Šmigová, *Princíp komplementarity v medzinárodnom trestnom práve* [Principle of complementarity in international criminal law] (Passau/Berlin/Prague/Waldkirchen: rw&w Science & New Media, 2019), at 57), it is not clear from the text of the Statute whether adjectives total/substantial relate to the collapse of judicial system

three scenarios fulfilled leads the Court to second consideration—whether the scenario is a root for the state being unable to either obtain the accused or the necessary evidence, testimonies, or it otherwise being unable to carry out its proceedings. Thus, once again the consideration under Art. 17(3) RS is a two-stage process, and both stages need to be fulfilled in order to make a conclusion that the state is unable to genuinely carry out investigation or prosecution.[71]

Unlike in case of unwillingness, the test of inability tends to be more objective[72] assessment of domestic judicial organs' capabilities to perform their functions. Consequently, it is not a surprise that inability within the sense of Art. 17 (3) RS is usually found in countries suffering from armed conflicts or going through post-conflict reconstruction periods. It may also relate to natural disasters or failed states situations.[73]

A total collapse of judicial system[74] indicates its complete failure in performing its functions, for example, because of its non-existence or malfunctioning.

A substantial collapse does not reach that far, but the judicial system is non-functioning to the extent that it is still unable to perform its functions fully. A collapse of judicial system is however not always easy to differentiate from the judicial system's unavailability.

A theoretical unavailability might be explained using an example of governments in exile, such as those during WW2. The occupied state's domestic judicial system exists and possibly even performs its functions but is located within territory under occupation by a foreign power. The government in exile thus does not have access to its judicial system; i.e., it is unavailable although not collapsed (neither totally nor substantially) to investigate and prosecute suspects.

In its practice, the ICC stated that issues determinative of the unavailability of domestic judicial system might be even human resources

only or to its unavailability as well. Nonetheless, the Court did not relate the unavailability to them in its practice as is seen below.

[71] *Gaddafi and Al-Senussi* (Judgment on the appeal of Mr. Abdullah Al-Senussi against the decision of Pre-Trial Chamber I of 11 October 2013 entitled "Decision on the admissibility of the case against Abdullah Al-Senussi"), *supra* note 64, § 265.

[72] Schabas and El Zeidy, *supra* note 1, at 1005; Holmes, *supra* note 3, at 677.

[73] M. Bergsmo and P. Webb, *supra* note 11, para. 16.

[74] While the text of Rome Statute refers to "judicial system," the term should be understood as encompassing even enforcement authorities such as police that enable the judicial system to perform its functions. Šmigová, *supra* note 70, at 58.

availability, the number of cases pending before the national courts, or shortage of judges[75] in combination with complexity of prosecution of certain crimes.[76] Thus, even severe predominantly financial and personnel obstacles might be grounds to create unavailability of judicial system.[77]

A less clear situation of unavailability that arguably touches very thin line to substantial collapse of judicial system, was found by the ICC in areas where the judicial system exists but faces 'substantial difficulties in exercising its judicial powers fully across the entire territory [of state due to which] national system cannot be yet applied in full in areas or aspects relevant to the case.'[78] For example, in a post-conflict situation where a judicial system (as well as entire state) is not yet fully capable of reaching entire territory (despite being operational in the rest), can the judicial system be denoted by the Court as unavailable? In the situation in Libya, the Court thus found the judicial system unavailable. And because even the second consideration was fulfilled—domestic judiciary was unable to obtain the accused due to his detention by militia in Zintan outside control of the central government[79]—it found the state to be unable to genuinely carry out investigation or prosecution.[80]

Thus, as total or substantial collapse of judicial system or its unavailability is only a first step in assessment, the next step is that the state must be unable to obtain the accused or the necessary evidence and testimony or otherwise unable to carry out its proceedings, in order to be found unable to genuinely carry out investigation or prosecution. If it was not so, any state, e.g., failing to apprehend an accused could be considered fulfilling the admissibility criterion under Art. 17(3) RS despite its judicial system otherwise perfectly functioning.[81]

[75] *Bemba Gombo* (Decision on the Admissibility and Abuse of Process Challenges), supra note 25, §§ 245–246.

[76] Ibid., § 246.

[77] Consequently, it may be claimed that unavailability of judicial system in fact necessarily leads to more cases admissible before the ICC when the concurrent domestic jurisdiction is of a state without robust judicial system not facing financial shortages.

[78] *Gaddafi and Al-Senussi* (Decision on admissibility of the case against Saif Al-Islam Gaddafi), *supra* note 55, § 205.

[79] Ibid., § 206.

[80] Ibid., § 216.

[81] N. N. Jurdi, 'The Complementarity Regime of the International Criminal Court in Practice: Is It Truly Serving its Purpose? Some Lessons from Libya,' 30 *Leiden Journal of International Law* (2017) 199, at 217.

Being unable to obtain the accused was, for example, found when the accused was held by militia outside the control of the government.[82] The Court also decided that the state was unable to obtain the necessary testimonies when it was incapable of controlling certain territory and guaranteeing sufficient witness protection.[83] And lack of appointment of legal representation guaranteed by domestic law was once found to be a ground for the state to being 'otherwise unable to carry out its proceedings'[84] (in *Gadaffi* case), and in the same situation in Libya, it was rejected as a ground for inability (in *Al-Senussi* case). The Appeals Chamber unconvincingly attempted to legitimize the distinction by pointing out that Libya was unable to obtain the accused in the *Gadaffi* case while in the *Al-Senussi* case, he was in custody of the governmental forces.[85] However, firstly that fact does not really speak favours to the finding that the lack of counsel does not render the state unable when the accused is in custody of

[82] *Gaddafi and Al-Senussi* (Decision on admissibility of the case against Saif Al-Islam Gaddafi), *supra* note 55, § 206. Compare with conclusions in relation to Mr. Al-Senussi (also in situation in Libya) whom the government had in custody; thus, the state was not unable to obtain the accused. Decision on the admissibility of the case against Abdullah Al-Senussi, *Prosecutor v. Saif Al-Islam Gaddafi and Abdullah Al-Senussi* (ICC-01/11-01/11-466-Red), Pre-Trial Chamber I, 11 October 2013, § 294.

[83] *Gaddafi and Al-Senussi* (Decision on admissibility of the case against Saif Al-Islam Gaddafi), *supra* note 55, § 209. Again, compare to the case of Mr. Al-Senussi (also situation in Libya) held in custody in governmental facility and in the case of which the state gathered evidence and 'there is no indication that collection of evidence and testimony has ceased or will cease because off unaddressed security concerns for witnesses [...] or due to the absence of governmental control over certain detention facilities.' *Gaddafi and Al-Senussi* (Decision on the admissibility of the case against Abdullah Al-Senussi), *supra* note 82, § 294. Particularly regarding the absence of witness protection that played differing roles in *Gaddafi* and *Al-Senussi* cases as to inability conclusions of the Pre-Trial Chambers, the Appeals Chamber stated that the cases relied on different facts and for the purposes of the *Al-Senussi* case, 'conclusion that the absence of witness protection programmes had not resulted in Libya's inability to obtain the necessary evidence was not unreasonable [...], because the Pre-Trial Chamber considered a variety of circumstances together, including the amount of evidence that had been gathered in the case as a whole.' *Gaddafi and Al-Senussi* (Judgment on the appeal of Mr. Abdullah Al-Senussi against the decision of Pre-Trial Chamber I of 11 October 2013 entitled "Decision on the admissibility of the case against Abdullah Al-Senussi"), *supra* note 64, § 295.

[84] *Gaddafi and Al-Senussi* (Decision on admissibility of the case against Saif Al-Islam Gaddafi), *supra* note 55, §§ 214–216.

[85] *Gaddafi and Al-Senussi* (Judgment on the appeal of Mr. Abdullah Al-Senussi against the decision of Pre-Trial Chamber I of 11 October 2013 entitled "Decision on the admissibility of the case against Abdullah Al-Senussi"), *supra* note 64, § 203.

the state. Quite contrarily. And secondly, the Appeals Chamber even admitted accepting prediction that in future, the lack of counsel could be remedied.[86] But admissibility consideration needs to be based upon the facts as they are, not as they (might!) be in the future.

6 Ne bis in idem/Prohibition of Double Jeopardy

Article 17(1)(c) RS envisages that 'a second trial for the "same conduct" is not permitted unless "the proceedings in the other court" were tainted with irregularities as reflected in Article 20(3)(a) and (b) of the Statute.'[87]

This widely recognized principle, sometimes called *ne bis in idem*, *non bis in idem*, or double jeopardy, logically made its way into the Rome Statute. Considering, however, its source being human rights and also taking into account the role of human rights protection within the system of the ICC stipulated in Art. 21(3) RS, it is also necessary to keep in mind how human rights treaties protect the principle. The International Covenant on Civil and Political Rights[88] prohibits the double jeopardy in Art. 14(7).[89] The Optional Protocol No. 7 to the European Convention on Human Rights[90] covers it in its Art. 4(1)[91] and the American Convention on Human Rights[92] in its Art. 8(4).[93] It is worth noting that unlike Art. 20(3) RS, the human rights treaty provisions require either finality of the decision or its non-appealable character in order to create the obstacle of

[86] Ibid., § 201.

[87] *Gaddafi* (Decision on the 'Admissibility Challenge by Dr. Saif Al-Islam Gadafi pursuant to Articles 17(1)(c), 19 and 20(3) of the Rome Statute'), *supra* note 25, § 34.

[88] International Covenant on Civil and Political Rights (adopted 16 December 1966, entered into force 23 March 1976), 999 UNTS 171.

[89] 'No one shall be liable to be tried or punished again for an offence for which he has already been finally convicted or acquitted in accordance with the law and penal procedure of each country.'

[90] Protocol No. 7 to the European Convention on Human Rights and Fundamental Freedoms (adopted 22 November 1984, entered into force 1 November 1988), ETS No. 117.

[91] 'No one shall be liable to be tried or punished again in criminal proceedings under the jurisdiction of the same State for an offence for which he has already been finally acquitted or convicted in accordance with the law and penal procedure of that State.'

[92] American Convention on Human Rights (adopted 22 November 1969, entered into force 18 July 1978), OAS Treaty Series No. 36.

[93] 'An accused person acquitted by a nonappealable judgment shall not be subjected to a new trial for the same cause.'

ne bis in idem, a notion that found its effects even in jurisprudence of the ICC as will be seen below.

The text of Art. 17(1)(c) RS establishes two cumulative elements of the principle (a trial already having occurred and sameness of conduct). The defence in the *Gaddafi* case suggested (and the trial chamber accepted) four elements that build upon the text and include those in Art. 20(3) RS. These elements must be proven by the challenging party to persuade the Court about inadmissibility of a case on the grounds of *ne bis in idem*. These cumulative elements are as follows:

1. that [the suspect] has already been tried by the [domestic courts];
2. that the national trial was with respect "to the same conduct" as that alleged in this case [...];
3. national proceedings were not for the purpose of shielding within the meaning of Article 20(3)(a) [...]; and
4. national proceedings were not otherwise lacking in sufficient independence or impartiality, nor did they involve egregious due process violations, to the extent that the proceedings were incapable of providing genuine justice within the meaning of Article 20(3)(b) [... footnote omitted].[94]

This ground for admissibility challenge must be sufficiently distinguished from the grounds under Art. 17(1)(b) RS. Therein, the challenge may be raised due to existence of a decision not to prosecute. That however concerns a preliminary stage of the entire proceedings. Under letter (c), the ground is based upon a meritory decision (conviction or acquittal), i.e., decision of the competent domestic body regarding guilt and sentence of the accused.

In general, the principle operates both ways of the vertical line. That means that it prevents second trial both by the international court as well as by domestic courts. Nonetheless, the Statute regulates it from the perspective of ICC and thus focuses on the inadmissibility of a case in front of it due to a genuine domestic decision.

An issue not explicitly mentioned in the RS but in fact required by the human rights treaties, case law, and subsequently even by the case law of the ICC, is that the decision must be final and create a *res iudicata*

[94] *Gaddafi* (Decision on the 'Admissibility Challenge by Dr. Saif Al-Islam Gadafi pursuant to Articles 17(1)(c), 19 and 20(3) of the Rome Statute'), *supra* note 25, § 26.

obstacle. Thus, a decision that may be subject to appeal or any other reversal is not sufficient to fulfil grounds for this admissibility challenge.[95]

Another issue that the Rome Statute does not address explicitly, is the entity that issued the decision to create an obstacle of *ne bis in idem*. It comes into question particularly with regard to a quasi-state entities, such as the so-called de facto states.[96] While in cases of the first two grounds of inadmissibility (Art. 17(1)(a) and (b) RS), the text of the Rome Statute refers explicitly to an investigation and/or prosecution by "a state," in case of the third ground, this reference is missing and the treaty "only" refers to a trial.[97] The PTChI just stated that in accordance with plain reading of the text, it must be another court to pass a decision in a trial to create the obstacle.[98] That might however also be a court of a de facto state, or a state still being created.[99] The issue remains to be settled by the ICC yet, but Judge Kovács was right that '[a] too categorical standpoint could lead to a policy running against the basic philosophy of the ICC.'[100] The author of this chapter agrees that under certain circumstances even if

> a *de facto* regime passed a proper sentence following the principles of due process of law against an accused person for one or more of the crimes falling within the jurisdiction of the Court, this could furnish a sufficient basis for an admissibility challenge [on the grounds of *ne bis in idem*].[101]

[95] Ibid., § 36. The PTChI then goes on in the subsequent paragraphs into analysis of the human rights treaties and case law of the ad hoc tribunals to persuasively confirm the conclusion.

[96] De-facto states are a heterogeneous group of entities that fulfil the constitutional elements of statehood (territory, population, power) but lack recognition for various reasons (either political, legal, or both). See, e.g., M. Lipovský, 'Podněstří – de facto stát? [Transnistria - A de facto state?],' in P. Šturma (ed.), *Mezinárodní právo a státní území* [International law and state territory] (Prague: Charles University, 2015).

[97] Nonetheless, El Zeidy and Schabas claim that 'it is certain that the plain language of Article 17 revolves around national proceedings conducted by the relevant organs/institutions of a "State".' Schabas and El Zeidy, *supra* note 1, at 980.

[98] *Gaddafi* (Decision on the 'Admissibility Challenge by Dr. Saif Al-Islam Gadafi pursuant to Articles 17(1)(c), 19 and 20(3) of the Rome Statute'), *supra* note 25, § 35.

[99] Separate opinion of Judge Péter Kovács to Decision on the Prosecutor's request for authorization of an investigation, *Situation in Georgia* (ICC-01/15-12-Anx-Corr), Pre-Trial Chamber I, 27 January 2016, § 65.

[100] Ibid., § 65.

[101] Ibid., § 66.

The circumstances that would need to be taken into account would certainly include the standpoint of the parent-state towards trials in the de facto states/regimes, i.e., whether their decisions could be considered final in case of reclaiming the territory by the parent-state.

This text focused primarily at the first element. The others (elaborate upon above) are present in other grounds for inadmissibility as well and must be read in the same fashion like there.[102] In any way, the case law of the ICC on *ne bis in idem* until now is rather limited and focuses primarily on the first elements.[103]

7 Conclusion

As it was expected already during negotiations of the Rome Statute, the principle of complementarity plays a significant role in proceedings before the International Criminal Court. As a tool to balance rights and duties of states on one side and of the Court on the other, it attracts a lot of attention.

The Court's practice regarding the principle established so far has added certain clarity to the text of the Statute but also added some elements not explicitly present therein. By doing so, the predictability of the proceedings in front of the ICC were at times increased and at other times unfortunately a bit blurred.

It is to be expected that the case law will develop further. Because there are also still certain aspects that need addressing for the first time, it would be beneficial if the Court addressed the legal issues in a predictable and unified way.

[102] See, e.g., *Gaddafi and Al-Senussi* (Judgment on the appeal of Mr. Abdullah Al-Senussi against the decision of Pre-Trial Chamber I of 11 October 2013 entitled "Decision on the admissibility of the case against Abdullah Al-Senussi"), *supra* note 64, § 222.

[103] Schabas and El Zeidy, *supra* note 1, at 978.

CHAPTER 5

Cumulative Charges and Convictions for War Crimes and Crimes against Humanity and the Promotion of Adherence to IHL

Yael Naggan

Cumulative charges and convictions are a prominent feature in international criminal law (ICL) practice. This chapter focuses on some of the issues that arise when considering this practice, with respect to instances where both war crimes and crimes against humanity charges are based on the same underlying conduct, from the perspective of the promotion of adherence to international humanitarian law (IHL), as one of the goals of the war crimes regime in ICL. The chapter examines ICL practice in this regard, and argues that the adoption of a strict policy for cumulative charges and convictions, based on a rigid, technical jurisprudential test, is not conducive to ensuring results that are sufficiently attuned to the particular circumstances of each and every case. It surveys the recent *Ongwen* proceedings in the ICC and discusses the Court's failure to provide more comprehensive doctrinal guidance in this regard. It then proposes the adoption of a more nuanced approach when contemplating cumulative

Y. Naggan (✉)
Georgetown University Law Center, Washington, DC, USA
e-mail: yn106@georgetown.edu

O. Svaček, M. Faix (eds.), *Prosecution of War Crimes before the ICC*, Global Issues, https://doi.org/10.1007/978-3-031-84216-0_5

charges for these two categories of crimes, which involves an in-depth examination of the "nexus to an armed conflict" requirement of war crimes.

1 Introduction

The ICC's judgement in the landmark *Ongwen* case[1] features various novel and important findings on issues such as sexual and gender-based international crimes, and the implications of earlier victimhood of perpetrators who were formerly child soldiers, which have justly received much scholarly attention.[2] One issue that has received far less attention is the defence's challenge, and the ICC Chambers' responses, to the fact that Mr. Ongwen was charged with "[o]verlapping war crimes and crimes against humanity," or, in other words, war crimes and crimes against humanity on the basis of the same underlying conduct.[3] The Court rejected the defence's argument, based on the longstanding test in the ad hoc tribunals' case law—adopted in earlier ICC jurisprudence as well—which allows for entering cumulative convictions for crimes on the basis of

[1] Judgement on the appeal of Mr. Ongwen against the decision of Trial Chamber IX of 4 February 2021 entitled "Trial Judgment," *Prosecutor v Dominic Ongwen* (ICC-02/04-01/15-A), Appeals Chamber, 15 December 2022 (hereafter *Ongwen* Appeals Judgement); Trial Judgement, *Prosecutor v Dominic Ongwen* (ICC-02/04-01/15-1762-Red), Trial Chamber IX, 4 February 2021 (hereafter *Ongwen* Trial Judgement); Sentence, *Prosecutor v Dominic Ongwen* (ICC-02/04-01/15-1819-Red), Trial Chamber IX, 6 May 2021.

[2] See, e.g., W. Nortje and N. Quénivet, "Fertile or Futile Grounds for Excluding Criminal Responsibility? A Critical Analysis of the *Ongwen* Judgment in Relation to the Claim of Coercive Environment," 23 *International Criminal Law Review* (2023) 675; L. Hiromoto and L.F. Sparr, "*Ongwen* and Mental Health Defenses at the International Criminal Court," 51 *Journal of the American Academy of Psychiatry and the Law* (2023) 61; S.S. Mera, "Fighters, Not Victims: On Victimhood Recognition and Gender Representations in the Enslavement Charges in the *Ongwen* Case," 23 *International Criminal Law Review* (2023) 782; M. Kersten, "The moral and legal correctness of Dominic Ongwen's conviction," Justice in Conflict, 10 February 2021, available at https://justiceinconflict.org/2021/02/10/the-moral-and-legal-correctness-of-dominic-ongwens-conviction/ (last visited 4 November 2023); S. van Campen, "A Legal First in International Criminal Justice: A Conviction for Forced Pregnancy in the Ongwen Case," IntLawGrrls, 18 May 2021, available at https://ilg2.org/2021/05/18/a-legal-first-in-international-criminal-justice-a-conviction-for-forced-pregnancy-in-the-ongwen-case/ (last visited 4 November 2023).

[3] *Ongwen* Trial Judgement, *supra* note 1, § 2818.

the same underlying conduct, if one crime requires proof of a fact not required by the other.[4]

This chapter seeks to examine the issue of cumulative charges and convictions for war crimes and crimes against humanity, from the perspective of promotion of adherence to international humanitarian law (IHL) through the war crimes regime in international criminal law (ICL). As part of this analysis, the chapter looks to challenge the aforementioned test, exclusively applied in international criminal jurisprudence over the last two decades, by highlighting several considerations that come to the fore when contemplating the cumulation of charges and convictions for these two categories of crimes.

The chapter will first provide, in Sect. 2, a broad overview of ICL practice regarding cumulative charges. Since the focus of this chapter is on the cumulation of charges for war crimes and crimes against humanity for the same underlying conduct, Sect. 3 will then briefly describe the relationship between these categories of crimes. Against this backdrop, Sect. 4 will highlight four potential challenges arising from cumulative charges and convictions that merit consideration when cumulatively charging or convicting defendants for these two categories of crimes, from the standpoint of promotion of adherence to IHL. Section 5 will then present the discussion in the *Ongwen* case, in view of these challenges. Finally, in light of the longstanding ICL practice of cumulation based on the same underlying conduct, the chapter will also propose a possible modification of the aforementioned jurisprudential test, to alleviate some of the concerns that arise. Section 7 concludes.

2 Cumulative Charges and Convictions in Modern ICL

Charging and convicting defendants for cumulative crimes on the basis of the same underlying conduct is common practice in international criminal tribunals.[5] Such cumulation may occur, for example, when an individual is

[4] Ibid., § 2820; *Ongwen* Appeals Judgement, *supra* note 1, § 1635.

[5] C. Stuckenberg, "Cumulative Charges and Cumulative Convictions," in C. Stahn (ed.), *The Law and Practice of the International Criminal Court* (Oxford: Oxford University Press, 2015) 840, at 841, 853. See, e.g., the *Kunarac*, *Kupreškić*, *Naletilić*, *Stakić*, *Vasiljević*, *Jelisic*, *Galić*, *Perišić* and *Tolimir* ICTY cases; *Akayesu*, *Ntakirutimana*, *Ntagerura*, *Nahimana*, *Simba* and *Musema* ICTR cases; and *Bemba*, *Ntaganda* and *Ongwen* ICC cases.

charged, and later convicted, with respect to a particular incident, for murder as both a war crime and a crime against humanity.

In modern international criminal tribunals, this practice was approved early on. While chambers in cases such as *Akayesu* in the International Criminal Tribunal for Rwanda (ICTR) and *Kupreškić* in the International Criminal Tribunal for the former Yugoslavia (ICTY) laid out several parameters for its lawful application, the longstanding legal test for cumulative convictions is the one put forth by the ICTY's Appeals Chamber in its 2001 judgement in the *Čelebići* case. According to the *Čelebići* test, multiple convictions based on the same underlying conduct are permissible if each criminal provision involved "has a materially distinct element not contained in the other." An element is materially distinct "if it requires proof of a fact not required by the other."[6]

This test was subsequently applied and followed by other ad hoc and hybrid tribunals,[7] as well as by the ICC, in cases such as *Bemba* and *Ntaganda*.[8] More recently, the ICC's Appeals Chamber reaffirmed the adoption of this test in its judgement in the *Ongwen* case, pursuant to the aforementioned challenges made by the defence.[9]

Cumulative charges and convictions are a subset of the wider criminal law concept of *concursus delictorum*—a term that describes all situations in which at least two offenses are adjudicated at once.[10] In this broader sense, *concursus delictorum* occurs in domestic legal systems as well, and those systems have developed various mechanisms to resolve situations of

[6] Judgement, *Prosecutor v Zdravko Mucić* et al. (IT-96-21-A), Appeals Chamber, 20 February 2001, § 412 (hereafter *Čelebići*). For a survey of earlier ad hoc tribunal jurisprudence on this issue, see: A. Bogdan, "Cumulative Charges, Convictions and Sentencing at the Ad Hoc International Tribunals for the Former Yugoslavia and Rwanda," 3 *Melbourne Journal of International Law* (2002) 1.

[7] The ICTR, the SCSL and the ECCC. See Stuckenberg, *supra* note 5, at 846.

[8] Judgement Pursuant to Article 74 of the Statute, *Prosecutor v Jean-Pierre Bemba Gombo* (ICC-01/05-01/08-3343), Trial Chamber III, 21 March 2016, §§ 750–751; Judgement Pursuant to Article 74 of the Statute, *Prosecutor v Bosco Ntaganda* (ICC-01/04-02/06-2359), Trial Chamber VI, 8 July 2019, § 1202. See also: Judgement Pursuant to Article 74 of the Statute, *Prosecutor v Germain Katanga* (ICC-01/04-01/07-3436-tENG), Trial Chamber II, 7 March 2014, § 1696; G. Mettraux, *International Crimes: Law and Practice: Volume II: Crimes Against Humanity* (Oxford: Oxford University Press, 2020) at 810.

[9] *Ongwen* Appeals Judgement, *supra* note 1, §§ 1631, 1635. See also *Ongwen* Trial Judgement, *supra* note 1, § 2818.

[10] Stuckenberg, *supra* note 5, at 841; K. Ambos, *Treatise on International Criminal Law, Vol. II: The Crimes and Sentencing* (Oxford: Oxford University Press, 2014) at 246 et seq.

concurrence for the same underlying conduct.[11] Indeed, the *Čelebići* test itself is based on domestic case law, and follows the US Supreme Court's ruling in the *Blockburger* case.[12]

Domestic criminal law has long been seen as one of the sources of ICL, especially in respect of the "general part" of this legal field.[13] However, international criminal tribunals deal with different categories of *international* crimes,[14] such as genocide, war crimes, and crimes against humanity. Thus, the suitability of this domestic test in international settings may be questioned,[15] in particular insofar as a comparative analysis does not focus on, or at least take into account, how international crimes are adjudicated in domestic settings.

Importantly, in ICL, cumulation can, and does, occur within the specific categories of international crimes, such as when charging or convicting a defendant for both rape and torture as crimes against humanity, on the basis of the same conduct.[16] The present inquiry focuses, however, on cumulation across the different categories of crimes.[17] Each category of crimes has its own set of contextual elements: war crimes require an armed conflict and that the alleged crimes occur in connection to that armed conflict (the nexus requirement)[18]; crimes against humanity are established

[11] Stuckenberg, *supra* note 5, at 841. See also: Judgement, *Prosecutor v Zoran Kupreškić* et al. (IT-95-16-T), Trial Chamber, 14 January 2000, §§ 680 ff.

[12] See *Čelebići* Judgement, *supra* note 6, § 409, referencing *Blockburger v US*, 284 US 299, 304 (1932).

[13] See, e.g., K. Ambos, "Remarks on the General Part of International Criminal Law," 4 *Journal of International Criminal Justice* (2006) 660, at 662; E. van Sliedregt, *Individual Criminal Responsibility in International Law* (Oxford: Oxford University Press, 2012) 15; Ambos Vol. II, *supra* note 10, at 246–247.

[14] See, e.g., M. Ch. Bassiouni, 'Crimes against Humanity' in M. Ch. Bassiouni (ed.), *International Criminal Law, Volume I: Sources, Subjects and Contents* (3rd edn., Leiden: Martinus Nijhoff, 2008) 437, 439.

[15] See, e.g., Appeal Judgement, *Prosecutor v Kaig Guek Eav "Duch"* (001/18-07-2007-ECCC/SC), Supreme Court Chamber, 3 February 2012, § 292 (hereafter *"Duch"*); Separate and Dissenting Opinion of Judge David Hunt and Judge Mohamed Bennouna, *Čelebići* Judgement, *supra* note 6, § 20. See also *Kupreškić*, *supra* note 11, § 697.

[16] G. Werle and F. Jeßberger, *Principles of International Criminal Law* (4th edn., Oxford: Oxford University Press 2020) at 328–329.

[17] See, e.g., Tolimir, Perišić, and Bemba cases. See also Mettraux (2020), *supra* note 8, at 807 (note 57).

[18] R. Cryer et al., *An Introduction to International Criminal Law and Procedure*, (3rd edn., Cambridge: Cambridge University Press, 2014) at 280–281; G. Werle and Jeßberger, *supra* note 16, at 473.

when particular prohibited acts are committed as part of a widespread or systematic attack against the civilian population.[19] Recalling the content of the aforementioned *Čelebići* test, these different contextual elements necessarily mean that the "proof of a fact not required by another"—or a materially distinct element—can be established in each case of cumulative charging, simply by virtue of those contextual elements.[20]

This ostensibly automatic fulfilment[21] of the *Čelebići* test through the contextual elements of international crimes may explain why, despite its consistent application in ICL practice, some commentators have noted that international law on the matter of cumulation does not seem to be sufficiently theorized,[22] and international jurisprudence in this regard has been criticized.[23] For example, in their separate and dissenting opinions in the *Čelebići* case, Judges Hunt and Bennouna noted that:

> the fundamental consideration arising from charges relating to the same conduct is that an accused should not be penalised more than once for the same *conduct*. The purpose of applying this test is therefore to determine whether the *conduct* of the accused genuinely encompasses more than one crime. For that reason, we believe that it is not meaningful to consider for this purpose legal prerequisites or contextual elements which do not have a bearing on the accused's conduct, and that the focus of the test should therefore be on the substantive elements which relate to an accused's conduct ....[24]

[19] Mettraux (2020), *supra* note 8, at 194 et seq.; Cryer et al., *supra* note 18, at 233 et seq.

[20] G. Mettraux, *International Crimes and the* ad hoc *Tribunals* (Oxford: Oxford University Press, 2005) at 323–324.

[21] *Čelebići* Judgement, *supra* note 6, Separate and Dissenting Opinion of Judges Hunt and Bennouna, § 31 (referring specifically to the contextual elements of war crimes and crimes against humanity, the judges state that "[a]pplying the majority's test, convictions would therefore necessarily and in every case be entered on both counts") and § 45 (calling the approach of the Majority "inflexible," "with the potential to produce outcomes which are, in the circumstances of any given case, arbitrary and artificial").

[22] Stuckenberg, *supra* note 5, at 842; Ambos Vol. II, *supra* note 10, at 246–247. See also: *"Duch"* Appeal Judgement, *supra* note 15, at § 290.

[23] Stuckenberg, *supra* note 5, at 847–848; Mettraux (2005), *supra* note 20, at 318–319; C.F. Estrada, "The International Criminal Court and the *Čelebići* Test: Convictions Based on the Same Set of Facts from a Comparative Perspective," 15 *Journal of International Criminal Justice* (2017) 689.

[24] Separate and Dissenting Opinion of Judges Hunt and Bennouna, *supra* note 6, § 26 (emphasis in the original).

Questions regarding theoretical considerations that may serve as guidance when contemplating cumulative convictions will be revisited in Sect. 4 below, and considerations regarding using the contextual elements of war crimes differently are proposed in Sect. 6. Since this chapter focuses on the cumulation of charges and convictions for the categories of war crimes and crimes against humanity on the basis of the same underlying conduct, and the consequences of such practice from the standpoint of the development and promotion of the adherence to IHL, the following section will briefly survey the relationship between war crimes and crimes against humanity.

3 War Crimes and Crimes Against Humanity: An Overview

"War crimes" and "crimes against humanity" are two of the core crimes at the centre of ICL. In the Rome Statute, these categories appear alongside the crime of genocide,[25] and the more recently incorporated crime of aggression.[26] While they are independent concepts in ICL, war crimes and crimes against humanity nonetheless have a shared history, which bears on the present analysis.

War crimes represent the criminalization of certain (but not all) violations of international humanitarian law (IHL).[27] On the national level, they were codified as early as the mid-nineteenth century, with the introduction of the Lieber Code (1863) during the American Civil War.[28] Internationally, while war crimes are considered to have become a "category of international offences" by the end of the First World War, they were first codified as such in Article 6(b) of the Nuremberg Charter of

[25] Rome Statute of the International Criminal Court (adopted 17 July 1998, entered into force 1 July 2002), 2187 UNTS 90 (hereafter Rome Statute), Art. 6.

[26] Rome Statute, *supra* note, Art. 8bis.

[27] F. Pocar, "The criminalization of the violations of international humanitarian law from Nuremberg to the Rome Statute," in Pocar et al. (eds.), *War Crimes and the Conduct of Hostilities: Challenges to Adjudication and Investigation* (Cheltenham: Edward Elgar, 2013) 3; Cryer et al., *supra* note 18, at 268.

[28] Werle and Jeβberger, *supra* note 16, at 444–445; B. B. Jia, "The Differing Concepts of War Crimes and Crimes against Humanity in International Criminal Law" in G. S. Goodwin-Gill and Stefan Talmon (eds.), *The Reality of International Law: Essays in Honour of Ian Brownlie* (Oxford: Oxford University Press, 1999) at 243, 245; M. Ch. Bassiouni, *Crimes Against Humanity in International Criminal Law* (2nd edn., Kluwer 1999) at 518–519.

1945.[29] A war crime is now commonly understood as a serious violation of international humanitarian law for which there is a criminal sanction.[30] Thus, while certainly not all IHL violations are criminal, all war crimes must consist of violations of IHL.[31]

The term "crimes against humanity" was first introduced as a legal concept in 1915, when the massacre of Armenians by Turkey was denounced as "crimes against civilization and humanity."[32] As an international category of crimes, it was initially proposed as a separate crime following the First World War. Nevertheless, this proposition was rejected at the time due to its novelty,[33] and subsequently crimes against humanity were also first codified in the Nuremberg Charter.[34]

In the course of the discussions leading up to Nuremberg,[35] some emphasized the need to criminalize conduct other than that strictly prohibited by the laws of war at the time, whereas others stressed that the basis for such criminalization could be found in the laws of war themselves—and particularly the Martens Clause which denounced violations of the laws of humanity and the dictates of public conscience.[36] This debate notwithstanding, it was clear at the time that crimes against humanity were introduced in Nuremberg in order to fill a *lacuna*: the "war crimes" provisions could be applied to atrocities committed against foreign civilians, but could not be applied to crimes committed against Germany's

[29] Jia, *supra* note 28, at 245, 255; Werle and Jeβberger, *supra* note 16, at 445, 451–452; Yves Sandoz, "Penal Aspects of International Humanitarian Law," in Bassiouni (ed.), *supra* note 14, 293, at 298; H. Lauterpacht, "The Law of Nations and the Punishment of War Crimes," 21 *British Yearbook of International Law* (1944) 58, at 77–78.

[30] Werle and Jeβberger, *supra* note 16, at 453–455.

[31] Decision on the Defence Motion for Interlocutory Appeal on Jurisdiction, *Prosecutor v Tadić* (IT-94-1), Appeals Chamber, 2 October 1995, § 94; R. Cryer, "War Crimes," in B. Saul and D. Akande (eds.), *The Oxford Guide to International Humanitarian Law* (Oxford: Oxford University Press, 2020) 339, at 342.

[32] D. Luban, "A Theory of Crimes against Humanity," 29 *Yale Journal of International Law* (2004) 85, at 86; Werle and Jeβberger, *supra* note 16, at 375.

[33] R. O'Keefe, *International Criminal Law* (Oxford: Oxford University Press, 2015) at 160-161; Mettraux (2020), *supra* note 8, at 5–7; Werle and Jeβberger, *supra* note 16, at 375.

[34] Charter of the International Military Tribunal (adopted 8 August 1945), 82 UNTS 279, Art 6(c); Mettraux (2020), *supra* note 8, at 1.

[35] Held under the auspices of the London International Assembly and later the United Nations War Crimes Commission.

[36] Mettraux (2020), *supra* note 8, at 8–10.

own citizens.[37] The crimes against humanity provision in the Nuremberg Charter did, however, include a requirement that there be a "nexus" between the crime and the armed conflict.[38] Nevertheless, this requirement was eventually severed in modern ICL,[39] and the crimes against humanity regime pertains to both times of peace and war.[40]

Thus, the category of crimes against humanity is a distinct one, created with a view to elaborating existing international crimes.[41] At the same time, the categories of war crimes and crimes against humanity significantly overlap at times, in terms of the conduct they criminalize.[42] Consequently, and in light of the evolution of crimes against humanity, some have stressed that such crimes should have a non-military purpose behind them—otherwise, the inhumane acts would be covered by the notion of war crimes.[43] Others have emphasized that at least some of the particular crimes against humanity capture notions of criminality pervasive in everyday aspects of life, and thus protect a broad set of interests in peacetime as well.[44]

In order to better understand the relationship between these categories of crimes for the purposes of cumulative charges, it may be worth

[37] Luban, *supra* note 32, at 93–94; L. N. Sadat, "Crimes Against Humanity in the Modern Age," 107 *American Journal of International Law* (2013) at 334, 337; Mettraux (2020), *supra* note 8, at 7–8, 10, 16, 805.

[38] M. Ch. Bassiouni, *Crimes Against Humanity: Historical Evolution and Contemporary Application* (New York: Cambridge University Press, 2011) at 33–34.

[39] *Tadić*, *supra* note 31, §31 141; Rome Statute, *supra* note 25, Art. 7. See also: Mettraux (2020), *supra* note 8, at 36, 53–54; Werle and Jeβberger, *supra* note 16, at 377; C. Greenwood, "The Development of International Humanitarian Law by the International Criminal Tribunal for the Former Yugoslavia," 2 *Yearbook of United Nations Law* (1998) 97, at 136. However, some states dispute this conclusion. See: International Law Commission, *Fourth report on crimes against humanity*, UN Doc. A. CN.4/725, 18 February 2019, § 49.

[40] L. N. Sadat, "Putting Peacetime First: Crimes Against Humanity and the Civilian Population Requirement," 31 *Emory International Law Review* (2017) 199, at 200.

[41] Trial Judgement, *US v Josef Altstoetter* et al. (Justice Case), Military Tribunal III, 4 December 1947. Trials of War Criminals before the Nuremberg Military Tribunals, Vol. III, at 972 (4 December 1947) (noting, regarding the prohibitions on crimes against humanity, that they "are not surplusage. They supplement the preceding sections on war crimes and include within their prohibition not only war crimes, but also acts not included within the preceding definitions of war crimes."); Jia, *supra* note 28, at 255–256; Mettraux (2020), *supra* note 8, at 16, 46.

[42] Mettraux (2020), *supra* note 8, at 41–42.

[43] Jia, *supra* note 28, at 267, 270.

[44] Mettraux (2020), *supra* note 8, at 42.

considering what are the protected values underlying the criminalization of each of them. In fact, prior to the adoption of the *Čelebići* test, ad hoc tribunal case law on cumulative convictions (in cases such as *Akayesu* and, to a lesser degree, *Kupreskić*) included the question of protected values of crimes as part of their considerations.[45]

Generally, both categories of crimes are considered as intended to safeguard fundamental human rights—such as life, dignity, and bodily integrity—as part of the broader perception of international criminal justice as guided towards the protection of human dignity and "fundamental legal values" concerning individuals, as well as humankind as a whole.[46] In line with this perception, both categories have also been linked to the protection of international peace. For crimes against humanity, this is based on their severity and the dangers that infringements of such basic notions of humanity entail when perpetrated on a large scale.[47] Regarding war crimes, the protection of peace and security is understood as related to a key interest at the heart of this regime—the enforcement and compliance with IHL that war crimes are intended to promote.[48]

Other than these shared broader protected values, particular crimes within each category have specific protected values of their own. As war crimes embody the criminalization of certain violations of IHL,[49] the protected values of particular war crimes also correspond to the object of the protection afforded by the relevant underlying IHL provision or principle (protected persons, protected objects, the prevention of unnecessary

[45] Judgement, *Prosecutor v Jean-Paul Akayesu* (ICTR-96-4-T), Trial Chamber, 2 September 1995, § 468; *Kupreškić, supra* note 11, §§ 693–695; Ambos Vol. II, *supra* note 10, at 258. This was also evident in the approach taken by Judges Hunt and Bennouna in their dissenting opinion in the *Čelebići* Judgement, *supra* note 6. See: Dissenting Opinion, at §18.

[46] K. Ambos, *Treatise on International Criminal Law, Vol. I: Foundations and General Part* (1st edn., Oxford: Oxford University Press, 2013) at 66; Werle and Jeβberger, *supra* note 16, at 379, 459; Mettraux (2020), *supra* note 8, at 40–41.

[47] Werle and Jeβberger, *supra* note 16, at 379; Ambos Vol. I, *supra* note 46, at 66–67; Mettraux (2020), *supra* note 8, at 145.

[48] Werle and Jeβberger, *supra* note 16, at 450, 452; Cryer et al., *supra* note 18, at 267; J. S. Pictet (ed.), *Commentary to the IV Geneva Convention Relative to the Protection of Civilian Persons in Time of War* (Geneva: International Committee of the Red Cross, 1958) at 583–585; Ambos Vol. I, *supra* note 46, at 66–67 and Ambos Vol. II, *supra* note 10, at 118.

[49] Pocar, *supra* note 27, at 3; Cryer et al., *supra* note 18, at 268.

suffering, etc.).[50] Thus while there are notable commonalities in both the conduct covered and the interests protected by each category of crimes, they are not identical in this regard, and they were, as noted, distinctly developed for different purposes.

The ICC Trial Chamber's judgement in the *Ongwen* case reflected this notion, when referring in particular to the issue of cumulative charges and convictions. The Chamber noted, when discussing the contextual elements of crimes under the jurisdiction of the Court, that

> [T]he statutory contextual elements of crimes, considered individually, encapsulate *distinct interests protected* by the corresponding incriminating provisions under the Statute. Indeed, and as far as the charges in the present case are concerned, the Chamber observes that war crimes give protection in criminal law to persons in times of armed conflict, whereas crimes against humanity protect persons where there is a widespread and systematic attack on a civilian population. *Thus, the two sets of crimes reflect (partly) different forms of criminality*, in that they complement, in terms of protected interests, the incrimination of the individual 'specific' crimes ....[51]'

However, some developments in ICL practice have contributed to a certain degree of opacity regarding the relationship between these categories of crimes. One example in this regard is the jurisdictional decision by the *Ntaganda* Appeals Chamber, according to which the war crimes of rape and sexual slavery can be committed against members of the same armed force or group.[52] Although this decision has been criticized for what is arguably an even greater error with respect to war crimes (in that the crimes at the focus of those proceedings are not based on a violation of IHL),[53] it may perhaps be seen as adding to the confusion between the

[50] Jia, *supra* note 28, at 246; Ambos Vol. II, *supra* note 10, at 118, 164ff; A. Cassese, "The Nexus Requirement for War Crimes," 10 *Journal of International Criminal Justice* (2012) 1395, at 1397.

[51] *Ongwen* Trial Judgement, *supra* note 1, § 2820 (emphasis added).

[52] Judgement on the appeal of Mr. Ntaganda against the "Second decision on the Defence's challenge to the jurisdiction of the Court in respect of Counts 6 and 9," *Prosecutor v Bosco Ntaganda* (ICC-01/04-02/06-1962), Appeals Chamber, 15 June 2017. See also *Ntaganda* Trial Judgement, *supra* note 8, § 965.

[53] K. J. Heller, "ICC Appeals Chamber Says a War Crime Does not have to Violate IHL," Opinio Juris, 15 June 2017, available at http://opiniojuris.org/2017/06/15/icc-appeals-chamber-holds-a-war-crime-does-not-have-to-violate-ihl/ (last visited 4 November 2023); A. Jachec-Neale, "The Unintended Consequences of International Court Decisions," Lieber

categories of crimes, when considering their development and that crimes against humanity were intended to fill a *lacuna* regarding the commission of crimes towards one's own nationals.[54] An exceptional war crime in this regard is that of enlistment or recruitment of child soldiers—but this crime was purposefully incorporated into the Rome Statute as a crime against one's own party to the conflict (and was considered a novel war crime at that).[55]

An even more telling indication of such obfuscation can be found in Judge Eboe-Osuji's partly concurring opinion in the *Ntaganda* appeal judgement. When contemplating the correct interpretation of the term "attack" for war crimes under Article 8 of the Rome Statute,[56] the Judge struggled to find an "actionable difference between the interest of humanity that the proscription of crimes against humanity seeks to achieve in forbidding 'attack directed' against a civilian population in Article 7, and the humanitarian interest that the proscription of war crimes seeks to achieve in proscribing 'directing attack' protected objects as provided in Article 8(2)(e)(iv)."[57] He further questioned how the distinction between

Institute, 19 November 2020, available at https://lieber.westpoint.edu/unintended-consequences-international-courts-decisions/ (last visited 4 November 2023) (adopting Heller's critique). This decision has also been criticized by commentators who agree with (some or all of) the Appeals Chamber's conclusions, who point to the flawed reasoning or substantiation underlying them. See, e.g., C. Kenny and Y. McDermott, "The Expanding Protection of Members of a Party's Own Armed Forces under International Criminal Law," 68 *International and Comparative Law Quarterly* (2019) 943; O. Svaček, "Brothers and Sisters in Arms As Victims of War Crimes: Ntaganda Case Before the ICC," 8 *Czech Yearbook of Public and Private International Law* (2017) 346.

[54] Mettraux (2020), *supra* note 8, at 808.

[55] Ambos Vol. II, *supra* note 10, at 118; M. Cottier and J. Grignon, "Article 8(2)(b)(xxvi)," in O. Triffterer and K. Ambos (eds.), *The Rome Statute of the International Criminal Court - A Commentary* (3rd edn., Munich: C. H. Beck, 2016) at 520–523; M. Bothe, "War Crimes," in A. Cassese, P. Gaeta and J. R. W. D. Jones (eds.), *The Rome statute of the International Criminal Court: A Commentary Vol. I* (Oxford: Oxford University Press, 2002) 379, at 417.

[56] See also: part 4.D below.

[57] Partly Concurring Opinion of Judge Eboe-Osuji, Judgement on the appeals of Mr. Bosco Ntaganda and the Prosecutor against the decision of Trial Chamber VI of 8 July 2019 entitled "Judgment," *Prosecutor v Bosco Ntaganda* (ICC-01/04-02/06-2666-Anx5-Corr), Appeals Chamber, 30 March 2021, § 113. For a broader assessment of the various judges' opinions on this matter: O. Pomson, "Ntaganda Appeals Chamber Judgment Divided on Meaning of 'Attack,"' Lieber Institute, 12 May 2021, available at https://lieber.westpoint.edu/ntaganda-appeals-chamber-judgment-divided-meaning-attack/ (last visited 4 November 2023).

the categories of crimes assists in "suppressing or preventing violations against human dignity in peacetime and in war?"[58] This opinion was published just several weeks after the aforementioned *Ongwen* trial judgement, but did not mention the Trial Chamber's observations in this regard.

The doctrinal and historical deficiencies of Judge Eboe-Osuji's broader message notwithstanding,[59] if the protected values of the two categories share much of the same substance (as mentioned above as well), plausible questions may arise as to why cumulative convictions for the same underlying conduct are required,[60] or at least whether their current application in practice merits re-examination. Against this backdrop, the next part will discuss some considerations which may be borne in mind when assessing the question of cumulative charges for both categories of crimes, on the basis of the same underlying conduct.

4 Contemplating Cumulative Charges and Convictions for the Same Underlying Conduct

Much of the discourse in ICL commentary surrounding cumulative charges has revolved around the rights of the defendant. In this regard, some have discussed the challenge of having to mount several defences vis-à-vis the same conduct,[61] and the ramifications of having two separate convictions for two crimes, especially if it is more accurate to describe the conduct as one type of crime rather than the other.[62] The following will

[58] Ibid., § 121.

[59] See part 4.D below.

[60] See, e.g., Jia, *supra* note 28, at 270.

[61] See, e.g., the approach of the ICC Pre-Trial Chamber in the *Bemba* case (Decision on the Prosecutor's Application for a Warrant of Arrest against Jean-Pierre Bemba Gombo, *Prosecutor v Jean-Pierre Bemba Gombo* (ICC-01/05-01/08-14-tENG), Pre-Trial Chamber, 10 June 2008, § 25.) See also Decision Pursuant to Article 61(7)(a) and (b) of the Rome Statute, *Prosecutor v Jean-Pierre Bemba Gombo* (ICC-01/05-01/08-424), Pre-Trial Chamber, 15 June 2009, § 202.

[62] See, for example, *Bemba* Judgement, *supra* note 8, § 745: "... the Chamber notes that the appeals chambers of the ICTY and Extraordinary Chambers in the Courts of Cambodia (ECCC) have found that multiple convictions create a very real risk of prejudice to an accused, including the stigma inherent in being convicted of additional crimes and practical consequences, such as a potential impact on sentencing in the same and subsequent proceedings ...." See also Appeals Judgement, *Prosecutor v Alex Tamba Brima* et al. (SCSL-2004-16-A), Appeals Chamber, 22 February 2008, § 202, discussing the offences of "outrages upon personal dignity" (as a war crime) and "other inhumane acts" (as a crime against humanity),

highlight several additional considerations and perspectives which may be taken into account when assessing the implications of cumulative charges and convictions for both war crimes and crimes against humanity.

It should be noted at the outset that the considerations that affect prosecutorial discretion in the choice of charges are a much broader topic, and this chapter does not intend or aim to address them in full. It merely seeks to highlight that considerations such as those described below may have a role to play when contemplating cumulative charges and convictions for the same underlying conduct.

4.1 Reflection of an Accurate Historical Record

While not uncontroversial,[63] one goal commonly associated with international criminal justice is the establishment of an historical record that accurately reflects the events that occurred.[64] This may be considered as a stand-alone goal, but it can likewise be connected to ensuring that victims' rights to truth and justice are upheld.[65] From this perspective, there is additional value in the outcome of international criminal trials accurately reflecting what has occurred.

When discussing the choice of charges and when setting out to convict defendants, one consideration may therefore be the extent to which the characterization of a particular act as falling within one category of crimes or another affects the historical narrative, by virtue of the criminal label

in relation to forced marriages: "there is no bar to entering cumulative convictions for both offences on the basis of the same facts. However, in this case the Appeals Chamber is inclined against entering such cumulative convictions. The Appeals Chamber is convinced that society's disapproval of the forceful abduction and use of women and girls as forced conjugal partners as part of a widespread or systematic attack against the civilian population is adequately reflected by recognising that such conduct is criminal and that it constitutes an 'Other Inhumane Act' capable of incurring individual criminal responsibility under international law." See also Ambos Vol. II, *supra* note 10, at 256.

[63] See, e.g., Barrie Sander, "History on Trial: Historical Narrative Pluralism Within and beyond International Criminal Courts," 67 *International and Comparative Law Quarterly* (2018) 547.

[64] See, e.g., Cryer et al., *supra* note 18, at 29, 38–40. See also T. Dias, *Beyond Imperfect Justice: Legality and Fair Labelling in International Criminal Law* (Leiden: Martinus Nijhoff, 2022) at 98.

[65] Werle and Jeβberger, *supra* note 16, at 47–48.

that is chosen.[66] For instance, is there value in reflecting that certain conduct took place as part of a military campaign, and would charging defendants for crimes against humanity alongside war crimes affect the war crimes narrative in any way?[67] On the other hand, there have been examples of military campaigns carried out for purposes which would be regarded as criminal, such as mass deportations or transfers,[68] and in such cases reflecting the historical narrative may very well require that the conduct be framed as a crime against humanity through cumulative charges.

4.2 *Fair Labelling*

Characterizations of crimes may affect not only the historical perspective (and that of victims' rights in that respect) but also the rights of the accused, through the issue of fair labelling.[69] Much of the discourse in ICL commentary surrounding cumulative charges has revolved around the rights of the defendant. This section will therefore limit its focus to this particular issue.

In criminal law more generally, fair labelling functions to ensure an accurate representation of the offender's wrongdoing. Such representation is seen as owed to the defendants, including for reputation and sentencing purposes. It is also viewed as owed to the victims, as an important recognition of their suffering.[70] Fair labelling also serves as a way of

[66] Cf. L. van den Herik, "A Quest for Jurisdiction and an Appropriate Definition of Crime – Mpambara before the Dutch Courts," 7 *Journal of International Criminal Justice* (2009) 1117, at 1126.

[67] An example of such a debate may be found in the discourse surrounding the Mpambara proceedings in The Netherlands, wherein, for jurisdictional reasons relating to Dutch law, the accused was tried for war crimes, and not for genocide, against the backdrop of conflicting accounts of the Rwandan genocide of 1994. See van den Herik, ibid., at 1125–1126.

[68] See, e.g., Jia, *supra* note 28, at 264; Mettraux (2005), *supra* note 20, at 158. See also Mettraux (2020), *supra* note 8, at 223–224.

[69] On the connection between the two see, e.g., van den Herik, *supra* note 66, at 1126–1127; T. de Souza Dias, "Recharacterisation of Crimes and the Principle of Fair Labelling in International Criminal Law," 18 *International Criminal Law Review* (2018) 788, at 806–807. See also D. Guilfoyle, "Responsibility for Collective Atrocities: Fair Labelling and Approaches to Commission in International Criminal Law," 64 *Current Legal Problems* (2011) 255, at 260.

[70] J. Chalmers and F. Leverick, "Fair Labelling in Criminal Law," 71 *The Modern Law Review* (2008) 217, at 224–239; A.P. Simester, *Fundamentals of Criminal Law: Responsibility, Culpability and Wrongdoing* (Oxford: Oxford University Press, 2021) at 338–339.

conveying information within and outside the criminal justice system, to the general public more broadly.[71]

In ICL, fair labelling is tied to the field's expressive function and to the raison d'être of defining international crimes as such, and society's moral condemnation of such conduct.[72] In her comprehensive study of fair labelling in ICL, Dias has put forth that "some of the purposes of international criminal law, such as retribution, criminal deterrence, and expressivism, may only be achieved through fair labels,"[73] and that "the various purposes of international criminal law show a profound reliance, if not dependence on fair labels."[74] Fair labelling applies to all stages of criminal proceedings, and international jurisprudence has addressed the need for reflection of the totality of the criminal conduct and culpability of the perpetrator when it comes to convictions and sentencing, recognizing the criminal label's indication of society's condemnation of the acts and the "stigmatizing effect" that it carries.[75]

The significance of the war crimes label has been stressed as a key component in the enforcement of IHL norms and prevention of violations.[76] It also bears noting that IHL takes into account that armed conflicts necessarily entail harm, death and destruction—and their occurrence does not in and of itself indicate illegality.[77] Some have thus stressed that war crimes should be strictly construed, and particularly that consideration should be given to the chaotic situation of conflict, requirements of military strategy, etc.[78]

[71] Dias (2022), *supra* note 64, at 93–94.

[72] Dias (2018), *supra* note 69, at 805; Dias (2022), *supra* note 64, at 88–89, 95.

[73] Dias (2022), *supra* note 64, at 95.

[74] Ibid., at 98.

[75] *Čelebići* Judgement, *supra* note 6, § 769 ff; *Akayesu, supra* note 45, § 468; Dias (2022), *supra* note 64, at 92; Dias (2018), *supra* note 69, at 805; Ambos Vol. I, *supra* note 46, at 70–71; Mettraux (2020), *supra* note 8, at 810; van den Herik, *supra* note 66, at 1126.

[76] M. Sassòli, "Humanitarian Law and International Criminal Law," in A. Cassese (ed.), *The Oxford Companion to International Criminal Justice* (Oxford: Oxford University Press, 2009) 111, at 113. See also: H. van der Wilt, "War Crimes and the Requirement of a Nexus with an Armed Conflict," 10 *Journal of International Criminal Justice* (2012) 1113, at 1128.

[77] Cryer et al., *supra* note 18, at 267; W. J. Fenrick, "Should Crimes Against Humanity Replace War Crimes?" 37 *Columbia Journal of Transnational Law* (1999) 767, at 783.

[78] Cryer et al., *supra* note 18, at 267.

As noted above, while much of the underlying conduct of the two categories of crimes is congruent,[79] the criminalization of the conduct cannot necessarily be considered identical. War crimes are meant to reflect serious violations of the laws or customs of war, and that is what this criminal label was meant to establish. Moreover, at least to some, the label of crimes against humanity carries a significant symbolic value of its own, which is not necessarily the same as that attached to war crimes.[80] Thus, cumulative charges and convictions, when applied in a technical manner, will not always necessarily result in the most accurate reflection of the criminal conduct of the perpetrator.

Of course, the reflection of criminality through fair labelling—like historical accuracy— cuts both ways. While in certain circumstances this consideration could lead to the conclusion that cumulative charging is misplaced, this will not always be the case, and the same conduct could plausibly form the basis of two crimes since military operations and attacks against a civilian population (as they are understood under crimes against humanity) could and have occurred simultaneously.[81] As noted by Dias, "labels can indicate whether certain crimes are sufficiently different. And it is this difference that justifies the cumulation of labels to reflect the totality of the accused's culpability."[82]

Yet, could the frequent practice of cumulative charges be perceived as indicating that the label connected to having committed a war crime is not strong enough by itself? This question relates to the next consideration, which involves the discussion surrounding the hierarchy between the categories of international crimes.

4.3 Preventing the Perception of a Hierarchy of Crimes

While earlier ad hoc tribunal jurisprudence was split on this matter,[83] the predominant approach nowadays is that there is no hierarchy between

[79] Mettraux (2020), *supra* note 8, at 809–810.

[80] Ibid., at 812.

[81] Mettraux (2020), *supra* note 8, at 223–224; Cryer et al., *supra* note 18, at 232. See also Stuckenberg, *supra* note 5, at 844; Werle and Jeßberger, *supra* note 16, at 582.

[82] Dias (2022), *supra* note 64, at 111. See also Partial Dissenting Opinion of Judge Shahabuddeen, *Prosecutor v Goran Jelisić* (IT-95-10-A), Appeals Chamber, 5 July 2001, § 42.

[83] M. Frulli, "Are Crimes against Humanity More Serious than War Crimes?" 12 *European Journal of International Law* (2001) 329, at 344–345; Mettraux (2020), *supra* note 8, at 810.

international crimes.[84] Nevertheless, some ICL commentary points to key differences between the categories of war crimes and crimes against humanity that render crimes against humanity as graver than war crimes.[85] This approach stems from the definitions of the crimes themselves,[86] as well as from certain provisions of the Rome Statute.[87] Some highlight the fact that crimes against humanity are policy crimes and, unlike war crimes, by virtue of their contextual elements cannot be committed "incidentally," therefore implying their inherently more serious nature. Others point to the fact that some particular crimes against humanity, such as extermination or persecution, are inherently of great gravity, whereas war crimes have a wider range of gravity within them.[88]

Insofar as there is a hierarchy among these categories of crimes, this could be seen as a consideration against cumulative charges: if elements for murder as both a war crime and a crime against humanity are fulfilled, a hierarchy could ostensibly mean that the lesser crime should be subsumed in the graver one.[89] Yet even under the leading approach of the tribunals, whereby there is no hierarchy, one could ask whether the very fact of cumulative charges and convictions for the same underlying conduct does not create such a hierarchy, or the illusion of one, as though one of the criminal labels is not sufficient on its own.

From the perspective of the promotion of adherence to IHL, this question ultimately relates to the position of war crimes, as the representation

[84] Ambos Vol. II, *supra* note 10, at 251–253; O'Keefe, *supra* note 33, at 160–161. See, e.g., Judgement, *Prosecutor v Milomir Stakić* (IT-97-24-A), Appeals Chamber, 22 March 2006, § 375; Judgement, *Prosecutor v Ferdinand Nahimana* et al.(ICTR-99-52-A), Appeals Chamber, 28 November 2007, § 1060.

[85] Mettraux (2020), *supra* note 8, at 812; Frulli, *supra* note 83. Though both authors present a nuanced position. For Frulli, this assessment was qualified as a tentative conclusion at the time of writing. Mettraux takes care to stress that on an individual level, there is no difference in the seriousness of a crime of rape, for instance, whether as a war crime or a crime against humanity. See also: Ambos Vol. II, *supra* note 10, at 252–253. For a more expansive approach to the issue of hierarchy of crimes, see O. Olusanya, *Double Jeopardy Without Parameters: Re-characterisation in International Criminal Law* (Antwerp/Oxford: Intersentia, 2004) at 250–251.

[86] Mettraux (2005), *supra* note 20, at 323; Frulli, *supra* note 83, at 334–335.

[87] Frulli, *supra* note 83, at 340; Ambos Vol. II, *supra* note 10, at 251–253.

[88] Mettraux (2020), *supra* note 8, at 812.

[89] Pursuant to one of the models of *concursus delictorum*. See, e.g., Ambos Vol. II, *supra* note 10, at 248–249; F. M. Palombino, "Should Genocide Subsume Crimes Against Humanity? Some Remarks in the Light of the *Krstić* Appeal Judgement." 3 *Journal of International Criminal Justice* (2005) 778.

of IHL, within ICL. A final consideration which also has to do with the relationship between these branches concerns the role that tribunals play in the interpretation of IHL standards.

4.4 Interpretation of IHL Standards

Starting with the earliest jurisprudence of the ICTY, the international tribunals' interpretations of either particular war crimes or the regime as a whole are considered to have had a profound impact on IHL.[90] Indeed, the interaction of ICL institutions with the enforcement, inter alia, of IHL violations that have been criminalized has significant consequences for this legal regime.[91] When considering the matter of cumulative charges and convictions, the question that arises is when war crimes and crimes against humanity are analysed in the same brushstroke,[92] without paying heed to particular aspects of an armed conflict or to where there is an actual overlap between the two types of crimes, and where there was none, could this also inadvertently lead to mistaken interpretations of IHL, or cause confusion or inconsistencies in this area of law?

A recent example of a misinterpretation of this sort can be found in Judge Eboe-Osuji's aforementioned partly concurring opinion in the *Ntaganda* appeal judgement. As noted, a central question in the proceedings involved the interpretation of the concept of "attack" in Article 8 war crimes under the Rome Statute, in light of how this term is understood under IHL.[93] Judge Eboe-Osuji's opinion rejected the Trial Chamber's finding in this regard—that was based on the IHL understanding that attacks in the war crimes under consideration are acts of violence against the adversary committed during the actual conduct of hostilities—by relying, inter alia, on an analysis that (albeit intentionally) conflated war crimes with crimes against humanity, and particularly how the term "attack" is understood under each category.

Specifically, Judge Eboe-Osuji invoked the crimes against humanity contextual element of "attack" as part of his reasoning for why the Trial

[90] For example, *Tadić, supra* note 31, §§31 66–70, 96–127; R. Bartels, "Dealing with the Principle of Proportionality in Armed Conflict in Retrospect: The Application of the Principle in International Criminal Trials," 46 *Israel Law Review* (2013) 271, at 277.

[91] Cryer (2020), *supra* note 31, at 341.

[92] See, e.g., *Bemba* Judgement, *supra* note 8, §§ 622–638.

[93] Order inviting expressions of interest as *amici curiae* in judicial proceedings, *Prosecutor v Bosco Ntaganda* (ICC-01/04-02/06-2554), Appeals Chamber, 24 July 2020, § 15.

Chamber's findings on "attack" for war crimes are too narrow, noting that various crimes against humanity do not involve "the actual infliction of acute violence in every case."[94] However, unlike the contextual element of "civilian population," for which the predominant approach is to generally interpret it in IHL terms,[95] "attack" as a contextual element *for crimes against humanity* is understood in much broader terms and is intentionally detached from its IHL counterpart, as indeed it does not require a military attack and it is not limited to the conduct of hostilities. An attack for the purposes of crimes against humanity may occur during peacetime, and need not, per se, be directed against an enemy or adversary.[96] Judge Eboe-Osuji seems to have rejected this approach—and, perhaps, the separation between the concepts of war crimes and crimes against humanity altogether—and called the different interpretations of attack for the two categories of crimes "artificially constructed" "silos of understanding."[97] Thus, while the risk of mistaken interpretations, or interpretations which are not in line with the *lex lata* of IHL, is not necessarily unique to instances of cumulative charges, this example demonstrates that insofar as terminology, elements or circumstances external to IHL provisions are injected into the analysis, this risk is perhaps exacerbated.

The discussion of the various considerations presented in this section—reflection of an accurate historical record, fair labelling, the perception of a hierarchy of crimes, and interpretation of IHL standards—is not exhaustive. This overview provides only an initial examination of what some critiquing the under-theorized practice of cumulation across categories of crimes in ICL may have had in mind, from the viewpoint of the promotion of adherence to IHL. The following section will explore in greater depth the discussion in the *Ongwen* case surrounding cumulative charges for war crimes and crimes against humanity on the basis of the same underlying conduct, in light of these considerations.

[94] Eboe-Osuji Opinion, *supra* note 57, § 112.

[95] Mettraux (2020), *supra* note 8, at 250–252; Cryer et al., *supra* note 18, at 240–241. But see: Sadat (2017), *supra* note 40 (arguing that the interpretation of civilian population should be detached from the IHL-focused interpretation, so as to better provide for circumstances of peace-time crimes against humanity).

[96] Mettraux (2005), *supra* note 20, at 157; O'Keefe, *supra* note 33, at 141.

[97] Eboe-Osuji Opinion, *supra* note 57, § 120.

5 The *Ongwen* Case: An Opportunity for Doctrinal Clarification Gone By?

In the *Ongwen* case, the defendant challenged the practice of cumulative charges and convictions for the same underlying conduct at both the trial and appellate levels. As part of the appellate proceedings, the Appeals Chamber invited the submissions of *amici curiae*, inter alia, on the question of cumulative convictions. Notably, some of the claims made by the *Ongwen* defence were raised in the earlier *Bemba* et al. case concerning offences against the administration of justice.[98] However, the discussion in the appellate judgement in that case was much more circumscribed than it was in *Ongwen*. More significantly, in *Ongwen* the challenges related specifically to the overlap of the Court's core offences, which are the focus of this chapter as well—war crimes and crimes against humanity—for the same underlying conduct.

In this sense, the *Ongwen* proceedings provided an excellent opportunity for the ICC to provide some doctrinal guidance regarding convictions based on these two categories cumulatively. While the Chambers engaged with Ongwen's claims, as with some of the claims made by *amici curiae* and the prosecution in this regard, they did not pick up the opportunity to provide much further insight beyond the application of the *Čelebići* test.

Ongwen was charged with counts of murder, torture, rape, sexual slavery and forced pregnancy as both war crimes and as crimes against humanity.[99] He argued that cumulative charges for war crimes and crimes against humanity on the basis of the same underlying conduct should be impermissible. Ongwen also argued that even if the Court does accept that charges based on both categories for the same underlying conduct are acceptable, it should not take into account the contextual elements of the crimes when assessing the parameters of the *Čelebići* test, but only the *actus reus* and *mens rea* elements of the particular crimes charged.[100] The prosecution stressed that the contextual elements are "mandatory

[98] Judgement on the appeals of Mr. Jean-Pierre Bemba Gombo, Mr. Aimé Kilolo Musamba, Mr. Jean-Jacques Mangenda Kabongo, Mr. Fidèle Babala and Mr. Narcisse Arido against the Decision of Trial Chamber VII entitled "Judgment pursuant to Article 74 of the Statute," *Prosecutor v Jean-Pierre Bemba Gombo* et al. (ICC-01/05-01/13-2275-Red), Appeals Chamber, 8 March 2018, §§ 740–751.

[99] *Ongwen* Trial Judgement, *supra* note 1, § 2819; *Ongwen* Appeals Judgement, *supra* note 1, §§ 1614–1616.

[100] *Ongwen* Trial Judgement, *supra* note 1, § 2818.

constituent components" which must form part of the analysis undertaken by the Court.[101]

As mentioned earlier, the Trial Chamber rejected the defence's argument. It noted in particular that murder and torture, under their respective war crimes and crimes against humanity manifestations, contain elements that differ beyond their contextual elements.[102] In relation to murder as a war crime, the Court ostensibly referred to the element requiring that the person or persons killed "were either *hors de combat*, or were civilians, medical personnel, or religious personnel taking no active part in the hostilities,"[103] which is not required for the crime against humanity. With regard to torture, the Chamber was ostensibly referring to the similar element requiring that the victims of torture were either *hors de combat*, civilians, or medical or religious personnel taking no active part in the hostilities,[104] and to the element requiring that "the perpetrator inflicted the pain or suffering for such purposes as: obtaining information or a confession, punishment, intimidation or coercion or for any reason based on discrimination of any kind."[105] More broadly, while the Trial Chamber repeated the *Bemba* et al. Appeals Chamber obiter dictum whereby "there may be situations in which crimes requiring *in abstracto* different elements may nevertheless be in impermissible concurrence, and bears this in mind in its analysis of the concrete questions posed in this case,"[106] it also stressed that it "does not consider that contextual elements are qualitatively different from the specific elements of the crimes" and that they should be set aside.[107]

As discussed in Sect. 3, the Trial Chamber also addressed the contextual elements of each category of crimes, and the protected values they aim to safeguard. In particular, the court held that:

> [T]he statutory contextual elements of crimes, considered individually, encapsulate distinct interests protected by the corresponding incriminating provisions under the Statute. Indeed, and as far as the charges in the present case are concerned, the Chamber observes that war crimes give protection

[101] Ibid.
[102] *Ongwen* Trial Judgement, *supra* note 1, § 2819.
[103] Rome Statute, *supra* note 25, ICC Elements of Crime, Article 8(2)(c)(i)-1, element 2.
[104] Rome Statute, *supra* note 25, ICC Elements of Crime, Article 8(2)(c)(i)-4, element 3.
[105] Rome Statute, *supra* note 25, ICC Elements of Crime, Article 8(2)(c)(i)-4, element 2.
[106] *Ongwen* Trial Judgement, *supra* note 1, § 2796.
[107] Ibid., § 2820.

> in criminal law to persons in times of armed conflict, whereas crimes against humanity protect persons where there is a widespread and systematic attack on a civilian population. Thus, the two sets of crimes reflect (partly) different forms of criminality, in that they complement, in terms of protected interests, the incrimination of the individual 'specific' crimes – which, in turn, are therefore distinct depending (also) on the relevant contextual elements. In these circumstances, neither of these two sets of crimes can thus be said to be subsumed or consumed in any way by the other.[108]

These observations are certainly correct, and in line with international criminal jurisprudence up to that point. The issue the present chapter takes with this judgement is its missed opportunity to provide further theoretical reasoning and address some of the merits behind the argument that crimes against humanity and war crimes should not *necessarily* be charged simultaneously for the same underlying conduct, even if the *Čelebići* test is fulfilled, regardless of whether they found the Ongwen defence's arguments compelling to that effect.

This wasted opportunity is even more apparent when considering the Appeals Chamber judgement, which, while devoting some 30 pages to dealing with the defence's challenges with respect to cumulative charges and convictions for overlapping war crimes and crimes against humanity, did not provide much further insight. Before considering the Appeals Chamber judgement itself, two additional circumstantial considerations surrounding that judgement that should have further incentivized the Court to provide additional doctrinal analysis bear mentioning. First, as noted earlier, given various arguments made by the defence in its appeal, the Appeals Chamber issued a decision calling for highly qualified scholars and/or practitioners of criminal procedure and/or of international law to submit their observations to the Court, as *amici curiae*, inter alia, on the question of cumulative convictions.[109] Second, the Appeals Chamber ostensibly had before it Judge Eboe-Osuji's aforementioned partly concurring opinion in the *Ntaganda* Appeals judgement, wherein he not only did not address the *Ongwen* Trial Chamber's finding in respect of the question of protected values of war crimes and crimes against humanity, but also seems to have directly contradicted it, in questioning the

[108] Ibid.

[109] Order inviting expressions of interest as *amici curiae* in judicial proceedings (pursuant to rule 103 of the Rules of Procedure and Evidence), *Prosecutor v Dominic Ongwen* (ICC-02/04-01/15-1884), Appeals Chamber, 25 October 2021.

distinction between the categories of crimes.[110] Despite addressing these matters as well, the *Ongwen* appeal judgement also did not take up the opportunity to clarify this apparent discord.

Ongwen raised three grounds of appeal with respect to the matter of cumulative charges: (1) the Trial Chamber should not have rejected the principle of *ne bis in idem* as a basis for guidance in its assessment of concurrences of crimes[111]; (2) challenges related to concurrence across categories of crimes—specifically that the Trial Chamber erred in imposing multiple convictions for war crimes and crimes against humanity based on the same underlying conduct given the complete overlap of facts in this case, and that the protected interests were identical in each overlapping pair of convictions[112]; and (3) challenges related to concurrences between specific crimes.[113] The prosecution argued that the Appeals Chamber should maintain the established test for "predictable and stable jurisprudence."[114]

Some of the submissions made by the *amici* expressed their support for the *Čelebići* test and thought that while the Trial Chamber's judgement was mostly correct in its implementation of that test, some of the charges merited a departure from the strict application of the test.[115] Regarding the relationship between the two categories of crimes, Paul Behrens, in his *amicus* brief, argued that "[w]ith regard to crimes against humanity and analogous war crimes, there is no relationship of specialty" given that the contextual element distinguishes these categories of crimes.[116]

[110] Eboe-Osuji Opinion, *supra* note 57, § 121.

[111] *Ongwen* Appeals Judgement, *supra* note 1, § 1600 et seq.

[112] Ibid., §§ 1639–1640.

[113] Ibid., § 1661 et seq.

[114] Ibid., § 1602.

[115] Ashraph et al. argued that the Trial Chamber erred in its legal characterization of criminal conduct of sexual slavery as a more specific form of enslavement, and should have entered a conviction for enslavement. See: *Amici Curiae* Observations on Sexual- and Gender-Based Crimes, Particularly Sexual Slavery, and on Cumulative Convictions Pursuant to Rule 103 of the Rules of Procedure and Evidence, *Prosecutor v Dominic Ongwen* (ICC-02/04-01/15-1934), Appeals Chamber, 23 December 2021, at §§ 12, 29–31. Behrens argued that specific charges for inhumane acts should be subsumed in charges of torture, as both a war crime and a crime against humanity, and also argued that enslavement and sexual slavery have a relationship of specialty. See *Amicus curiae* observations on issues raised in the Appeals Chamber Order of 25 October 2021 inviting expressions of interest as *amici curiae* in judicial proceedings (pursuant to Rule 103 of the Rules of Procedure and Evidence), *Prosecutor v Dominic Ongwen* (ICC-02/04-01/15-1943), Appeals Chamber, 23 December 2021, at §§ 34–35.

[116] Behrens *amicus* brief, *supra* note 115, at § 33.

However, the *amicus* brief filed by the Association of Defence Counsel Practising before the International Courts and Tribunals (the ADC-ICT)[117] argued that the Appeals Chamber should reject the *Čelebići* test, as it allows for "improper and unnecessarily punitive cumulative convictions."[118] The ADC-ICT relied on dissenting opinions of ICTY and ICTR judges criticizing the *Čelebići* test as inflexible, arbitrary and artificial, and argued that it could lead to irrational and unfair outcomes.[119] The ADC-ICT also argued that "[t]he ICC has an opportunity to develop a fairer test, more attentive to the rights of the accused."[120] This test, the ADC-ICT suggested, should rely on Judges Hunt and Bennouna's aforementioned dissent in *Čelebići*, and consider only elements that form part of the *actus reus* and *mens rea* of the particular crimes, without the contextual elements. They quote the dissenting opinion in stating that "[t]he purpose of applying this test is ... to determine whether the *conduct* of the accused genuinely encompasses more than one crime."[121] The ADC-ICT also points to Judge Dolenc's dissenting opinion in the ICTR's *Semanza* case, wherein he suggested that the analysis does include the contextual elements, but such "comparison must include a substantive assessment of whether the contextual elements of each article are of such significance that they considerably change the nature or gravity of the crimes in question and therefore justify cumulative convictions for the ideal concurrence of crimes under several articles."[122] Both these alternative tests, the ADC-ICT argues, focus on conduct rather than elements, and should underlie the approach followed by the ICC.[123]

Both Ongwen's challenge and the ADC-ICT arguments relate to considerations of fair labelling. This can be gleaned, inter alia, from Ongwen's invocation of the protected interest of each crime, the ADC-ICT's invocation of Judge Dolenc's dissent concerning the need for a substantive

[117] Observations of the Association of Defence Counsel Practising Before the International Courts and Tribunals (ADC-ICT) As *Amicus Curiae* Regarding Questions Posed by the Appeals Chamber in *Prosecutor v. Ongwen, Prosecutor v Dominic Ongwen* (ICC-02/04-01/15-1937), Appeals Chamber, 23 December 2021.

[118] Ibid., at § 19.

[119] Ibid., at §§ 26–27.

[120] Ibid., at § 29.

[121] Ibid., § 32.

[122] Ibid., § 33, quoting Separate and Dissenting Opinion of Judge Pavel Dolenc, Judgement, *Prosecutor v Laurent Semanza* (ICTR-97-20-T), Trial Chamber III, 15 May 2003, § 23.

[123] Ibid., § 34.

assessment of whether the contextual elements of each crime are of significance, and its assertion that the *Čelebići* test is inflexible, artificial and arbitrary. Though not discussed directly, the ADC-ICT's argument may also be seen as reflective of the expressive function of ICL and in that sense as advocating for an accurate historical record.

In its judgement, the Appeals Chamber once again confirmed the *Čelebići* test, explaining that its rationale is "in the need to reflect the full culpability of an accused person, given that each provision has a 'materially distinct' element protects different legal interests. What the legal interests protected by each crime are, can only be discerned by reference to the elements of that specific crime."[124] The Chamber also agreed with the prosecution's view, that "any remaining concerns arising from overlapping facts can be addressed in the determination of the sentence," and held that this approach "strikes a careful balance between the need to reflect the full culpability of an accused person while safeguarding his or her rights and ensuring that the person is not being unlawfully punished."[125]

While the punishment aspect is certainly of significant importance insofar as the rights of the accused are concerned, focusing on this aspect of the consequences of cumulative convictions fails to take into account other considerations, such as those described above, including the expressivist function of international criminal law and fair labelling and its multiple consequences.

With regard to Ongwen's direct challenge of his conviction for war crimes and crimes against humanity for the same underlying conduct, the Appeals Chamber upheld the Trial Chamber's aforementioned conclusions on this matter as well, and quoted its statement whereby "crimes against humanity and war crimes 'reflect (partly) different forms of criminality, in that they complement, in terms of protected interests, the incrimination of the individual 'specific' crimes – which, in turn, are therefore distinct depending (also) on the relevant contextual elements."[126] The Appeals Chamber continued to state that "[f]or instance in relation to murder both as a crime against humanity and as a war crime, while some of the legal interests protected may coincide (e.g., the right to life), the protected interests discerned from the contextual elements do reflect

[124] *Ongwen* Appeals Judgement, *supra* note 1, § 1635.
[125] Ibid., § 1636.
[126] Ibid., § 1654.

different forms of criminality, and consequently, distinct crimes,"[127] and that "the inclusion of the contextual elements as constitutive elements of the crimes allows the identification of the legal interests protected by each provision which, given the materially distinct contextual elements contained therein, indicate that they protect different legal interests."[128]

Again, while these statements by the Appeals Chamber are definitely true, they do not address the concern raised herein, whereby the difference in contextual elements ultimately leads to the automatic permissibility of cumulative convictions in particular cases. The application of the *Čelebići* test does not require a genuine inquiry into the context of each charge, whether it was connected to the armed conflict in question, or to a widespread attack on the civilian population, or indeed to both. It thus fails to recognize what this omission may mean in terms of the historical record, the consequences for the accused for bearing the stigma for both crimes without a meticulous analysis as to whether the particular case so warrants, the consequences— even if implicit—for the perception of a hierarchy of crimes, and the meaning of a conviction for both categories of crimes from the perspective of each category.

6 The War Crimes "Nexus" Requirement: An Existing Tool for a New Approach?

The considerations described in Sect. 4 underscore that the fact that both types of crimes can occur during times of armed conflict does not in and of itself imply that charges should be brought forward under both categories for the same underlying conduct in each case. Conversely, the fact that cumulative charges and convictions are not necessarily carried out in international criminal practice in a way that is sufficiently sensitive to the unique characteristics of each case does not mean they should necessarily be prohibited.[129] The pertinent questions are therefore whether cumulation should be such an automatic course of action, as reliance on the *Čelebići* test ultimately leads to,[130] is the current test satisfactory in light of the

[127] Ibid.

[128] Ibid., § 1656.

[129] But see Jia's more principled position in this respect, whereby "as long as it is generally accepted that the two crimes are different, cumulative charges should be avoided." Jia, *supra* note 28, at 271.

[130] Stuckenberg, *supra* note 5, at 848. See also: Fenrick *supra* note 77, at 785. Moreover, as mentioned above, the ICC's Trial Chamber rejected the *Ongwen* defence's challenge to

challenges described, and whether there are other ways to differentiate between cases in which it should be applied and cases in which it should not.

One approach that was raised in this regard was that of a *lex specialis* rule.[131] While such a rule may be applied in several ways, put simply, under this proposition, war crimes would be the *lex specialis* to crimes against humanity in situations where both would seem to apply, and alleged perpetrators would be charged for the former when the elements of both types of crimes are fulfilled for the same underlying conduct. This idea is intuitively appealing. However, it also carries the risk of being too sweeping a solution, and could raise challenges with respect to some of the considerations discussed before, such as accurately reflecting the criminality in the perpetrator's conduct, and preventing the perception of a hierarchy of crimes. Moreover, automatically charging a suspect for allegedly perpetrating a war crime rather than a crime against humanity may be equally arbitrary as automatically charging for both types of crimes with respect to the same underlying conduct.[132]

Perhaps then the solution does not lie with one fixed approach, especially when considering that the ICC is a multi-situational court that will have to deal with a large variety of scenarios and circumstances throughout the years. Thus, the suggestion put forth below does not necessarily replace the *Čelebići* test but rather seeks to modify it, by adding another layer of analysis. This layer focuses on the contextual elements of war crimes, namely that they be committed in the context of an armed conflict.

Under the proposed approach, each instance of cumulative charges for a war crime and a crime against humanity, on the basis of the same underlying conduct of the defendant, would require that an analysis of the nexus element in relation to that particular conduct be carried out. Such an analysis would replace what is currently mixed practice in ICC case law,

the Court's adoption of the *Čelebići* test, which suggested, inter alia, that insofar as the Court does apply this test it does not take into consideration the contextual elements, but only compare the *actus reus* and *mens rea* elements. See *Ongwen* Trial Judgement, *supra* note 1, §§ 2818, 2820.

[131] See, e.g., P. Akhavan, "Reconciling Crimes Against Humanity with the Laws of War: Human Rights, Amed Conflict, and the Limits of Progressive Jurisprudence," 6 *Journal of International Criminal Justice* (2008) 21, which discusses IHL in its entirety, as the *lex specialis*. It should be noted that case law has specifically determined that genocide is not *lex specialis* in relation to crimes against humanity or to war crimes. See Werle and Jeβberger, *supra* note 16, at 328, 439.

[132] See also Akayesu, *supra* note 45, § 470 and *Ongwen* Trial Judgement, *supra* note 1, § 2820, both implicitly rejecting this idea.

wherein in some cases the chambers carry out a single examination of the nexus element with regard to all of the war crimes charges in a specific case, and in other cases, while a more particularized approach is undertaken, the analysis of the nexus element remains a terse one at best.[133]

As mentioned, the nexus requirement between the alleged conduct and an armed conflict is a distinct feature of war crimes,[134] and distinguishes them from both ordinary domestic offences and other international crimes.[135] In this sense, there is nothing new with the proposed approach, as this is an element that needs to be examined in any case. The proposal merely seeks to put additional emphasis on this element when deciding if the cumulative charges or convictions are warranted in each particular case, in light of considerations such as those discussed earlier. In other words, it seeks to utilize this existing element as a filter which will allow a particularized approach for every charge contemplated. This approach may also be reflective of Judge Dolenc's aforementioned position in the *Semanza* case.

However, assessments of the nexus element in the jurisprudence of international criminal tribunals thus far, most notably articulated by the *Kunarac* Appeals Chamber,[136] have been criticized in several respects. For example, one of the criteria put forth by the Chamber in that case was that a nexus would be established when the perpetrator acted "in furtherance of" or "under the guise" of an armed conflict. This was seen as too broad a characterization since it also covered those perpetrators who take advantage of the chaos that is a common feature of times of conflict. Likewise, other criteria that were indicated, such as the fact that the perpetrator was a combatant or that the victim was a non-combatant, were also seen as

[133] Compare *Ongwen* Trial Judgement, *supra* note 1, §§ 2689–2693 and *Bemba* Judgement, *supra* note 8, §§ 664–665, with *Katanga*, *supra* note 8, §§1231–1234 and *Ntaganda supra* note 8, § 742. The exception to this observation may be found in §§ 983–986 of the *Ntaganda* Judgement, which may be due to the fact that this analysis concerned the novel finding regarding rape and sexual slavery within one's own party to the conflict.

[134] Jia, *supra* note 28, at 246.

[135] Van der Wilt, *supra* note 76, at 1116; Ambos Vol. II, *supra* note 10, at 140–141; van den Herik, *supra* note 66, at 1124.

[136] Judgement, *Prosecutor v Dragoljub Kunarac* et al. (IT-96-23 & IT-96-21/1-A), Appeals Chamber, 12 June 2002, §§ 58–59. This articulation of the nexus to an armed conflict element was adopted in ICC case law as well. See *supra* note 8, *Katanga*, § 1176; *Bemba*, §§ 142–144; *Ntaganda*, §§ 731–732; and *Ongwen* Trial Judgement, *supra* note 1, § 2689.

insufficient, since ordinary crimes by or against persons of that status may equally take place.[137]

Thus, in order for the nexus to an armed conflict to work as an additional filtering layer in decisions regarding cumulative charging, how it is interpreted or applied may very well need to be tweaked. Commentators have suggested several directions in this regard, such as focusing on the fact that the armed conflict facilitates the commission of the war crime, in the sense that it could not have been committed in the same way during peacetime, and looking at whether the acts can be characterized as perversion of accepted military practices.[138] Cassese has discussed, in this regard, a requirement that a war crime be "occasioned by and linked to the armed conflict" and that "the offence must be committed to pursue the aims of the conflict or, alternatively, be carried out with a view to somehow contributing to attain the ultimate goals of a military campaign or, at a minimum, in unison with the military campaign."[139]

However, challenges to the analysis of the nexus requirement may arise even upon modification of the *Kunarac* dictum. An example in this regard is that of the crime of rape, when committed by soldiers on their own initiative during an armed conflict. Such a crime is occasioned by and linked to the conflict, but framing such conduct as serving the ultimate goal of a military campaign would be highly dubious. On the other hand, such a crime could not necessarily have been committed the same way during peacetime, and it could be characterized as a perversion of accepted military practices.[140]

In any event, for present purposes the aim is not to propose a bright line rule for the nexus to the armed conflict requirement, but only to demonstrate that this element can provide another level of analysis through which cumulative charges or convictions should be looked at, the deficiencies of how this element has been interpreted thus far notwithstanding.[141] The benefit of this approach is that it would not rule out, a priori, cumulative charges, and when a case merits charges of both types of crimes, those

[137] Van der Wilt, *supra* note 76, at 1127–1128.

[138] Ibid.; Ambos Vol. II, *supra* note 10, at 142–143.

[139] Cassese, *supra* note 50, at 1397. But see Jia, *supra* note 28, at 270.

[140] See, e.g., Cassese, *supra* note 50, at 1406–7; van der Wilt, *supra* note 76, at 1127–1128.

[141] In this regard, the analysis of the nexus requirement in ICC jurisprudence thus far has been far from satisfactory. See, e.g., *supra* note 8: *Katanga*, § 1176; *Bemba*, §§ 142–144, 664–665; *Ntaganda*, §§ 731–732; and *Ongwen* Trial Judgement, *supra* note 1 §§ 2689, 2813–2815.

would be pursued. Rather, it encourages an inquiry into whether the conduct in question *can be* more accurately described using the framework of either war crimes or crimes against humanity, requiring an assessment on the facts of the case, and not just relying on the fact that each category of crimes has different contextual elements which require proof of a fact not required by the other.[142]

It bears noting that such an approach may draw certain criticisms as well. One such critique may question its utility in situations such as internal/intra-state NIACs, in two respects. First, when considering the origin of crimes against humanity, and the fact that this category came into being in order to allow the prosecution of crimes against nationals of the same country as the perpetrators. In internal NIACs that would always be the case, so it could be asked whether a meticulous application of cumulative charging is more challenging, or should be conducted with particular caution in this regard. Second, internal NIACs may take different forms, and it would not necessarily always be easy to discern the goals of the military campaign in order to differentiate between war crimes and crimes against humanity.[143]

While these are surely factors that merit consideration when contemplating a modification of how cumulative charges and convictions are applied, additional aspects may also be taken into account. First, while significant differences remain,[144] war crimes in NIACs are nowadays much more developed and elaborate—something that presumably may be of assistance when considering the gap that crimes against humanity were originally meant to fill.[145] In this regard, of course, crimes against humanity can equally be committed in international and not just intra-state contexts. Second, and more broadly, the discussion presented in this chapter concerns a legal policy choice regarding how to adjudicate conduct that rises to the level of war crimes.[146] The considerations behind this policy choice equally apply to circumstances of internal NIACs. In other words, if examining cumulative charges would require not only meeting the "distinct elements" *Čelebići* test—be it for reasons of cementing the status of war crimes, or reasons of historical narratives or fair labelling—this decision

[142] Cf. Mettraux (2005), *supra* note 20, at 324.
[143] See, e.g., Cassese, *supra* note 50, at 1404.
[144] Werle and Jeßberger, *supra* note 16, at 458.
[145] Mettraux (2020), *supra* note 8, at 806.
[146] Cf. van den Herik, *supra* note 66, at 1126.

is pertinent to internal NIACs as well. The promotion of adherence to IHL, by repudiating war crimes, is no less significant in those contexts.

Thus, while using the nexus to the armed conflict element as an additional lens through which the decision whether or not to employ cumulative charges and convictions may be assessed might be more challenging when it comes to internal NIACs, it is by no means a futile exercise.

7 Conclusion

Cumulative charges and convictions feature prominently in ICL practice, and the ICC is no different in this regard. This chapter focused on some of the issues that arise when considering this practice, with respect to instances where both war crimes and crimes against humanity charges are based on the same underlying conduct, and sought to explore how this practice may affect the promotion of adherence to IHL—one of the goals of the war crimes regime of ICL.

Was the ICC, as the main vehicle through which this regime may be upheld in coming years, correct in adopting, as is, the test developed for situations of cumulation in the ad hoc tribunals? While it is beyond the scope of this chapter to provide a comprehensive answer to this question, it has highlighted several relevant considerations when contemplating the cumulation of charges and convictions for war crimes and crimes against humanity for the same underlying conduct, going forward. What the analysis above demonstrates is that adopting a strict policy, based on a technical test, will not necessarily lead to results that are sufficiently attuned to the particular circumstances of each and every case. A more nuanced approach, such as the proposal put forth to take into account the war crimes nexus requirement when determining cumulative charges and convictions, would require an in-depth analysis of the war crimes context for each and every charge.

Insofar as we have entrusted ICL institutions with the enforcement of IHL violations that have been criminalized, their interactions with, and application of, IHL will influence this legal regime, and significant implications may follow. If they provide sound and reasoned decisions when convicting for war crimes, including when doing so cumulatively with crimes against humanity, they will contribute to the enforcement of IHL and compliance with it, in line with the aims of the war crimes regime.

CHAPTER 6

Digital Evidence in the Practice of the International Criminal Court: What Future for Proceedings on War Crimes Committed in Ukraine?

Khrystyna Gavrysh

1 Introduction

Although criminal proceedings typically rely on witness testimony, the principle of orality provides only a limited view of the entire experience of international criminal tribunals. As emphasized by the International Criminal Court (ICC) regarding the proceedings conducted by the International Criminal Tribunal for the former Yugoslavia (ICTY) aimed at determining the international criminal responsibility of individuals in the Balkan conflict, "(…) the more access the Prosecution had to official documents of the entities involved or to audio or video evidence, the lesser

K. Gavrysh (✉)
Department of Law, University of Ferrara, Ferrara, Italy
e-mail: gvrkry@unife.it

O. Svaček, M. Faix (eds.), *Prosecution of War Crimes before the ICC*, Global Issues, https://doi.org/10.1007/978-3-031-84216-0_6

weight was placed on the evidence given by witnesses."[1] This is even more evident nowadays, as social media platforms such as Facebook, X/Twitter, YouTube, Instagram, and Telegram have become *de facto* repositories for storing evidence of the most heinous crimes.

Even the International Criminal Court, despite its clear commitment to respecting the importance of testimony in international criminal proceedings,[2] has accepted its crisis, which is also accentuated by an increasing difficulty in finding credible witnesses.[3] More and more often, indeed, the need has emerged in its practice to exclude some testimonies due to their contradictory statements.[4] This reflects more generally the crisis of the regime of evidence within the Court. It is well known that the Prosecutor faces difficulties in gathering sufficient evidence to overcome the confirmation of charges stage before the Pre-Trial Chamber, leading to the total or partial rejection thereof.[5] The difficulties also stem from the need to establish close cooperation with the state where the crimes under examination were committed, which does not always prove to be fully cooperative, especially due to the prior position of the accused at the top

[1] Corrigendum to the Decision on Evidentiary Scope of the Confirmation Hearing, Preventive Relocation and Disclosure under Article 67(2) of the Statute and Rule 77 of the Rules, *Prosecutor v. Germain Katanga Mathieu Ngudjolo Chui* (ICC-01/04-01/07-428-Corr), Pre-Trial Chamber, 25 April 2008, § 76.

[2] Art. 69(2) of the Rome Statute of the International Criminal Court (adopted 17 July 1998, entered into force 1 July 2002), 2187 UNTS 90 (hereafter Rome Statute): "[t]he testimony of a witness at trial shall be given in person (…)."

[3] On the practice of the International Tribunal for Rwanda, the Special Court for Sierra Leone, and the East Timor Tribunal see N. Combs, *Fact-Finding Without Facts. The Uncertain Evidentiary Foundations of International Criminal Convictions* (Cambridge: Cambridge University Press, 2010). See also P. Murphy, 'Excluding Justice or Facilitating Justice? International Criminal Law Would Benefit from Rules of Evidence,' 12 *The International Journal of Evidence and Proof* (2008) 15.

[4] N. Combs, "Evidentiary Deficiencies in International Criminal Law: Tracing the Trajectory from Ignored to Integral to Irrelevant," 22 *International Criminal Law Review* (2022) 835, at 838 f.

[5] See, for instance, Decision on the Confirmation of Charges, *Prosecutor v. Bahr Idriss Abu Garda* (ICC-02/05-02/09-243-Red), Pre-Trial Chamber, 8 February 2010; Decision on the Confirmation of Charges, *Prosecutor v. Callixte Mbarushimana* (ICC-01/04-01/10-465-Red), Pre-Trial Chamber, 16 December 2011; Decision on the Confirmation of Charges Pursuant to Article 61(7)(a) and (b) of the Rome Statute, *Prosecutor v. William Samoei Ruto* et al. (ICC-01/09-01/11-373), Pre-Trial Chamber, 23 January 2012; Decision on the Confirmation of Charges Pursuant to Article 61(7)(a) and (b) of the Rome Statute, *Prosecutor v. Francis Kirimi Muthaura* et al. (ICC-01/09-02/11-382-Red), Pre-Trial Chamber, 23 January 2012.

of the state organization. Furthermore, practice shows that the personnel employed by the Court to investigate crimes on-site often consists of few officials with relatively short terms of duty.[6]

Therefore, the Prosecutor needs to have access to all the available resources. In particular, digital evidence may fill some gaps, considering the peculiarities of international criminal proceedings, which are aimed at determining events with wide-ranging consequences, involving various actors of the international community. In other words, it may be necessary to use all that evidence that may contribute to a description of the events under investigation, and especially of the context of the armed conflict where such events occurred. In fact, the expansion of online services has generated vast quantities of data that private entities collect, store, and process. This data can serve as crucial digital evidence in criminal cases, such as IP addresses identifying suspects or geolocation data pinpointing crime scenes. This holds true in international criminal justice as well, where commercial satellite imagery might reveal mass graves, or online propaganda could establish a perpetrator's intent to commit genocide.[7] Therefore, the concept of digital evidence encompasses any information

[6] For example, during the investigation against *Gbagbo*—later acquitted of the charges of crimes against humanity committed during the wave of post-electoral violence in 2010–2011 in Ivory Coast—eight investigators in total were utilized, alternating in groups of two. Also, in the investigation the situation in Libya, a group of eleven individuals was deployed, and in the investigation against Lubanga Dyilo—convicted of war crimes committed during the Second Congo War between 2002 and 2003—a total of twelve were used, a number considered insufficient even by Prosecutor Lavigne, as emerged from his statements during the trial. C.M. De Vos, "Investigating from Afar: The ICC's Evidence Problem," 26 *Leiden Journal of International Law* (2013) 1009. See also Transcripts, *Prosecutor v. Thomas Lubanga Dyilo* (ICC-01/04-01/06-Rule68Deposition-Red2-ENGWT), Chamber, 16 November 2010, 16. These strategic choices are primarily linked to the need to contain the costs of proceedings while also ensuring procedural efficiency. However, the price to pay often lies in the insufficiency of the evidentiary framework to support the prosecution in court. War Crimes Research Office, Investigative Management, Strategies, and Techniques of the International Criminal Court's Office of the Prosecutor (2012). S. SáCouto and K. C. Thompson, "Investigative Management, Strategies, and Techniques of the ICC's OTP," in C. Stahn (ed.), *The Law and Practice of the International Criminal Court* (Oxford: Oxford Academic, 2015).

[7] Europol, *SIRIUS EU Digital Evidence Situation Report - 2nd Annual Report* (2020), available at https://www.europol.europa.eu/cms/sites/default/files/documents/sirius_desr_2020.pdf (last visited 15 October 2024); L. Freeman, "Digitally Disappeared: The Struggle to Preserve Social Media Evidence of Mass Atrocities," 23 *Georgetown Journal of International Affairs* (2022) 105.

or data stored on, transmitted, or received by an electronic device, mostly a computer or smartphone, or made available via the web, including CDs, DVDs, MP3s, USBs, and digital broadcast radio.[8] Open-source data, namely publicly available information, may play a crucial role in this context, given the widespread use of smartphones worldwide and their utility in documenting relevant details within armed conflicts and sharing them though social media. Nowadays, user-generated evidence represents a significant advancement in international criminal justice.[9]

Nevertheless, the use of digital evidence in international criminal proceedings faces certain shortcomings. This chapter aims at analyzing both the increasing importance of such evidence in international criminal law practice and its limits. Specifically, the analysis will focus on the ongoing conflict between Russia and Ukraine.

2 Rules on Evidence in the Case Law of the International Criminal Court

Before analyzing digital evidence specifically, we need first to briefly address evidentiary rules within the ICC Statute (Statute) and its pertinent case law. The International Criminal Court enjoys a certain degree of autonomy in admitting and evaluating evidence. The evidentiary regime is governed by Articles 64 and 69 of the Statute and Articles 63–75 of the Rules of Procedure and Evidence, adopted by the Assembly of States Parties (pursuant to Article 51 of the Statute), which is the body representing all states that have ratified the Statute and exercising legislative power over it.[10] These rules are supplemented by the Court's Regulations, adopted by the Court itself (pursuant to Article 52 of the Statute).

[8] T.R. Kirabira, "Technology as a Key Tool for the Prosecution of International Crimes: Lessons from Uganda," 22 *International Criminal Law Review* (2022) 1143, at 1145; R. B. da Silva, "Updating the Authentication of Digital Evidence in the International Criminal Court," 22 *International Criminal Law Review* (2022) 941; R.V. Segate, "Cognitive Bias, Privacy Rights, and Digital Evidence in International Criminal Proceedings: Demystifying the Double-Edged ai Revolution," 21 *International Criminal Law Review* (2021) 242, at 248–249; E. Casey, *Digital Evidence and Computer Crime* (Cambridge: Academic Press, 2011) 12.

[9] R.J. Hamilton, "Social Media Platforms in International Criminal Investigations," 52 *Case Western Reserve Journal of International Law* (2020) 213, at 215; R. Hamilton, 'User-Generated Evidence,' 57 *Columbia Journal of Transnational Law* (2018) 1.

[10] A. Cassese, 'The Statute of the International Criminal Court: Some Preliminary Reflections,' 10 *European Journal of International Law* (1999) 144.

Pre-Trial and Trial Chambers may both decide on the admission of evidence. In fact, while the primary role of the former is to confirm the charges if there are "substantial grounds to believe" that the alleged facts were committed in accordance with the prosecution's theory, it may also find itself in the position of assessing the admissibility—albeit with a non-binding decision on the Trial Chamber[11]— of the evidence presented at the confirmation hearing.[12] Indeed, although Article 69 is located in Part VI of the ICC Statute, which pertains to the trial, Article 63(1) of the Rules of Procedure specifies that the rules regarding evidence, including Article 69 of the Statute, apply to all the chambers of the Court.[13]

After the confirmation of the charges, the management of the proceedings shifts to the Trial Chamber, which, pursuant to Article 64(3)(a) of the Statute, adopts the necessary procedures to facilitate the fair and expeditious conduct of the trial. Before the Trial Chamber, the parties submit the evidence relevant to the case. Where such evidence appears insufficient, the Trial Chamber may also order "the production of evidence in addition to that already collected prior to the trial or presented during the trial by the parties" (Article 64(6)(d) of the Statute). Then the Trial Chamber rules on the prima facie admissibility of the evidence presented,[14] as set forth by Article 69(4) of the Statute, which states that "[t]he Court may rule on the relevance or admissibility of any evidence, taking into account, *inter alia*, the probative value of the evidence and any prejudice that such

[11] Decision on the Prosecution's and Defence's applications for leave to appeal the Decision on the confirmation of charges, *Prosecutor v. Thomas Lubanga Dyilo* (ICC-01/04-01/06), Pre-Trial Chamber, 24 May 2007, § 75.

[12] A. Novak, *The International Criminal Court. An Introduction* (Heidelberg: Springer, 2015) at 65–68.

[13] B. Krzan, "Admissibility of Evidence and International Criminal Justice," 7 *Revista brasileira de direito processual penal* (2021) 170. In the same fashion, see Decision on the Evidence Disclosure System and Setting a Timetable for Disclosure between the Parties, *Prosecutor v. Jean-Pierre Bemba Gombo* (ICC-01/05-01/08-55), Pre-Trial Chamber, 31 July 2008, §§ 8–11. Conversely, see Decision on the Set of Procedural Rights Attached to Procedural Status of Victim at the Pre-Trial Stage of the Case, *Prosecutor v. Germain Katanga and Mathieu Ngudjolo Chui* (ICC-01/04-01/07-474), Pre-Trial Chamber, 13 May 2008, §§ 107–113.

[14] M. Nerenberg and W. Timmermann, "Documentary Evidence," in K.A.A. Kham, C. Buisman and C. Gosnell (eds), *Principles of Evidence in International Criminal Justice* (Oxford: Oxford University Press, 2010) at 443 ff.; B. Krzan, *supra* note 13, at 172. Corrigendum to Decision on the admissibility of four documents, *Prosecutor v. Thomas Lubanga Dyilo* (ICC-01/04-01/06-1399-Corr), Trial Chamber, 21 January 2011, § 27.

evidence may cause to a fair trial or to a fair evaluation of the testimony of a witness (…).”[15]

This assessment pertains to the relevance and probative value of the evidence presented. The first requirement entails that the evidence concerns the charges,[16] namely that it is logically connected to one of the facts subject to the criminal proceedings. In other words, according to the Court, “[i]f the evidence tendered makes the existence of a fact at issue more or less probable, it is relevant.”[17] On the other hand, the analysis of the probative value of the elements presented pertains to the reliability and weight to be assigned to each of them.[18] Such assessment implies an evaluation of the intrinsic coherence of each piece of evidence in light of the overall evidentiary framework.[19] Lastly, the probative value of the admitted evidence must outweigh any prejudice it may cause to the fair conduct of the trial. This principle could be violated in cases where, for example, such evidence proves to be redundant, thus excessively prolonging the duration of the proceeding,[20] or where the evidence was obtained in violation of the Statute or internationally recognized human rights. In any case, such violation must undermine the reliability of the evidence itself or its admission must cause serious prejudice to the integrity of the proceed-

[15] H. Brady, “The System of Evidence in the Statute of the International Criminal Court,” in F. Lattanzi and W. A. Schabas (eds.), *Essays on the Rome Statute of the International Criminal Court* (1st edn., Fagnano Alto: Il Sirente, 1999) at 286 ff.; M. Klamberg, *Commentary on the Law of the International Criminal Court* (Bruxelles: Torkel Opsahl Academic EPublisher, 2017) at 532 ff.

[16] Decision on the Prosecution’s Application for Admission of four documents from the bar table pursuant to Article 64(9), *Prosecutor v. Thomas Lubanga Dyilo* (ICC-01/04–01/06), Trial Chamber, 20 January 2011, § 27.

[17] Decision on the Bar Table Motion of the Defence of Germain Katanga, *Prosecutor v. Germain Katanga and Mathieu Ngudjolo Chui* (ICC-01/04-01/07-3184), Trial Chamber, 21 October 2011, § 16. In the same fashion, see also Judgement, *The Prosecutor v. Milutinović* et al. (IT-05-87-T), Trial Chamber, 26 February 2009, § 36.

[18] Decision on the confirmation of charges, *Prosecutor v. Germain Katanga and Mathieu Ngudjolo Chui* (ICC-01/04-01/07), Pre-Trial Chamber, 30 September 2008, § 78.

[19] Ibid., § 77: “(…) In the view of the Chamber, this means that the Chamber must look at the intrinsic coherence of any item of evidence, and to declare inadmissible those items of evidence of which probative value is deemed prima facie absent after such an analysis. Any other assessment of the probative value of any given item of evidence will be made in light of the whole body of evidence introduced at the confirmation hearing.”

[20] Decision on the Prosecution’s Application for Admission of Materials into Evidence Pursuant to Article 64(9) of the Rome Statute, *Prosecutor v. Jean-Pierre Bemba Gombo* (ICC-01/05-01/08) Pre-Trial Chamber, 6 September 2012, § 8.

ings (Article 69(7) of the Statute). The Court will assess such prejudice in light of the probative weight of the evidence presented: the lower the weight, the more likely it is that the prejudice caused will lead to the exclusion of the evidence.[21]

It is quite common for the Chamber to assess the overall evidentiary framework, instead of focusing on the admissibility of single pieces of evidence,[22] at the moment of the final decision on the responsibility of the accused.[23] Therefore, evidence can be excluded at every stage of the proceeding. As highlighted in the *Bemba* case,

> [t]he Majority decision to admit into evidence all of the materials included by the prosecution in its List of Evidence, is based on making a *prima facie* finding of the admissibility of this evidence. It is important to distinguish this from the Chamber's future determination of the probative value to be given to the evidence (…) at the end of the case when making its final judgement.[24]

[21] B. Krzan, *supra* note 13, at 172. See also *Lubanga Dyilo, (Corrigendum)*, *supra* note 13, § 29: "Whilst it is trite to observe that all evidence that tends to incriminate the accused is also 'prejudicial' to him, the Chamber must be careful to ensure that it is not unfair to admit the disputed material, for instance because evidence of slight or minimal probative value has the capacity to prejudice the Chamber's fair assessment of the issues in the case". The need to safeguard the principle of fair trial in assessing the probative value of the evidence presented has characterized the activities of ad hoc Tribunals as well. In application of this principle, during the proceedings against *Kvočka* et al., the ICTY excluded from the evidentiary record a newspaper article concerning the Omarska concentration camp due to unfounded and defamatory assertions that could have prejudiced the defense's efforts. Decision on Zoran Zigic's Motion for Rescinding Confidentiality of Schedules Attached to the Indictment Decision on Exhibits, *The Prosecutor v. Miroslav Kvočka* et al. (IT-98-30/1-T), Trial Chamber, 19 July 2001.; W. A. Schabas, *The UN International Criminal Tribunals. The Former Yugoslavia, Rwanda and Sierra Leone* (Cambridge: Cambridge University Press, 2006) at 452 ff.

[22] Judgment on the appeals of Mr. Jean-Pierre Bemba Gombo and the Prosecutor against the decision of Trial Chamber III entitled "Decision on the admission into evidence of materials contained in the prosecution's list of evidence," *Prosecutor v. Jean-Pierre Bemba Gombo* (ICC-01/05-01/08-1386), Appeals Chamber, 3 May 2011, § 60.

[23] Decision on the admission into evidence of materials contained in the prosecution's list of evidence, *Prosecutor v. Jean-Pierre Bemba Gombo* (ICC-01/05-01/08-1022), Trial Chamber, 19 November 2010, § 24.

[24] Ibid., § 9. See also § 10: "The Majority considers that a ruling on admissibility is not a pre-condition for the admission of any evidence, as it only implies a prima facie assessment of the relevance of any material, on the basis that it appears to be a priori relevant to the case. Apart from what is provided for in Article 69(7)(*a*) and (*b*) of the Statute and Rule 71 of the Rules, no evidence is per se inadmissible, and the uncontested jurisprudence of the Court

Moreover, it is undebatable that the Trial Chamber may decide on the admissibility of evidence at any stage of the criminal proceedings, as set forth by Article 69(4) of the Statute.

The International Criminal Court has outlined that there are two different approaches to the admissibility stage. According to the first approach, the Trial Chamber may "recognize the submission of such item of evidence by a party without a prior ruling on its relevance and/or admissibility and consider its relevance and probative value as part of the holistic assessment of all evidence submitted when deciding on the guilt or innocence of the accused." Alternatively, it may "rule on the relevance and/or admissibility of such item of evidence as a pre-condition for recognizing it as 'submitted' (…) and assess its weight at the end of the proceedings as part of its holistic assessment of all evidence submitted."[25]

Regardless of the approach to be chosen, it is important that an evaluation of single pieces of evidence is conducted before the final decision on the case.[26] To this end, the Court should consider the specific probative weight each piece of evidence may acquire according to the principle of "holistic evaluation and weighing of all the evidence taken together in relation to the fact at issue",[27] in order to establish international criminal

determines that any evidence may be 'admitted (…) unless [it] is expressly ruled inadmissible (…) by the Chamber upon a challenge by any of the participants at the hearing.'" R. Gallmetzer, "The Trial Chamber's Discretionary Power to Devise the Proceedings Before It and Its Exercise in the Trial of Thomas Lubanga Dyilo," in C. Stahn and G. Sluiter (eds), *The Emerging Practice of the International Criminal Court* (Leiden/Boston: Martinus Nijhoff, 2009) at 508 ff.

[25] Judgment, *Prosecutor v. Dominic Ongwen* (ICC-02/04-01/15), Trial Chamber IX, 4 February 2021, § 234.

[26] This is evident from the proceeding against Bemba Gombo, where the Appeals Chamber deemed the Trial Chamber's choice to admit the entire body of evidence prima facie "outside the legal framework of the Court." However, the Trial Chamber did not assess the probative value of individual pieces of evidence even at the time of the final decision. Such a choice prevented the parties from raising objections to the admissibility or relevance of the evidence under Article 64(1) of the Court's Rules of Procedure. *Bemba Gombo (Judgment on the Appeals), supra* note 22, §§ 2, 37 e 57.; C. Schuon, "The Appeals Decision in the ICC's Case on the Trial on the Appeals Decision Jean-Pierre Bemba Gombo Chamber's 'Decision Admission into Evidence of Materials Contained in the Prosecution's List of Evidence,'" 25 *Leiden Journal of International Law* (2012) 511; D. F. Sorvatzioti, "Free Evaluation of Evidence: Does the ICC Need a Law of Evidence?" 22 *International Criminal Law Review* (2021) 895.

[27] Judgment pursuant to Article 74 of the Statute, *Prosecutor v. Jean-Pierre Bemba Gombo* (ICC-01/05-01/08-3343), Trial Chamber III, 21 March 2016, § 223: "(…) the Chamber's

responsibility beyond a reasonable doubt.[28] It has been stated that "[t]he reasonable doubt standard cannot consist of imaginary or frivolous doubt – it must have a rational link to the evidence, lack of evidence or inconsistencies in the evidence."[29] In other words, "the proof must be such as to exclude not every hypothesis or possibility of innocence, but every fair or rational hypothesis which may be derived from the evidence, except that of guilt."[30] Such analysis is conducted according to the principle of the international criminal judge's free evaluation of evidence,[31] having due regard for the criteria of reliability and credibility of the evidence presented in light of the entire body of evidence.[32]

3 Digital Evidence in International Criminal Justice

Although the widespread dissemination of digital evidence has only occurred recently, its usage traces back to the experience of the Nuremberg Tribunal established in 1945 by the London Agreement for prosecuting those responsible for atrocities committed during World War II. In fact, the Chief Prosecutor heavily relied on first types of such evidence, thus considering data stemming from early IBM computers, where Nazis

admissibility inquiry has no bearing on the Chamber's final determination of the weight that it will give to any particular item of evidence (...)[which] is to be performed at the end of the case when the Chamber assesses the evidence as a whole." A. Giannini, "Theories of Evaluation of Evidence and the International Criminal Court Practice," *SSRN Electronic Journal* (2017) 1.

[28] D. Marchesi, 'Intercepted Communications in the Ongwen Case: Lessons to Learn on Documentary Evidence at the ICC,' 22 *International Criminal Law Review* (2021) 920. *Contra* P. Murphy, "No Free Lunch, No Free Proof: The Indiscriminate Admission of Evidence is a Serious Flaw in International Criminal Trials," 12 *Journal of International Criminal Justice* (2010) 539.

[29] Judgment on the Prosecutor's appeal against the decision of Trial Chamber II entitled "Judgment pursuant to Article 74 of the Statute," *Prosecutor v. Mathieu Ngudjolo Chui* (ICC-01/04-02/12-271-Corr), Appeals Chamber, 7 April 2015, § 109.

[30] Judgment, *Prosecutor v. Dusko Tadić* (IT-94-1-A), Appeals Chamber, 15 July 1999, § 174.

[31] Sorvatzioti, *supra* note 26, at 896.

[32] Judgment pursuant to Article 74 of the Statute, *Prosecutor v. Thomas Lubanga Dyilo* (ICC-01/04-01/06), Trial Chamber, 14 March 2012, § 94; Judgment pursuant to Article 74 of the Statute, *Prosecutor v. Germain Katanga* (ICC-01/04-01/07), Trial Chamber, 7 March 2014, § 79; Judgment pursuant to Article 74 of the Statute, *Prosecutor v. Mathieu Ngudjolo Chui* (ICC-01/04-02/12-3-t), Trial Chamber, 26 December 2012, § 45.

tracked lists of Jewish names, photographs, and hours of film taken by war correspondents.[33]

In the same fashion, International ad hoc Tribunals for the former Yugoslavia (ICTY) and for Rwanda (ICTR), established by the Security Council respectively with Resolutions 827 (1993) and 955 (1994), dealt with specific types of digital evidence. In particular, ICTR prosecutors led the way in leveraging novel forms of evidence to bolster groundbreaking charges. This especially happened in the case *Prosecutor v. Nahimana* et al., also known as "media case."[34] In this instance, the prosecution presented radio broadcasts as evidence to substantiate the accusation of inciting genocide by promoting violence over public airwaves. At the ICTY, the prosecution submitted aerial images to depict areas of disrupted soil, indicating mass graves in cases involving *Krstić*, *Blagojević*, *Popović* et al., and *Tolimir*.[35] These images, submitted to the prosecution by the US government, additionally depicted structures, vehicles, sizable groups of detainees, and corpses, aligning with witness testimonies and aiding the judges in understanding pertinent geographic contexts, such as the proximity of the mass graves to Srebrenica.

The establishment of the International Criminal Court coincided with the rise of the Internet, especially social media (like Instagram, Facebook, Telegram, and TikTok), the increasing availability of smartphones and other mobile devices equipped with cameras and GPS, the emergence of drone technologies, and accessibility and dropping cost of satellite imagery.[36] Therefore, in the meantime, the amount of digital data to process during international criminal proceedings has drastically grown. Even though the ICC still hasn't had to deal with trials mostly based on digital evidence, since its initial investigations concerning situations in the Democratic Republic of Congo and Uganda, it relied respectively upon

[33] L. Freeman, 'Digital Evidence and War Crimes Prosecutions: The Impact of Digital Technologies on International Criminal Investigations and Trials,' 41 *Fordham International Law Journal* (2018) 283, at 285–286.

[34] Judgment and Sentence, *The Prosecutor v. Ferdisand Nahimana* et al. (ICTR-99-52-T), Trial Chamber I, 3 December 2003.

[35] Judgement, *Prosecutor v. Zdravko Tolimir* (IT-05-88/2-T), Trial Chamber II, 12 December 2012, § 67 ff.; Judgement, *Prosecutor v. Vujadin Popovid* et al. (IT-05-88-T), Trial Chamber II, 10 June 2010, § 72 ff.; Judgement, *Prosecutor v. Vidoje Blagojević and Dragan Jokić* (IT-02-60-T), Trial Chamber I, 17 January 2005, § 312 ff.; Judgement, *Prosecutor v. Radislav Krstic* (IT-98-33-T), Trial Chamber, 2 August 2001, §§ 64, 114, 202, 222 etc.

[36] Freeman, *supra* note 33.

video evidence,[37] audio recordings of radio intercepts,[38] and sometimes even on open-source evidence posted on social media.[39]

After all, as confirmed by the Trial Chamber in the case against Lubanga Dyilo:

> [T]he Chamber has concluded that it enjoys a significant degree of discretion in considering all types of evidence. This is particularly necessary given the nature of the cases that will come before the ICC: there will be infinitely variable circumstances (...) in which those involved will have been killed or wounded, and the survivors or those affected may be untraceable or unwilling – for credible reasons – to give evidence.[40]

Photographs, aerial and satellite images, audio and video recordings, call records, emails, open-source materials, namely those publicly available online, user-generated evidence, and other electronic communications or records are only some examples of vast digital materials that may be submitted by the Prosecutor. Since 24 May 2023, such material may also be collected through the ad hoc application at the Prosecutor's Office (OTP), namely the OTPLink, for the purpose of "allowing the Office to handle larger information volumes utilizing Artificial Intelligence (AI) and Machine Learning (ML)."[41] Therefore, witnesses may enter into direct contact with the OTP, ensuring the conservation of material relevant for future proceedings. This application may represent a turning point in the collection of user-generated content by the OTP, since its capture from social media is sometimes impossible due to its removal by the relevant company for the violation of terms of service, given the violent content of

[37] *Lubanga Dyilo* (Judgment pursuant to Article 74 of the Statute), *supra* note 32, § 93.

[38] Judgment, *The Prosecutor v. Dominic Ongwen* (ICC-02/04-01/15), Trial Chamber IX, 4 February 2021, §§ 666, 879, 1019, 1107 etc.

[39] Public Warrant of Arrest, *The Prosecutor v. Mahmoud Mustafa Busayf Al-Werfalli* (ICC-01/11-01/17), Pre-Trial Chamber I, 15 August 2017, § 12.

[40] Decision on the admissibility of four documents, *The Prosecutor v. Thomas Lubanga Dyilo* (ICC-01/04-01/06), Trial Chamber I, 13 June 2008, § 24.

[41] See https://otplink.icc-cpi.int. See also 'ICC Prosecutor Karim A.A. Khan KC announces launch of advanced evidence submission platform: OTPLink,' International Criminal Court, 24 May 2023, available at https://www.icc-cpi.int/news/icc-prosecutor-karim-aa-khan-kc-announces-launch-advanced-evidence-submission-platform-otplink (last visited 15 October 2024). T. Mimran and L. Weinstein, "Digitalize It: Digital Evidence at the ICC," Lieber Institute, 14 August 2023, available at https://lieber.westpoint.edu/digitalize-it-digital-evidence-icc/ (last visited 15 October 2024).

such material.[42] In this case, only upon request, the company will take a copy of the relevant content as provided for by Section 2703(f) of the Electronic Communications Privacy Act adopted in the USA in 1986 for the purpose of regulating US-based online service providers to curate or remove content.[43] For instance, Facebook deleted content concerning the situation in Myanmar – which is also under investigation before the ICC – because it was linked to incitement of violence against the Rohingya minority.[44]

However, the complexity of digital evidence may put the respect of the principle of the equality of arms set forth by Article 67 of the Statute at risk. It is thus important that the prosecution promptly discloses both the original materials and the methodology applied to analyze them, so that the defense may effectively react against it. For instance, if the prosecution plans to present a report detailing specific call records and associated IP addresses, and the defense wasn't involved in selecting the relevant data, defense attorneys must not only have access to all other call records to demonstrate the irrelevance of the presented data, they must also be able to evaluate the methodology employed by the prosecution in order to compare their own findings.[45]

Digital evidence is classified as documentary evidence and is thus assessed using the same criteria as traditional paper documents.[46] This means that the admission of digital evidence—as any other type of evidence—depends on its relevance, its probative value, and any prejudice that such evidence may cause to a fair trial. Furthermore, under Article 69(7) of the Statute, pieces of evidence may be excluded, if they are unreliable or their admission would be antithetical, which might happen if the evidence was obtained in violation of the right to privacy.[47]

[42] Freeman, *supra* note 7, at 106 ff.; Hamilton, *supra* note 9, at 213–214.

[43] See www.oas.org.

[44] "Removing Myanmar Military Officials from Facebook," Meta, 28 August 2018, available at https://about.fb.com/news/2018/08/removing-myanmar-officials/ (last visited 15 October 2024); see also United Nations, Report of the Human Rights Council, 42nd session (2019), available at https://digitallibrary.un.org/record/3900742/files/A_74_53_Add.1-EN.pdf?ln=en (last visited 15 October 2024).

[45] M. de Arcos Tejerizo, "Digital evidence and fair trial rights at the International Criminal Court," 36 *Leiden Journal of International Law* (2023) 749.

[46] Freeman, *supra* note 33; Segate, *supra* note 8, at 249. Generally, on admissibility of documentary evidence, see K. Gavrysh, "La circolazione probatoria nella giustizia penale internazionale (*judicial notice*)," 1 *Rivista di diritto internazionale* (2024) 31.

[47] Tejerizo, *supra* note 45, at 762.

In particular, the probative value of evidence is established based on criteria such as reliability, credibility, origin, and genuineness, to be proved by the party seeking its admission.[48] In other words, the Chamber must examine its authenticity, namely the "provenance, source or author, as well as their role in the relevant events, the chain of custody from the time of the item's creation until its submission to the Chamber, and any other relevant information."[49] According to ICC case law, if the parties submit digital material as evidence from the bar table, they are required to provide accompanying information that substantiates its authenticity and reliability.[50]

Application of these criteria dates back to the activity of international ad hoc tribunals. For instance, during the *Milošević* proceeding before the ICTY, the prosecution presented in court some excerpts of footage purportedly showing the Serbian wartime unit Scorpions callously executing prisoners from Srebrenica. The defendant alleged that the video presented in court had been edited and manipulated. He noted that much of the tape lacked dates and that the location of the murders was a village located 160 km from Srebrenica.[51] Consequently, the Chamber declined to admit the footage as evidence.[52] On the other hand, issuing the arrest warrant of Al-Werfalli, the ICC decided that footage shared on social media depicting the shooting of victims by the accused satisfied the standard of 'reasonable grounds to believe,' considering that it was corroborated by "an expert report on the authentication of the video, prepared by a renowned, independent institute."[53] Unfortunately, the case did not provide any further guidance on the admissibility of digital evidence, since it was closed for the passing of the accused.

Authentication of digital material is even more important in relation to open-source evidence, considering that it might be easily accessible

[48] See *Bemba* (Judgment pursuant to Article 74 of the Statute), *supra* note 27, § 247.

[49] Ibid.

[50] Decision on the Prosecution's Application for Admission of Materials into Evidence Pursuant to Article 64(9) of the Rome Statute, *Prosecutor v. Jean-Pierre Bemba Gombo* (ICC-01/05-01/08), 8 October 2012, § 159.

[51] Transcripts, *Prosecutor v. Slobodan Milošević* (IT-02-54-T), 8 June 2005, 40734 ff.

[52] V. Petrović, "A Crack in the Wall of Denial: The Scorpions Video in and out of the Courtroom," in D. Zarkov, M. Glasius (eds.), *Narratives of Justice In and Out of the Courtroom* (Berlin: Springer, 2014) at 89; Segate, *supra* note 8, at 65.

[53] Second Warrant of Arrest, *The Prosecutor v. Mahmoud Mustafa Busayf Al-Werfalli* (ICC-01/11-01/17), Pre-Trial Chamber I, 4 July 2018, § 18. Mimran, Weinstein, *supra* note 41, at 4–5.

through unlawful means and easily alterable, thus creating so-called deep fakes, namely falsified videos that are sophisticated enough to deceive most viewers.[54] It is thus important that the admissibility is subjected to the analysis of metadata by experts for identifying the date, time, geolocation, and author of the material to be admitted.[55] For instance, in the *Bemba* et al. case, the defense contested the admission of screenshots of photographs from Facebook, tendered by the prosecution as evidence, on the grounds of the lack of forensic verification of the metadata.[56] However, in its final ruling, the Trial Chamber did not deliberate on their admissibility. Instead, it determined that the facts were adequately established through alternative evidence, rendering the screenshots not directly pertinent to the decisive reasoning of the case.[57]

Moreover, video evidence is easy to manipulate, since "videos represent the effect of a number of subjective choices",[58] namely what scenes and from what angle and perspective to record, cutting those considered as not necessary for a specific type of narration. Therefore, the ICC must balance the probative value of such evidence with its negative effects, in order to avoid prejudice to a fair trial. For this purpose, UC Berkeley adopted the Berkeley Protocol, which consolidates standards and guidelines for investigators and civil society pertaining to the identification, collection, preservation, verification, and analysis of digital open-source information. It aims at ensuring the efficient utilization of such information in international criminal and human rights investigations.[59] The same

[54] Hamilton, *supra* note 9, at 218; L. Freeman, "Hacked and Leaked: Legal Issues Arising from the Use of Unlawfully Obtained Digital Evidence in International Criminal Cases," 25 *UCLA Journal of International Law and Foreign* Affairs (2021) 45.

[55] K. Hellwig, "The Potential and the Challenges of Digital Evidence in International Criminal Proceedings," 22 *International Criminal Law Review* (2022) 965.

[56] Defence Response to Prosecution's Third Request for the Admission of Evidence from the Bar Table, *Prosecutor v. Jean-Pierre Bemba Gombo* et al. (ICC-01/05-01/13), Trial Chamber, 9 October 2015, §§ 83–86. Da Silva, *supra* note 8, at 953.

[57] Tejerizo, *supra* note 45, at 760.

[58] Segate, *supra* note 8, at 255.

[59] New York and Geneva, Human Rights Center and OHCHR, Berkeley Protocol on Digital Open Source Investigations: A Practical Guide on the Effective Use of Digital Open Source Information in Investigating Violations of International Criminal, Human Rights and Humanitarian Law (2020). Similarly, the Leiden Guidelines concerning the utilization of digitally derived evidence in international criminal courts and tribunals delineate crucial factors practitioners need to contemplate prior to presenting such evidence. See Kalshoven-Gieskes Forum, Leiden University, *Leiden Guidelines on the Use of Digitally Derived Evidence in International Criminal Courts and Tribunals* (2021), available at https://leiden-guide-

purpose is pursued by the Guidelines for Civil Society Organisations adopted by the European Union Agency for Criminal Justice Cooperation (Eurojust) and the ICC in 2022, which "are intended to further assist you in your efforts to collect and preserve information that may ultimately become admissible evidence in court."[60]

Once the evidence is admitted according to the mentioned criteria, the international criminal judge focuses on assessing its probative weight. Such a process requires first the separate evaluation of each piece of evidence, always in light of the entire evidentiary body. Second, it requests a comprehensive assessment of both inculpatory and exculpatory evidence, in order to establish whether the entire body of evidence is sufficient to convict the accused beyond reasonable doubt.[61] This examination takes into account the circumstances of the specific case on a case-by-case basis. Furthermore, regardless of the procedure chosen for the admissibility of evidence,[62] "a determination of the guilt or innocence of the accused requires an assessment on the part of a trial chamber of the relevance and reliability of all evidence submitted that has not been excluded in the course of the trial."[63] To this end, requirements already applied in the admissibility phase may come into play, namely the source of the document, the chain of custody from its creation to its presentation to the Court, and its relevance to the events under scrutiny. The ICC thus performs a second check on the reliability of the documents submitted by the parties, which may also lead to their exclusion from the body of evidence.[64]

lines.com/assets/Leiden%20Guidelines%20on%20the%20Use%20of%20DDE%20in%20ICCTs_20220404.pdf (last visited 15 October 2024).

[60] 'Documenting International Crimes and Human Rights Violations for Accountability Purposes: Guidelines for Civil Society Organisations,' Eurojust, 21 September 2022, available at https://www.eurojust.europa.eu/publication/documenting-international-crimes-and-human-rights-violations (last visited 15 October 2024).

[61] Judgement, *Prosecutor v. Andre Ntagerura* et al. (ICTR-99-46-A), Appeals Chamber, 7 July 2006, § 174; Judgement, *Prosecutor v. Sefer Halilović* (IT-01-48), Appeals Chamber, 16 October 2007, § 125. M. Klamberg, *Evidence in International Criminal Trials. Confronting Legal Gaps and the Reconstruction of Disputed Events* (Leiden/Boston: Martinus Nijhoff, 2013) 161. Y. McDermott, "Strengthening the Evaluation of Evidence in International Criminal Trials," in J. Nicholson, *Strengthening the Validity of International Criminal Tribunals* (Leiden/Boston: Martinus Nijhoff, 2018) 181.

[62] See *infra* § 2.

[63] *Ongwen* (Trial Judgment), *supra* note 38, § 244.

[64] Judgement, *Prosecutor v. Vidoje Blagojevic* et al. (IT-02-60-T), Trial Chamber I (Section A), 17 January 2005, § 29: "In order to assess the authenticity of documents, the Trial Chamber considered evidence as to the source and chain of custody. The Trial Chamber did

In fact, the weight given to digital evidence could be minimal if judges fail to grasp its importance or if it lacks proper sourcing or authentication.[65] In this perspective—although this does not exclude the possibility that a submitted element may acquire independent probative value (Article 63(4), of the procedural rules)—digital evidence that is corroborated by other evidentiary sources gains greater significance in supporting a particular occurrence or element of the crime.[66] However, as it has been stated in the *Bemba* case, "there is no strict requirement that every document be authenticated officially or by a witness in court."[67]

Application of these principles is evident in the *Lubanga* case, where the prosecution submitted video footage showing the accused inspecting troops who seemed to be under the age of fifteen, along with an expert report on X-ray examinations of bones and teeth. While this supplementary evidence had limited probative value, it contributed to corroborating elements of witness testimony and ultimately to securing a conviction.[68] The proceedings against Al-Mahdi, affiliated with an Islamic terrorist group sentenced for the war crime of destroying cultural property in Timbuktu (Mali) between June and July 2012, represent another useful example of the growing importance of digital evidence.[69] Even though the accused made an admission of guilt and agreed to the admission of evidence, the Chamber had to examine the evidence presented pursuant to Article 65(2) of the ICC Statute, namely—among others—satellite images from before and after the destruction, audio recordings found on the Internet containing statements from members of armed groups, and video recordings on the Internet showing the destruction at the time of the

not consider unsigned, undated or unstamped documents, a priori, to be void of authenticity. Even when the Trial Chamber was satisfied of the authenticity of a particular document, it did not automatically accept the statements contained therein to be an accurate portrayal of the facts. The Trial Chamber evaluated this evidence within the context of the trial record as a whole."

[65] Freeman, *supra* note 33.

[66] *Bemba* (Judgment pursuant to Article 74 of the Statute), *supra* note 27, § 237; Katanga (Judgment), *supra* note 32, § 91. Klamberg, *supra* note 61, at 179 ff.

[67] Bemba Gombo (Decision on the Prosecution's Application for Admission of Materials into Evidence Pursuant to Article 64(9) of the Rome Statute), *supra* note 20, § 9. See also, Judgement, The Prosecutor v. Boškoski et al. (IT-04-82), Trial Chamber II, 10 July 2008, §§ 262–265.

[68] *Lubanga Dyilo* (Judgment pursuant to Article 74 of the Statute), *supra* note 32, § 70.

[69] Freeman, *supra* note 33, at 314 ff.

attack, with geolocation reports.[70] Therefore, "[t]he Chamber f[ound] beyond reasonable doubt that the admission of guilt, together with the additional evidence presented, satisfies the essential facts to prove the crime charged and that there are no viable affirmative defences."[71]

4 The Ukrainian Case

The ongoing international armed conflict between Russia and Ukraine could represent an important step in enhancing the use of digital evidence in international criminal proceedings, considering the growing community of volunteers and professionals who gather user-generated evidence and open-source intelligence.[72] In fact, since the invasion of Ukraine, the public has had access to numerous videos, satellite images, and photographs, and especially user-generated content shared on social media (in particular, TikTok, Telegram, and X/Twitter), concerning the atrocities committed by the armed forces in the Ukrainian territories. Therefore, such a conflict could also serve as a pivotal examination of whether evidence generated through these methods can significantly contribute to securing convictions.[73]

The amount of digital material reporting possible violations of international criminal law stems both from the activity of Ukrainian citizens and from the commitment of civil society. In fact, Ukrainian authorities have repurposed widely used government applications—such as e-Enemy,

[70] Transcripts, *Prosecutor v. Ahmad Al Faqi Al Mahdi* (ICC-01/12-01/15-T-4-Red-ENG), Trial Chamber VIII, 22 August 2016, 28–29.

[71] Judgment and Sentence, *The Prosecutor v. Ahmad Al Faqi Al Mahdi* (ICC-01/12-01/15), Trial Chamber VIII, 27 September 2016, § 43.

[72] L. Carrée, "The Role of Technology in the Exposition of War Crimes in Ukraine: How the Use of Cutting-Edge Technologies and Open-Sources Investigations Can Expose Human Rights Violations," LSE Human Rights, 2 February 2023, available at https://blogs.lse.ac.uk/humanrights/2023/02/02/the-role-of-technology-in-the-exposition-of-war-crimes-in-ukraine-how-the-use-of-cutting-edge-technologies-and-open-sources-investigations-can-expose-human-rights-violations/#:~:text=With%20the%20development%20of%20new,alleged%20perpetrators%20and%20victims%2Fsurvivors (last visited 15 October 2024). See also S. Aalto-Setälä and M. F. Jaramillo Gomez, "ICC Investigations in Ukraine: How Digitally Derived Evidence Can Make a Difference," leidenlawblog, 19 May 2022), available at https://www.leidenlawblog.nl/articles/icc-investigations-in-ukraine-how-digitally-derived-evidence-can-make-a-difference (last visited 15 October 2024).

[73] J. Hendrix, "Ukraine May Mark a Turning Point in Documenting War Crimes," Just security, 28 March 2022, available at https://www.justsecurity.org/80871/ukraine-may-mark-a-turning-point-in-documenting-war-crimes/ (last visited 15 October 2024).

launched in 2020 for the purpose of conserving digital identifying documents of Ukrainians—enabling citizens to record and document war crimes. Additionally, new tools have been introduced to the application in order to assist users in geo-tagging and time-stamping their footage, with the aim of aiding authorities in attributing responsibility to perpetrators.[74] Moreover, the office of Ukraine's Prosecutor General set up a website, warcrimes.gov.ua, for properly documenting war crimes and crimes against humanity committed by the Russian military in Ukraine. On this website citizens may fill in a simple form with details concerning possible violations along with their geolocation and digital evidence. For this purpose, the former Ukrainian Prosecutor General Iryna Venediktova publicly declared that her office had adopted the Berkeley Protocol to improve societal engagement in digital evidence collection.[75]

On the other hand, a coalition of civil society groups swiftly mobilized to document potential war crimes, dubbing themselves the 5 AM Coalition.[76] This coalition was established by over thirty organizations, including humanitarian groups like Crimea-SOS, human rights defenders such as the ZMINA Center for Human Rights, investigators like Truth Hounds, journalists represented by the Public Interest Journalism Lab, and analysts and lawyers such as the Ukrainian Legal Advisory Group. They aimed at ensuring justice for Ukrainian citizens, sharing crucial information with international bodies, providing law enforcement agencies with potential evidence to strengthen legal accountability for both domestic and international crimes, and influencing both Ukrainian and international media to galvanize a global response.[77] Similar initiatives, such as eyeWitness to Atrocities, established by the International Bar Association, offer documenters mobile applications enabling the capture and transmission of digital evidence to a secure repository, along with

[74] V. Bergengruen, "How Ukraine Is Crowdsourcing Digital Evidence of War Crimes," Time, 18 April 2022, available at https://time.com/6166781/ukraine-crowdsourcing-war-crimes/ (last visited 15 October 2024).

[75] Tweet by Iryna Venediktova, X, 9 March 2022, available at https://x.com/VenediktovaIV/status/1501596904009912320 (last visited 15 October 2024).

[76] See "Ukraine 5 Am Coalition," 5:00 Am Coalition, available at https://www.5am.in.ua/en (last visited 15 October 2024).

[77] A. Koenig, "From 'Capture to Courtroom' Collaboration and the Digital Documentation of International Crimes in Ukraine," 20 *Journal of International Criminal Justice* (2022) 829.

tailored training.[78] By early March 2022, the eyeWitness app had facilitated the capture of over 20,000 pieces of footage related solely to the invasion of Ukraine.

All these instruments may gather evidence necessary for pursuing international investigations against those responsible for international crimes committed in Ukraine. As is well known, currently two proceedings are pending before the International Criminal Court for crimes committed in Ukraine during the invasion and occupation by Russia. In fact, even though Ukraine ratified the ICC Statute only on 21 August 2024 with law No. 3909-IX,[79] it has accepted the jurisdiction of the Court under Article 12(3) of the Statute through two declarations deposited respectively on 9 April 2014, concerning any crimes committed on Ukrainian territory between 21 November 2013 and 22 February 2014, and on 8 September 2014, regarding all those potentially committed from 20 February 2014 onwards. Within this proceeding, six arrest warrants have already been issued. The first two were delivered on 17 March 2023 against Russian President Vladimir Putin and Russian Commissioner for Children's Rights Maria Lvova-Belova, both charged with deportation and forced transfer of minors from the occupied territories under Articles 8(2)(a)(vii) and 8(2)(b)(viii) of the Statute.[80] The other two arrest warrants were issued more recently, namely on 5 March 2024, against Sergei Ivanovich Kobylash, a Lieutenant General in the Russian Armed Forces, and Viktor Nikolayevich Sokolov, an Admiral in the Russian Navy. According to the ICC, "there are reasonable grounds to believe that the two suspects bear responsibility for missile strikes carried out by the forces under their command against the Ukrainian electric infrastructure from at least 10 October 2022 until at least 9 March 2023", thus being allegedly responsible for the war crime of directing attacks at civilian objects under Article 8(2)(b)(ii) of the Rome Statute and the war crime of causing excessive incidental harm to civilians or damage to civilian objects under Article 8(2)(b)(iv) of the Rome

[78] See 'eyeWitness to Atrocities,' available at https://www.eyewitness.global (last visited 15 October 2024).

[79] The text is available only in Ukrainian at: www.itd.rada.gov.ua (last visited 30 September 2024).

[80] "Statement by Prosecutor Karim A. A. Khan KC on the issuance of arrest warrants against President Vladimir Putin and Ms. Maria Lvova-Belova," International Criminal Court, 17 March 2023, available at https://www.icc-cpi.int/news/statement-prosecutor-karim-khan-kc-issuance-arrest-warrants-against-president-vladimir-putin (last visited 15 October 2024).

Statute, and the crime against humanity of inhumane acts under Article 7(1)(k) of the Rome Statute. Finally, the last two arrest warrants were issued more recently, namely on 25 June 2024, against Sergei Kuzhugetovich Shoigu, Minister of Defence of the Russian Federation at the time of the alleged conduct, and Valery Vasilyevich Gerasimov, Chief of the General Staff of the Russian Federation's Armed Forces, and First Deputy Minister of Defence of the Russian Federation. According to the Pre-Trial Chamber II, there are reasonable grounds to believe that both individuals bear individual criminal responsibility for the war crime of directing attacks against civilian objects (art. 8(2)(b)(ii) of the ICC Statute), the war crime of causing excessive incidental harm to civilians or damage to civilian objects (art. 8(2)(b)(iv) of the ICC Statute) and the crime against humanity of inhumane acts under article 7(1)(k) of the ICC Statute.[81]

Currently, all the documentation concerning arrest warrants is issued in 'secret' in order to protect witnesses and to safeguard the investigations. While it is difficult to imagine which type of digital evidence may underlie the first set of proceedings, for what concerns the consistent bombing of electric infrastructure, web and social networks contain numerous images and videos. It is thus highly likely that this proceeding will benefit from the effort of civil society to collect digital evidence. This is also true for future trials that may be initiated before the ICC concerning the situation in Ukraine. For instance, other arrest warrants may be issued in future with regard to such incidents as: the Mariupol theater airstrike perpetrated on 16 March 2022 against the Donetsk Academic Regional Drama Theater in Mariupol, whose evidence could be represented by satellite images of Mariupol, which shows the Russian word 'children' written on each side of the theater before its bombing[82]; or the Bucha massacre per-

[81] "Situation in Ukraine: ICC judges issue arrest warrants against Sergei Ivanovich Kobylash and Viktor Nikolayevich Sokolov," International Criminal Court, 5 March 2024, available at https://www.icc-cpi.int/news/situation-ukraine-icc-judges-issue-arrest-warrants-against-sergei-ivanovich-kobylash-and (last visited 15 October 2024); "Situation in Ukraine: ICC judges issue arrest warrants against Sergei Kuzhugetovich Shoigu and Valery Vasilyevich Gerasimov", International Criminal Court, 25 June 2024, available at https://www.icc-cpi.int/news/situation-ukraine-icc-judges-issue-arrest-warrants-against-sergei-kuzhugetovich-shoigu-and. (last visited 20 February 2025) F. Capone, 'The Wave of Russian Attacks on Ukraine's Power Infrastructures: An Opportunity to Infuse Meaningfulness into the Notion of 'Dual-use Objects'?' 8 *European Papers* (2023) 741.

[82] See K. Vlamis, "Satellite images show the destruction of a Mariupol theater that had 'CHILDREN' written outside — before and after it was bombed by Russia," *Insider*, 20

petrated in March 2022, which may also be proved by satellite images of bodies on the streets of Bucha,[83] among others.

Moreover, relevant judicial authorities may also receive support from the joint investigation team set up on alleged core international crimes committed in Ukraine. It is composed by members of seven states[84] and a participant from the Office of the Prosecutor of the International Criminal Court and it operates under the auspices of the European Union Agency for Criminal Justice Cooperation (Eurojust).[85] The involved states also entered into a ***memorandum of understanding*** with the United States Department of Justice on 3 March 2023, in order to coordinate their efforts in their respective investigations.[86] The evidence collected by the participants in the joint investigative team is intended to be stored at the Core International Crimes Evidence Database (CICED), whose activity started in February 2023.[87] The database aims at securely storing, cataloging, and analyzing evidence of the most heinous crimes, thus preventing its duplication,[88] and ensuring its authenticity for the purposes of future

March 2022, available at https://www.businessinsider.com/satellite-images-show-destruction-of-mariupol-theater-bombed-by-russia-2022-3 (last visited 15 October 2024); Carrée, *supra* note 72.

[83] Aalto-Setälä, Jaramillo Gomez, *supra* note 72.

[84] Lithuania, Poland, Ukraine, Estonia, Latvia, Slovakia, and Romania.

[85] The relative agreement is not available online. See, however, the press release issued on 28 March 2022, available at: www.eurojust.europa.eu (last visited 27 January 2024); Y. Tan and S. Yang, "The Joint Investigation Team in Ukraine: An Opportunity for the International Criminal Court?" 22 *Chinese Journal of International Law* (2023) 103; M. Plachta, 'European Union Steps Up Effort to Bring Russia for Accountability for Aggression Against Ukraine,' 39 *International Enforcement Law Reporter* (2023) 107.

[86] See the press release issued on 4 March 2023, available at: www.eurojust.europa.eu (last visited 27 January 2024). "The United States Promotes Individual Criminal Accountability for Aggression and Atrocity Crimes Committed by Russians in Ukraine," 117 *American Journal of International Law* (2023) 516.

[87] The outlined cooperation system can currently benefit from another specialized entity focused on the crime of aggression, the International Centre for the Prosecution of the Crime of Aggression against Ukraine (ICPA), established at Eurojust. Its purpose is to collect evidence for potential future proceedings, support the activities of state judicial authorities in ongoing investigations, and enhance their cooperation in the exchange of evidence and the formulation of common strategies in the exercise of criminal prosecution. See the press release issued on 5 March 2023, available at: www.eurojust.europa.eu (last visited 27 January 2024). B. Zagaris, International Center for the Prosecution of the Crime of Aggression against Ukraine Opens, 39 *International Enforcement Law Reporter* (2023) 248.

[88] See the press release issued on 23 February 2023, available at: https://www.eurojust.europa.eu (last visited 27 January 2024).

submission as evidence before international and domestic tribunals. Receiving evidence from CICED might thus guarantee an easy admissibility phase.

5 Concluding Observations

The International Criminal Court enjoys broad powers and high flexibility as to the admission of evidence tendered by the parties. Such flexibility entails the possibility to declare admissible not only classic forms of evidence, like testimony, but also new ones, including digital evidence and especially open-source evidence. In fact, these types of evidence are increasingly important in international criminal proceedings, considering the widespread use of technology worldwide and the possibility to share digital material on social media. However, the criteria of credibility requested for its admission entail the obligation of analyzing its authenticity, which may be difficult to assess as it requires specific scientific knowledge. Therefore, this might run counter to the principle of equality of arms. For this reason, the prosecution must promptly disclose both the original materials and the methodology employed for their analysis. Moreover, the ICC must engage experts to analyze the metadata of the material submitted so as to verify its date, time, geolocation, and author, thus avoiding the risk of admission of so-called deep fakes.[89] It may also be useful to train ICC judges on digital evidence, so as to develop their skills with regard to the authentication of digital material.[90]

However, since the beginning of its activity, the ICC has had to deal with digital evidence in a very few cases. Just like its predecessors, it had to analyze video evidence, audio recordings of radio intercepts,[91] and satellite images.[92] Moreover, more recently even open-source evidence, such as that shared on social media, came into play,[93] but with limited outcomes.

[89] Freeman, *supra* note 33, at 318; Tejerizo, *supra* note 45, at 752 and 765.

[90] See International Criminal Court, *Independent Expert Review of the International Criminal Court and the Rome Statute System: Final Report* (2020), § 555, available at https://asp.icc-cpi.int/sites/asp/files/asp_docs/ASP19/IER-Final-Report-ENG.pdf (last visited 15 October 2024). Da Silva, *supra* note 8, at 961.

[91] *Lubanga Dyilo* (Judgment pursuant to Article 74 of the Statute), *supra* note 32; *Ongwen* (Trial Judgment), *supra* note 38.

[92] *Al Mahdi* (Transcripts), *supra* note 70.

[93] *Al-Werfalli* (Public Warrant of Arrest), *supra* note 39; *Al Mahdi* (Transcripts), *supra* note 70.

As demonstrated in the *Lubanga* and *Al-Mahdi* cases, the ICC is more confident to consider the digital evidence only if corroborated by other types of evidence relevant to the facts of the case. Therefore, it seems that this type of evidence has not yet had a real opportunity to enhance the prosecution of war crimes before the ICC.

The situation, however, might change amid the ongoing armed conflict between Russia and Ukraine, considering the high involvement of civil society in recording and sharing evidence of events mainly perpetrated by the Russian armed forces. After the issuance of four arrest warrants by the ICC—which are still being kept secret—it is highly likely that the Court will need to analyze a huge amount of user-generated evidence, collected though apposite applications, both at the national and international levels, and more generally open-source evidence. It is hoped that the establishment of CICED will help the ICC to quickly obtain the material necessary to pursue the pending proceedings and to open new ones. Moreover, the risk associated with the removal of the content concerning international crimes by social media appears to be limited here. After all, unlike previous international armed conflicts under investigation before the ICC, the invasion of Ukraine created great cooperation and commitment within the international community with a view to ensure justice for Ukrainian victims as soon as possible.

Be this as it may, a huge amount of evidence is expected to be processed by the OTP. Thus, it will be interesting to see how artificial intelligence, recently introduced by the OTP, will influence the selection of material to tender before the Court and whether the Court will use digital evidence only if corroborated by other types of material.[94]

[94] Segate, *supra* note 8, at 264.

CHAPTER 7

Reparations at the International Criminal Court: Dangled Carrot or Path to Healing?

Laurie A. Morgan

1 Introduction

Under international law, states are responsible for ensuring that citizens and others within their jurisdiction may freely enjoy their human rights and are afforded an "effective remedy" when their rights are violated.[1] One way in which states try to rectify violations of international humanitarian law and human rights law is through holding the violators criminally liable for their actions. Many states have turned to the ICC to facilitate holding alleged criminals accountable for human rights violations.

The purpose of international humanitarian law is to reduce the harm suffered as a result of armed conflict. The ICC attempts to fulfill this purpose in part by providing reparations to some of the victims of the atrocities addressed by the court under its reparations mandate. However, this approach appears to give significantly greater emphasis to the alleged

[1] International Covenant on Civil and Political Rights (adopted 16 December 1966, entered into force 23 March 1976) 92 U.S.T. 908, Art. 2.

L. A. Morgan (✉)
Commercial Law Development Program (CLDP), Washington, DC, USA
e-mail: lam338@georgetown.edu

O. Svaček, M. Faix (eds.), *Prosecution of War Crimes before the ICC*, Global Issues, https://doi.org/10.1007/978-3-031-84216-0_7

perpetrators of atrocities than to the victims of crimes to which the 'effective remedy' is owed.

Reparations may provide an 'effective remedy' to victims of human rights violations, potentially alongside other mechanisms of restorative justice. One way that the ICC provides reparations is through its Trust Fund for Victims (TFV). However, this system has two major flaws: reparations are often given only to a select group of victims and are not given in a timely manner. Therefore, this chapter proposes that the assistance mandate, an ICC process separate from the TFV's reparations mandate, be strengthened to provide reparations to victims before the end of a trial, weakening the tie between the reparations and the perpetrator. This recommendation will be discussed in the context of an analysis of reparations in general, the ICC TFV system at large, and four TFV reparations case studies: *Lubanga*, *Katanga*, *Al Mahdi*, and *Bemba*.

2 Background

This section first introduces reparations generally to prepare the reader to learn about how the ICC uses reparations as a tool of transitional justice with its TFV. Second, this section focuses on the ICC's TFV in greater detail.

2.1 Reparations, Generally

Reparations have two purposes: (1) to recognize harm done to the person or group receiving the reparations and (2) to repair at least some of the harm done to the recipient group.[2] Reparations typically, though not always, serve as an acknowledgment that a reparations provider had a duty to prevent the harm from occurring, whether it was done by the provider themselves or a third party.[3] Although, like all restorative justice measures, reparations are imperfect, they can nonetheless serve an important role in uplifting victims of atrocities.

Reparations can come in many different forms to address several different types of harm which may have occurred. Forms of reparations include: financial reparations, the restoration of certain civil and political rights, erasure of unfair criminal convictions, physical rehabilitation,

[2] "Reparations" International Centre for Transitional Justice, available at https://www.ictj.org/our-work/transitional-justice-issues/reparations (last visited 13 October 2024).

[3] *Ibid.*

acknowledgment of harm, and apologies. [4] This section will address each of these forms in turn.

First, financial reparations can either take the form of individual reparations to particular victims or community-based reparations which benefit a larger group of people affected by the type of harm the reparations seek to address.[5] An example of individual financial reparations is the one-time payment of about 3000 USD to identified victims of gross human rights violations during Apartheid in South Africa.[6] Collective financial reparations may include, for example, the building and financing of a new school or community center in a community known to have suffered human rights abuses.[7]

Second, reparations may involve the restoration of civil and political rights. This form of reparation seeks to place the victim in the position they would have been in had the wrong not occurred, a notion which is borrowed from tort law.[8] An example of this is the voting rights accorded to women in the United States after being forbidden to exercise the right to participate in government on account of their sex for centuries.[9]

Third, the erasure of unfair criminal convictions is another mechanism by which states can attempt to place a victim in the position they would have had, but for the harm caused to them. This was a popular form of reparations in European states following the fall of communism.[10]

Fourth, reparations may consist of physical rehabilitation. The Inter-American Court of Human Rights has recognized physical harm as a harm to be redressed.[11] This rehabilitation can take place via direct access to

[4] *Ibid.*

[5] *Ibid.*

[6] P. de Grieff, *The Handbook on Reparations* (Oxford: Oxford University Press, 2006) at 177.

[7] An example of collective reparations is the Luxembourg Agreement, in which the Federal Republic of Germany provided the State of Israel with 3 billion Deutsche Mark in 1952 in acknowledgment of the harms done to Jewish people during the Holocaust. See Agreement between the State of Israel and the Federal Republic of Germany (adopted 10 September 1952, entered into force 27 March 1953), 206 UNTS 2137.

[8] N. Roht-Arriaza, "Reparations Decisions and Dilemmas" 27 *Hastings Int'l & Comp. L. Rev.* (2004) 157, at 160.

[9] US Const. Amend. XIV.

[10] Former political prisoners in Czechoslovakia, Hungary, and Albania received erasure of their convictions and compensation for time served in prison. Roht-Arriaza, *supra* note 8, at 173.

[11] Judgment, *Velasquez-Rodriguez v. Honduras*, (ser. C) No. 4, July 29, 1988, at paras. 156, 175, 187.

medical clinics or reimbursement for the costs associated with healthcare, for example.[12]

Finally, specific acknowledgment of harm and apologies are also an important form of symbolic reparations. Apologies have been offered by individuals, states, and groups in societies and countries emerging from periods of repression or violence at different stages of their transitional justice processes.[13] Most have been offered years, and even decades, after atrocities happened, often after the conclusion of criminal, civil, or truth-seeking processes, as in Chile, Indonesia, and South Africa.[14]

In addition to which form(s) or reparation should be given, the question of which entity should provide reparations is often in debate. There are three main sources of reparations: states, perpetrators, and third parties.

The International Center for Transitional Justice (ICTJ) advocates that states should be the main source of reparations.[15] The ICTJ argues that, because the state is responsible for protecting its citizens from all gross violations of human rights, the state should bear the responsibility of providing reparations for their victimized citizens, even when the wrongs are committed by non-state actors.[16] This was the approach taken by the government of Peru during the operation of its Truth and Reconciliation Commission between 2001 and 2003, which investigated human rights abuses committed by state forces and insurgents between 1980 and 2000.[17]

The view that violators should pay for the harm resulting from their actions was partially taken in Colombia in the 2016 peace agreement,

[12] J. P. Perez-Leon Acevedo, "Realising the Right to Health for Victims of International Crimes. The Case of Medical Rehabilitation Reparations Ordered by International Courts: Challenges, Possibilities and Ways of Improvement," 3 *Groningen Journal of International Law* (2015) 17, at 28.

[13] R. Carranza and C. Correa, E. Naughton, *More Than Words: Apologies as a Form of Reparation* (2015), International Center for Transitional Justice, available at https://www.ictj.org/sites/default/files/ICTJ-Report-Apologies-2015.pdf (last visited 13 October 2024).

[14] *Ibid.*

[15] S. Baldo and L. Magarrell, *Reparation and the Darfur Peace Progress: Ensuring Victims' Rights* (2007), International Center for Transitional Justice, available at https://www.ictj.org/sites/default/files/ICTJ-Sudan-Darfur-Reparations-2007-English_0.pdf (last visited 13 October 2024).

[16] *Ibid.*

[17] R. Barrantes Segura, *Reparations and Displacement in Peru* (2012), International Center for Transitional Justice, available at https://www.ictj.org/sites/default/files/ICTJ-Brookings-Displacement-Reparations-Peru-CaseStudy-2012-English.pdf (last visited 13 October 2024).

which provided that perpetrators who had partaken in the truth-telling processes would face special sanctions that would include reparative work.[18] The view that perpetrators should directly partake in restorative processes is often taken by courts which charge criminals with both prison time and financial liability for their crimes.[19]

Finally, several third parties also contribute to the reparations process.[20] For example, several states as well as the United Nations have created trust funds with the aim of restoring peace and justice to victims and victimized communities outside of their own communities.[21] All of the existing trust funds suffer from "severe underfunding."[22] Nonetheless, there is value in allocating resources for victims of extreme human rights violations even if there is no direct connection between the source of the funds and the beneficiaries. The next section discusses the trust fund created by the International Criminal Court to financially address the harm the Court also addresses from a criminal liability perspective.

2.2 *Reparations at the International Criminal Court: The Trust Fund for Victims*

The TFV has voiced its strategic goals as providing "tangible reparative value to victims, their families, and their communities,"[23] "facilitating assistance and reparations," providing "advocacy for victims," and promoting "good governance, accountability, and transparency."[24]

Article 75 of the Rome Statute provides: "The Court shall establish principles relating to reparations to, or in respect of, victims, including restitution, compensation and rehabilitation."[25] The intent to provide

[18] D. Suarez Vargas and L. Moffett, "Reparations in Colombia: Redressing Civilian Harm in the Midst of Armed Conflict," Lieber Institute, 5 September 2024, available at: https://lieber.westpoint.edu/reparations-colombia-redressing-civilian-harm-midst-armed-conflict/ (last visited 13 October 2024).

[19] This is the case at the International Criminal Court, the Inter-American Court for Human Rights, and the Extraordinary Chambers in the Courts of Cambodia. *Ibid.*, at 17.

[20] Roht-Arriaza, *supra* note 8, at 175.

[21] *Ibid.*

[22] *Ibid.*

[23] The Trust Fund for Victims, *Foreword* to *Annual Report* (2016), at 3, available at https://www.trustfundforvictims.org/sites/default/files/imce/Annual%20Report-2016_Online_Revised.pdf (last visited 13 October 2024).

[24] *Ibid.*, at 9.

[25] Rome Statute of the International Criminal Court (adopted 17 July 1998, entered into force 1 July 2002), 2187 UNTS 90 (Rome Statute), Art. 75(1).

reparations to victims is actualized under Article 79 of the Rome Statute, which establishes the TFV itself "for the benefit of victims of crimes within the jurisdiction of the Court."[26] As established under Article 79, the TFV initially had a reparations mandate that applied only to victims in relation to "specific judicial proceedings before the Court that result in conviction," though, as is further described below, a second "assistance mandate" was later established to afford victimized communities additional assistance.[27] To be considered a victim for the purposes of the reparations mandate, pursuant to Rule 85(a) of the Rules of the Court, "reparations may be granted to direct and indirect individual victims, provided that the harm they suffered is personal."[28]

The funds for reparations under the reparations mandate come from two sources: the perpetrators themselves and from voluntary contributions by states, individuals, institutions, and interest.[29] Between July 2017 and June 2018, 23 states contributed more than 2.5 million euros, in payments between 4049 euros and 999,740 euros.[30]

The Court may give collective or individual reparations in accordance with "the scope and extent of any damage, loss or injury."[31] The Court may appoint experts to inform the Court's decision on these factors.[32] Since 2016, there have been six cases which have made it to the reparations stage: the *Lubanga* case, the *Katanga* case, the *Al Mahdi* case, the *Bemba* case, the *Ntaganda* case, and the *Ongwen* case.[33]

The limitation that the TFV's reparations mandate may only provide reparations to benefit the victims of crimes specifically within the Court's jurisdiction has been considered problematic by commentators.[34] This

[26] *Ibid.*, Art. 79(1).

[27] "Reparation implementation," The Trust Fund for Victims, available at https://www.trustfundforvictims.org/en/what-we-do/reparation-orders (last visited 13 October 2024).

[28] Reparations Order, *Prosecutor v. Ahmad Al Faqi Mahdi* (ICC-01/12-01/15), Trial Chamber VIII, 17 August 2017, at 40.

[29] International Criminal Court, *Report to the Assembly of States Parties on the projects and the activities of the Board of Directors of the Trust Fund for Victims for the period 1 July 2017 to 30 June 2018* (ICC-ASP/17/14), Assembly of States Parties, 23 July 2018.

[30] The largest donor was Sweden, and the smallest donor was the Philippines. *Ibid.*

[31] International Criminal Court, *Rules of Procedure and Evidence* (2002), Rule 97(1), available at https://www.icc-cpi.int/sites/default/files/RulesProcedureEvidenceEng.pdf (last visited 13 October 2024).

[32] *Ibid.*, at Rule 97(2).

[33] "Reparation implementation," *supra* note 27.

[34] W. Wakabi, "Bemba's Acquittal Raises Concerns on Reparations to Victims in the Central African Republic," International Justice Monitor, 18 July 2018, available at https://

means, for example, if there are two victims of the same atrocity crime, like genocide one victim would not be eligible for reparations because their perpetrator was of a nationality not covered under ICC jurisdiction. Furthermore, as cases such as the *Bemba* case face acquittals, victims who participated in these hearings may no longer be eligible for reparations under the reparations mandate.[35]

If necessity is the mother of invention, the problematic narrowness of the reparations mandate was the mother of the ICC's assistance mandate, which is also run by the TFV.[36] The TFV's assistance mandate was established to enable "victims of [atrocity] crimes [...] and their families who have suffered physical, psychological and/or material harm as result of war crimes, to receive assistance separately from, and prior to, a conviction by the Court."[37] This means that reparations which arise out of the assistance mandate have the potential to be provided on the ground in a more expeditious manner than reparations grounded in the reparations mandate. This chapter refers to funds and services allocated under the assistance mandate as reparations because they serve the same fundamental purpose as reparations under the reparations mandate: to repair harm suffered by victims of atrocity crimes.[38]

The assistance mandate covers three main forms of support: physical rehabilitation, psychological rehabilitation, and material support to improve the economic status of victims.[39] The assistance mandate is currently activated in the following countries: the Democratic Republic of the Congo (DRC), Uganda, the Central African Republic, Cote d'Ivoire, Mali, Georgia, and Kenya.[40]

There are two main problems that the reparations mandate has that the assistance mandate proposes to address. First, the assistance mandate addresses the lengthy period of time it takes for the TFV to actually provide resources to victims under the reparations mandate. Second, the assistance mandate addresses the limited scope of the reparations mandate by

www.ijmonitor.org/2018/07/bembas-acquittal-raises-concerns-on-reparations-to-victims-in-the-central-african-republic/ (last visited 13 October 2024).

[35] *Ibid.*

[36] "Assistance Mandate," The Trust Fund for Victims, available at https://www.trustfundforvictims.org/en/about/two-mandates-tfv/assistance (last visited 13 October 2024).

[37] *Ibid.*

[38] *Ibid.*

[39] *Ibid.*

[40] "Assistance programmes," The Trust Fund for Victims, available at https://www.trustfundforvictims.org/en/what-we-do/assistance-programmes (last visited 13 October 2024).

placing less emphasis on whether the victim is a victim of one of the specific crimes that the Court is addressing or has addressed. Most importantly, the assistance mandate does not require that the funds go only to victims of crimes committed by people being tried by the Court. Furthermore, the TFV earmarks a specific portion of the assistance mandate's funds for victims of sexual and gender-based violence.[41]

However, the assistance mandate is far from perfect. In its use so far, it is largely only used after a trial has ended, which does not entirely fix the timing problem posed by the reparations mandate. Furthermore, logistical concerns can prevent the assistance mandate from reaching all victims even by the time the trial is complete.[42]

3 Analysis

This section uses four case studies to analyze the successes and failures of the TFV: the *Lubanga* case, the *Al Mahdi* case, the *Katanga* case, and the *Bemba* case. For a brief, side-by-side comparison of the cases, please refer to **Annex I**.

3.1 Lubanga *Case (Democratic Republic of the Congo)*

On 14 March 2012, the ICC convicted Thomas Lubanga Dyilo, a leader of the Union of Congolese Patriots, a rebel group in the Democratic Republic of the Congo.[43] Lubanga was found guilty of conscripting and enlisting child soldiers under the age of fifteen to "participate actively in hostilities."[44] This case study highlights two main problems with the reparations proceedings: narrowness and timeliness.

In the *Lubanga* case, the TFV plans to award both symbolic and service-based collective reparations.[45] The symbolic reparations will come in the

[41] "Assistance Mandate," *supra* note 36.

[42] As will be explained further later in the chapter, in the *Katanga* case, many victims had already left the country by the time reparations were being discussed. This meant that they were largely ineligible for reparations. See W. Wakabi, "Trust Fund Unveils Reparations Plan for Katanga Victim,", International Justice Monitor, 6 September 2017), available at https://www.ijmonitor.org/2017/09/trust-fund-unveils-reparations-plan-for-katanga-victims/ (last visited 13 October 2024).

[43] Judgment, *Prosecutor v. Thomas Lubanga Dyilo* (ICC-01/04-01/06), Trial Chamber I, 14 March 2012.

[44] *Ibid.*

[45] "Reparation implementation," *supra* note 27.

form of three permanent community centers and one mobile center operating with the aim to reduce the stigma and discrimination against former child soldiers.[46] As a collective reparation, the TFV plans to "provide physical and psychological rehabilitation, as well as vocational training and income-generating activities" in the DRC.[47]

To cover the cost of the reparations of this case, the TFV will provide one million euros of its own funding.[48] Lubanga has been held liable for ten million dollars, all of which would go toward reparations.[49]

The charges in the *Lubanga* case were the subject of heavy criticism, with critics accusing the Court of neglecting evidence that women and girls were harmed by Lubanga in the so-called rape capital of the world.[50] For example, Lubanga stated that "[t]he beautiful girls were not treated in the same way as the boys" in response to a question by prosecutor Nicole Samson regarding whether boys he recruited were treated the same way as the girls he recruited.[51] Despite evidence that Lubanga instructed his soldiers to use rape as a means of warfare and enlisted women and girls to the military as sex slaves,[52] the Court did not charge Lubanga with any sexual or gender-based crimes.[53]

[46] *Ibid.*

[47] *Ibid.*

[48] This funding comes from voluntary contributions by states, individuals, institutions, and interests. *Ibid.*; International Criminal Court, *supra* note 29, at 19.

[49] W. Wakabi, "Lubanga's Financial Liability for Reparations Set at US$ 10 Million," International Justice Monitor, 15 December 2017), available at https://www.ijmonitor.org/2017/12/lubangas-financial-liability-for-reparations-set-at-us-10-million/ (last visited 13 October 2024).

[50] K'Shaani O. Smith, "Prosecutor v. Lubanga: How the International Criminal Court Failed the Women and Girls of the Congo," 54 *Howard Law Journal*, 467, 468 (2011).

[51] International Justice Monitor, "Lubanga Trial: Victims Recount UPC Brutality, Seek Reparations," International Justice Monitor, 15 January 2010), available at https://www.ijmonitor.org/2010/01/lubanga-trial-victims-recount-upc-brutality-seek-reparations/ (last visited 13 October 2024).

[52] In Congolese culture, women are viewed as leaders within their communities. Therefore, women of all ages were particularly vulnerable to gender-based attacks as a means of terrorizing local communities. Victims of these gender-based and sexual attacks are often shamed into silence. However, 103 victims, including victims of gender-based and sexual crimes, testified to the atrocities they faced under Lubanga's control. Smith, *supra* note 50, at 471, 473, 474.

[53] The second prosecutor of the ICC, Fatou Bensouda, has since made the prosecution of sexual and gender-based crimes a policy priority in order to "[a]ffirm the commitment of the Office to paying particular attention to sexual and gender-based crimes." Decision on Confirmation of Charges, *Prosecutor v. Thomas Lubanga Dyilo* (ICC-01/04-01/06-803-

Limiting this case only to child soldiers also has implications for reparations. Namely, only victims tied to the case against Lubanga specifically on this particular issue of child soldiers may be the recipients of individual reparations under the TFV's reparations mandate. This means, for example, that a victim who suffered sexual slavery under Lubanga when she was seventeen would not be eligible for individual reparations, even if she participated in the case. One author notes that the selectivity of the reparations mandate in contexts like this may result in "fictive conceptions of victimhood or hierarchies among victims."[54]

Another problem with the reparations to be given in connection with the *Lubanga* case is timeliness. Many of the victims involved in this case gave their testimonies years before the reparations proceedings began.[55] Indeed, while the trial began in 2009, reparations still, at the time of writing, have not been fully implemented.[56] The proceedings on reparations began more than fifteen years ago in 2009.[57] In the time between, the Court and the TFV may need to gather further information on the victims for the purposes of the case or reparations, which may over time lead to victim fatigue with the Court, if the length of the trial itself has not already.[58] Furthermore, Lubanga has had the opportunity to refute and appeal elements of the reparations process, which has caused a further delay in the release of the funds for reparations.[59]

Widespread victim fatigue could have negative effects for the Court, which may find it more difficult to garner the support it needs from victims for the purposes of evidence gathering. Victims that lose hope in the

tEN), Pre-Trial Chamber I, 29 January 2007); The Office of the Prosecutor, *Policy Paper on Sexual and Gender-Based Crimes* (2014), International Criminal Court, available at https://www.icc-cpi.int/sites/default/files/iccdocs/otp/OTP-Policy-Paper-on-Sexual-and-Gender-Based-Crimes%2D%2DJune-2014.pdf (last visited 13 October 2024).

[54] C. Stahn, "Reparative Justice after the *Lubanga* Appeal Judgment: New Prospects for Expressivism and Participatory Justice or 'Juridified Victimhood' by Other Means?" 13 *Journal of International Criminal Justice*, (2015) 801, at 812.

[55] *Ibid.*, at 811.

[56] International Criminal Court, *supra* note 29, at 44; See also "The Lubanga Case," The Trust Fund for Victims, available at https://www.trustfundforvictims.org/what-we-do/reparation-orders/lubanga (last visited 13 October 2024).

[57] *Ibid.*

[58] Stahn, *supra* note 54, at 811.

[59] International Criminal Court, *Case Information Sheet: the Prosecutor v. Thomas Lubanga Dyilo* (2021) at 1, available at https://www.icc-cpi.int/sites/default/files/CaseInformationSheets/LubangaEng.pdf (last visited 13 October 2024).

reparations proceedings may feel that their interests in the proceedings were not realized (particularly when women's and girls' victimhood was not addressed in the indictment).[60] This may, in turn, result in an increase in crime-related psychological harm.[61]

3.2 Katanga *Case (Democratic Republic of the Congo)*

On 17 March 2014, Germain Katanga was convicted of one count of crimes against humanity and four counts of war crimes: murder, attacking a civilian population, destruction of property, and pillaging.[62] His trial was opened on 29 November 2009, more than four years before the trial ended.[63] While the Office of the Prosecutor originally charged Katanga with using children under fifteen years of age in attacks as well as crimes of sexual violence, he was found not guilty on both of these charges.[64] Therefore, victims who participated in the trial specifically with regard to these crimes are not eligible for individual reparations under the reparations mandate of the TFV.[65]

The Trial Chamber of the ICC ordered Katanga to pay one million USD in reparations.[66] However, Katanga does not currently have enough funds to pay this amount.[67] Nonetheless, the order to pay remains so that if his financial situation were to change, Kantanga can bear financial responsibility in the amount that it would take to address the harm caused by his crimes.[68] The TFV has decided to use one million USD of its own funds to help with reparations costs.[69] Some of the funds the TFV will be using to fund the reparations come from a voluntary contribution from

[60] Smith, *supra* note 50, at 487.

[61] *Ibid.*

[62] *Ibid.*

[63] International Criminal Court, *Case Information Sheet: the Prosecutor v. Germain Katanga* (2021), https://www.icc-cpi.int/sites/default/files/CaseInformationSheets/KatangaEng.pdf (last visited 13 October 2024).

[64] Open Society Justice Initiative, *Fact Sheet: ICC Katanga Reparations*, Open Society Foundation, available at https://www.justiceinitiative.org/uploads/d473c39a-26c6-44dd-b47d-a29b0058355c/Katanga%20Reparations%20Factsheet%20-%20032317_0.pdf (last visited 13 October 2024).

[65] *Ibid.*

[66] "Reparation implementation," *supra* note 27.

[67] Open Society Justice Initiative, supra note 64.

[68] *Ibid.*

[69] "Reparation implementation," *supra* note 27.

the Netherlands which was specifically earmarked for use in relation to this case.[70]

The TFV has decided that the reparations funds will be used in five ways.[71] First, each of the 297 victims who participated in the trial for crimes that Katanga was actually convicted for will receive a reparation in the amount of 250 USD.[72] In addition, the TFV will provide collective awards in the following four forms: housing assistance, education assistance, income-generating activities, and psychological rehabilitation.[73]

One critique of the collective reparations in this case is their narrowness.[74] The collective reparations institutions will all be located near Bogoro, where the attack that Katanga was convicted for took place.[75] Victims of mass atrocities in other parts of the country will largely not be able to benefit from the reparations.[76] Furthermore, seventeen direct victims of the attacks by Katanga in Bogoro are refugees in Uganda; and their refugee status may prevent them from obtaining the specific forms of reparations offered by the TFV.[77] The TFV also considers that there will be no collective reparations for fifteen victims who are now refugees in Europe or the United States.[78]

Since the war began in the early 2000s, victims have reported that they were waiting for reparations to help them resume their lives.[79] One woman lost all of her children and her home in attacks associated with Katanga, and now lives alone, exposed to the elements.[80] She has stated with regard

[70] *Ibid.*

[71] *Ibid.*

[72] *Ibid.*

[73] *Ibid.*

[74] Wakabi, *supra* note 42.

[75] *Ibid.*

[76] *Ibid.*

[77] *Ibid.*

[78] Draft implementation plan relevant to Trial Chamber II's order for reparations of 24 March 2017 (ICC-01/04-01/07-3728), *Prosecutor v. Germain Katanga* (ICC-01/04-01/07-3751-Red), Trial Chamber II, 25 July 2017), at § 59.

[79] Radio Canal Révélation, "Reactions from the local population to collective reparations in the Katanga case," Coalition for the International Criminal Court, 20 July 2017, available at https://www.coalitionfortheicc.org/news/20170720/reactions-local-population-collective-reparations-katanga-case (last visited 13 October 2024).

[80] *Ibid.*

to reparations: "I am alone in the world ... I am still waiting for this reparation. All I am hoping for is a house in which to shelter."[81]

In addition, the application processes for reparations were challenging for some of the victims. Nicolas Kuyaku, the Public Information and Outreach Assistant with the ICC office in Bunia, the Democratic Republic of the Congo, stated that:

> [S]ome people did not fill out the forms correctly. Also, from the outset, some people who were targeted, neglected the invitation from the victims' department thinking that nothing could be done.[82]

One way the TFV has sought to address people who have not sought direct reparations or were otherwise unable to benefit from direct reparations is through collective reparations, which will not require an application process.[83]

3.3 Al Mahdi *Case (The Republic of Mali)*

Ahmad Al Faqi Al Mahdi's trial began on 22 August 2016, and he was convicted of intentionally destroying cultural heritage sites in Timbuktu on 27 September 2016.[84] This was the ICC's fastest trial yet, in part due to Al Mahdi's guilty plea. Despite this, as of the time of writing, the reparations have not been awarded.[85]

In its Reparations Order, the Appeals Chamber advocates for the following reparations: rehabilitating protected sites so that another attack does not occur, individual financial compensation only for people whose livelihoods depended solely on these buildings and for people whose ancestors' burial sites were damaged by the attack, and collective reparations for mental health of the community.[86] The collective reparations for the mental health of the community can be in the form of psychological services or a symbolic representation of the harm Al Mahdi caused, such

[81] *Ibid.*
[82] *Ibid.*
[83] "Reparation implementation," *supra* note 27.
[84] *Al Mahdi* (Reparations Order), *supra* note 28.
[85] "Reparation implementation," *supra* note 27.
[86] A*l Mahdi* (Reparations Order), *supra* note 28.

as a monument.[87] The Reparations Order did not seek to rebuild the damaged sites because this was already done by UNESCO.[88]

Notably, the Appeals Chamber did not endorse reparations for bodily harm or for damage to personal property.[89] Their reasoning for this explicit non-endorsement is that the Court did not attribute these crimes directly to Al Mahdi.[90]

In addition, the TFV does not have the necessary funding to meet its reparations goals. The TFV website provides:

> The TFV calls upon individuals, institutions and States Parties to support the TFV in successfully carrying out its mission of alleviating the harm of victims by making reparative justice a reality for them. The TFV has been able to complement half of the award [for the Al Mahdi Case] and is currently seeking for contributions for the remaining 1.35 million euros.[91]

3.4 Bemba *Case (Central African Republic)*

On 21 March 2016, Jean-Pierre Bemba Gombo was convicted of murder and rape as crimes against humanity; and murder, rape, and pillaging as war crimes. On 8 June 2018, more than eight years after his trial began, Bemba was acquitted of all charges.[92] This acquittal had a great effect on the reparations procedures, which resulted with Bemba being freed from all personal financial liability to victims.[93]

The Trial Chamber acknowledged that victims who participated in the trial felt "disappointed and have lost faith in the justice process" after Bemba's acquittal.[94] The Trial Chamber also recognized that the "climate of total impunity" in the Central African Republic made the ICC the only

[87] *Ibid.*

[88] *Ibid.*, at 63; "Reparation implementation," *supra* note 27.

[89] *Al Mahdi* (Reparations Order), *supra* note 28, at 98, 102.

[90] *Ibid.*

[91] "The Al Mahdi Case," The Trust Fund for Victims, available at https://trustfundforvictims.org/what-we-do/reparation-orders/al-madhi (last visited 13 October 2024).

[92] International Criminal Court, *Case Information Sheet: the Prosecutor v. Jean-Pierre Bemba Gombo* (2019), available at https://www.icc-cpi.int/sites/default/files/CaseInformationSheets/BembaEng.pdf (last visited 13 October 2024).

[93] Final decision on the reparations proceedings, *Prosecutor v. Jean-Pierre Bemba Bombo* (ICC-01/05-01/08-3653), Trial Chamber III, 3 August 2018, § 3.

[94] *Ibid.*, at 6.

avenue for justice for victims.[95] The Trial Court emphasized that it would not "make concrete findings on the extent and scope of victimization," and that a wider scope of victims than those who participated in the trial should be considered victims for the purposes of the TFV's assistance mandate.[96] After the Bemba acquittal, the TFV announced that it would hasten the launch of a fourth assistance mandate mission in the Central African Republic, in part to aid the 5229 victims who took part in the *Bemba* trial.[97] As mentioned, because the assistance mandate does not require a conviction, reparations under the assistance mandate can be allocated in a more expeditious manner than reparations under the reparations mandate.[98]

Nonetheless, the acquittal has resulted in many victims becoming ineligible for reparations under the reparations mandate.[99] Apart from what would have been Bemba's financial liability contribution, the Office of the Prosecutor considered other options to raise funds for victims under the reparations mandate.[100] These options included trial of other members of Bemba's militia who allegedly perpetrated the crimes, domestic criminal proceedings against Bemba in the DRC, and domestic civil proceedings against perpetrators in the DRC or in the Central African Republic.[101] Further trials at the ICC would likely be time-consuming and are, like the *Bemba* trial was, uncertain.

[95] The establishment of a hybrid criminal court in the Central African Republic which has since been established may alter the opportunity for victims to seek accountability outside of the ICC. *Ibid*; P. Labuda, "The Special Criminal Court in the Central African Republic," American Society of International Law, 22 January 2018, available at https://www.asil.org/insights/volume/22/issue/2/special-criminal-court-central-african-republic (last visited 13 October 2024).

[96] *Bemba*, *supra* note 93, at 6.

[97] "Following Mr Bemba's acquittal, Trust Fund for Victims at the ICC decides to accelerate launch of assistance programme in Central African Republic," International Criminal Court, 13 June 2018, available at https://www.icc-cpi.int/news/following-mr-bembas-acquittal-trust-fund-victims-icc-decides-accelerate-launch-assistance (last visited 13 October 2024); Wakabi, *supra* note 34.

[98] "Assistance Mandate," *supra* note 36.

[99] *Bemba*, *supra* note 93, at 3.

[100] W. Wakabi, "Judges Close Reparations Proceedings in Bemba's War Crimes Trial," International Justice Monitor, 15 August 2018, available at https://www.ijmonitor.org/2018/08/judges-close-reparations-proceedings-in-bembas-war-crimes-trial/ (last visited 13 October 2024).

[101] *Ibid*.

4 Recommendations for the TFV

This section discusses the problems identified in the case studies and advocates for an additional solution to the problems posed in the case studies: a greater emphasis on well-being, security, and peace for victims as opposed to the current emphasis placed on accountability for perpetrators.

Each of the case studies exhibited two main problems with the reparations process: timeliness and selectivity. The fact that people who lost their family, their house, their ability to work, and their overall health in a conflict in 2003 and still, in 2024, do not have reparations for crimes committed against them, as was the case for victims of Lubanga, is a clear indication that the system is not working as it should.[102] Similarly, should victims of crimes that were formerly attributed to Bemba before his acquittal continue suffering without the reparations they had expected only two years ago, for crimes that occurred seventeen years ago, be collateral damage in the fight against impunity? Victims of crimes that the Court decided not to pursue, despite evidence that crimes have occurred, as in the case in Afghanistan,[103] should also be considered when evaluating the selectivity of which victims are deemed eligible for reparations.

This section focuses on one main shift that can help to address these problems that the Court and the TFV have faced in its first twenty years of operation: shifting the focus of the TFV from criminals to victims. Instead of emphasizing the connection between victims and perpetrators of atrocity crimes, the TFV should emphasize the connection between victims and atrocity crimes generally. This can be done through greater reliance on the assistance mandate closer to the outset of a trial, instead of waiting to see whether the reparations mandate would be an option.

The well-being of victims, security, and peace should be prioritized because it is the purpose for which the ICC was established. The preamble of the Rome Statute for the International Criminal Court provides that the Statute was established for people who "have been victims of unimaginable atrocities that deeply shock the conscience of humanity," and for the fact that "grave crimes threaten the peace, security and well-being of the world."[104] Furthermore, shifting the priorities of the TFV does not inherently affect proceedings at the ICC: perpetrators of atrocity crimes still can

[102] *Lubanga*, *supra* note 43.

[103] P. P. Singh, "In Afghanistan, the ICC Abandons the Field," Human Rights Watch, 23 April 2019, available at https://www.hrw.org/news/2019/04/23/afghanistan-icc-abandons-field (last visited 13 October 2024).

[104] Rome Statute, *supra* note 25.

be held to account criminally and financially, no matter when reparations are given. However, with a shift to a more victim-centered approach, victims will have a greater opportunity to heal from atrocious crimes.

This shift from prioritizing accountability to prioritizing well-being, security, and peace in the TFV can address both the issues of timeliness and selectivity. For example, decisions on reparations once victims of atrocity crimes are identified can be made closer to the outset of proceedings, as opposed to after a criminal is charged definitively, which often takes several years.

The Rome Statute does not require that reparations must come after the actual proceedings. Article 75 of the Rome Statute states [emphasis added]: "The Court ***may*** make an order directly against a ***convicted person*** specifying appropriate reparations to, ***or in respect of***, victims, including restitution, compensation and rehabilitation."[105] Although the funds which come from the convicted persons themselves may not be received until after the conviction, in the past, most of the funds used by the TFV came from the TFV itself because the convicted persons did not have enough assets to cover their liability.

Furthermore, if the TFV sets aside funding for reparations toward the outset of an investigation or criminal proceedings and there are convictions related to those reparations, the convicted person's assets can be given directly to the TFV 'in respect of' the victims on whose behalf the TFV has served.[106] Then, this money could be used for additional reparations to the same group of victims, or could be retained by the TFV in repayment of the services the TFV has already provided for the victims of the convicted person, and used for other victims for whom criminal proceedings are still ongoing.

It would be difficult to have a timelier reparations process exclusively under the reparations mandate because the reparations mandate requires a conviction first, which tends to take several years in ICC proceedings. Even if the process occurred rapidly after a conviction was finalized, people would still have suffered from the harm incurred by the convicted person's crimes for the duration of the trial. Furthermore, many people may have fled their homes during the time between the investigation and the end of the trial, thus creating the risk that these victims will be ineligible for reparations, as was the case for many refugees associated with the *Katanga* case.[107]

[105] *Ibid.*, Art. 75.

[106] *Ibid.*

[107] Wakabi, *supra* note 42.

As with the current reparations proceedings under the reparations mandate, identifying victims will still take some time. However, if this process is initiated at the outset of the recognition that an atrocity crime has left victims in its wake, the process will be much more efficient than at the conclusion of the trial, when victims may be difficult to locate, or no longer alive.[108]

An additional benefit of involving victims from the beginning of the reparations procedure is a greater opportunity for increased victim participation in designing the reparations to be allocated. This process, in addition to the reparations themselves, could also have reparative value for victims.

In summary, a shift in focus for reparations processes would provide that at least some of the needs of victims of atrocity crimes are addressed in a timelier matter. Furthermore, if victims of atrocity crimes are identified without regard to specific perpetrators, there is a lesser likelihood that certain groups of victims would be excluded for lack of evidence connecting their victimhood to certain alleged criminals. This means that in cases like the *Lubanga* case, women and girls who suffered harm as a result of gender-based and sexual crimes would not be excluded despite evidence that they did suffer from atrocity crimes.

5 Conclusion

From the establishment of the modern system of international criminal justice in the twentieth century to the continuous work of the ICC and other transitional justice projects, society at large has come a long way in terms of advocating for victims of international atrocity crimes. Nonetheless, victims of crimes that shake the conscience of humanity deserve the best that society can offer to them. More inclusive and cohesive advocacy in the reparations process at the ICC can contribute to furthering the purposes of international humanitarian law: reducing the harm caused by armed conflict.

[108] The WHO provided that the life expectancy for people born in 2016 was between 59 and 62 years old. Even assuming that people born before this had the same life expectancy, people who were only 42 at the start of the ICC's investigation are likely to have passed away before the reparations actually hit the ground. Particularly when considering the unaddressed health problems which may have occurred as a result of the atrocity crimes, fifteen years is too long to wait for reparations. Also see "Democratic Republic of the Congo," World Health Organization, available at https://www.who.int/countries/cod/ (last visited 13 October 2024).

Annex I

A Comparative Look at the Reparations Granted Under the Reparations Mandate

	Katanga	*Lubanga*	*Al Mahdi*	*Bemba*
When were the reparations given?	Ongoing[a]	Not yet[b]	Not yet[c]	Never[d]
What were the reparations?	$250 to each victim of crimes that Katanga was convicted for; collective reparations (housing assistance, education assistance, income generating activities, and psychological rehabilitation)[e]	Collective reparations (not yet specified)[f]	Rehabilitating protected sites so that another attack does not occur; individual financial compensation for people whose livelihoods depended solely on the destroyed buildings and for people whose ancestors' burial sites were damaged by the attack; collective reparations for mental health of community (symbolic or otherwise)	No reparations under reparations mandate
Who got the reparations?	Victims of crimes that Katanga was convicted for; victims living near Bogoro[g]	Not yet specified[h]	All of humankind, vis-à-vis the local population[i]	No one[j]
How were the reparations financed?	Katanga is liable for 1M USD; TFV will provide 1M USD; Netherlands earmarked a donation specifically for this case[k]	Lubanga is liable for €10M; TFV will contribute 3M euros[l]	Al Mahdi is liable for 2.7M euros; TFV will contribute 800,000 euros[m]	N/A

	Katanga	*Lubanga*	*Al Mahdi*	*Bemba*
Other comments	Refugees now living in other countries due to the conflict will not receive any reparations[n]	Women and girls were largely excluded from the verdict and are expected to be excluded from reparations[o]	Many victims assert they were physically harmed or had personal property harmed by the attack, but because Al Mahdi was not tried for these crimes, reparations are not available to them[p]	Assistance mandate will be used to compensate victims who previously expected reparations under the reparations mandate[q]

[a] The *Katanga* reparations proceedings are still in their implementation phase. While the programming for collective reparations is underway, it is unclear whether reparations have physically been provided to beneficiaries. Individual reparations have not yet gone out. See International Criminal Court, *supra* note 29, at 43, 47

[b] The *Lubanga* reparations proceedings are still in their implementation phase. Reparations have not yet been provided to beneficiaries. *Ibid*., at 50

[c] The *Al Mahdi* reparations proceedings are in the draft implementation plan phase. *Ibid*.

[d] In response to Bemba's acquittal, the ICC has closed the reparations proceedings. Previously, the reparations proceedings were in the final observations phase, which occurs after all victims and their legal representatives submit their claims. *Ibid*., at 56; Wakabi, *supra* note 100

[e] "Reparation implementation," *supra* note 27

[f] *Ibid*.

[g] Wakabi, *supra* note 42

[h] "Reparation implementation," *supra* note 27

[i] Cultural Property has been regarded as "of great importance to the cultural heritage of every people." Therefore, the preservation of this property is of benefit to all people. Convention (IV) Respecting the Laws and Customs of War on Land (adopted 18 October 1907), 36 Stat. 2277, Art. 1

[j] International Criminal Court, *supra* note 29, at 56

[k] *Ibid*., at 48

[l] *Ibid*., at 42, 47

[m] *Ibid*., at 51, 54

[n] Wakabi, *supra* note 42

[o] Smith, *supra* note 50, at 468

[p] *Al Mahdi* (Reparations Order), *supra* note 28, at 98, 102

[q] "Following Mr Bemba's acquittal, Trust Fund for Victims at the ICC decides to accelerate launch of assistance programme in Central African Republic," International Criminal Court, 13 June 2018, available at https://www.icc-cpi.int/news/following-mr-bembas-acquittal-trust-fund-victims-icc-decides-accelerate-launch-assistance (last visited 13 October 2024)

CHAPTER 8

The ICC's Crucial Role in Ensuring Respect for IHL: Obligations Under the Geneva Conventions for States to Cooperate with the ICC

Emma Brandon

1 Introduction

As other chapters in this volume have indicated, the International Criminal Court (ICC) plays a crucial role in prosecuting war crimes and enforcing international humanitarian law (IHL). Because it does not have its own police force, it cannot do this without the cooperation of states in every aspect of the prosecution process.[1] This chapter argues that, because the ICC plays such a crucial role in ensuring the prosecution of violators of the Geneva Conventions, the Geneva Conventions themselves can serve as an additional source of obligations to cooperate with the ICC. This

[1] See, e.g., O. Bekou and D. Birkett, "Introduction," in O. Bekou and D. Birkett (eds.) *Cooperation and the International Criminal Court: Perspectives from Theory and Practice* 1 (Leiden/Boston: Martinus Nijhoff, 2016) 1, at 1.

E. Brandon (✉)
International Nuremberg Principles Academy, Nuremberg, Germany
e-mail: Emma.Brandon@nurembergacademy.org

O. Svaček, M. Faix (eds.), *Prosecution of War Crimes before the ICC*, Global Issues, https://doi.org/10.1007/978-3-031-84216-0_8

additional source of a cooperation obligation is relevant both to ground the cooperation obligations of all states in universally ratified treaties like the Geneva Conventions and to create additional obligations for states who are not state parties to the Rome Statute but are state parties to the Geneva Conventions. This chapter will focus on the question of whether the Geneva Conventions can create obligations for states who are not parties to the Rome Statute to cooperate with the ICC.

The issue of non-state party cooperation with the ICC has become particularly acute with the February 2022 invasion of Ukraine by Russia. In an echo of the arrest warrants for former Sudanese President Omar al-Bashir, the ICC Prosecutor has issued an arrest warrant for Russian President Vladimir Putin.[2] As the Sudanese situation has demonstrated, successful prosecution of such a case will require the cooperation of the non-state party run by the indicted leader, as well as many other state and non-state parties.[3]

Two provisions of the Geneva Conventions are particularly relevant to cooperation with the ICC. The first is the specific prosecution obligation in the grave breaches provisions.[4] The second relevant provision is Common Article 1's obligation to ensure respect for the Conventions.[5]

[2] See "Situation in Ukraine: ICC judges issue arrest warrants against Vladimir Vladimirovich Putin and Maria Alekseyevna Lvova-Belova," International Criminal Court, 17 March 2023, available at https://www.icc-cpi.int/news/situation-ukraine-icc-judges-issue-arrest-warrants-against-vladimir-vladimirovich-putin-and (last visited 14 October 2024).

[3] See, e.g., "75 Trips to 22 Countries in 7 Years: An Indicted War Criminal's Travels," Nuba Reports, 7 March 2016, available at https://nubareports.org/bashir-travels/ (last visited 14 October 2024).

[4] Geneva Convention for the Amelioration of the Condition of the Wounded and Sick in Armed Forces in the Field (adopted 12 August 1949, entered into force 21 October 1950), 75 UNTS 31 (hereafter Geneva I), Art. 49; Geneva Convention for the Amelioration of the Condition of the Wounded, Sick, and Shipwrecked Members of Armed Forces at Sea (adopted 12 August 1949, entered into force 21 October 1950), 75 UNTS 85 (hereafter Geneva II), Art. 50; Geneva Convention Relative to the Protection of Civilian Persons in Time of War (adopted 12 August 1949, entered into force 21 October 1950) 75 UNTS 287 (hereafter Geneva III), Art. 129; Geneva Convention Relative to the Treatment of Prisoners of War (adopted 12 August 1949, entered into force 21 October 1950), 75 UNTS 216 (hereafter Geneva IV), Art. 156; Protocol Additional to the Geneva Conventions of 12 August 1949, and Relating to the Protection of Victims of International Armed Conflicts (adopted 8 June 1977, entered into force 7 December 1978) 1125 UNTS 3 (hereafter AP I), Art. 85.

[5] Geneva I, *supra* note 4, Art. 1; Geneva II, *supra* note 4, Art. 1; Geneva III, *supra* note 4, Art. 1; Geneva IV, *supra* note 4, Art. 1; AP I, *supra* note 4, Art. 1.

This chapter begins with an analysis of the grave breaches provisions and the obligations that they create in relation to the ICC and continues on to a similar analysis of Common Article 1. It concludes with the overall obligations that states who are parties to the four 1949 Geneva Conventions have to cooperate with the ICC.

2 Obligations Under the Grave Breaches Provisions

All four Geneva Conventions and AP I contain nearly identical provisions relating to "grave breaches" of the Conventions or Protocol. The ordinary meaning of these provisions makes clear that all state parties to the four Geneva Conventions are obligated to look for any individuals alleged to have committed these violations of the Conventions.[6] Once a state has found and taken into custody the suspect, the state is obligated to either prosecute that individual domestically or to transfer the individual to another state party that will prosecute him.[7] It is clear from the wording that that state must intend to prosecute the individual and that the custodial state must not have good reason to doubt the recipient state's intentions. The transfer must be "for trial" and the recipient state must have gone so far in the investigation of the individual as to make "out a '*prima facie*' case."[8] In other words, extradition to a state that did not intend to prosecute the suspect in a manner that satisfied the Geneva Conventions would violate state parties' obligations under the grave breaches provisions of the Geneva Conventions.

2.1 Can States Transfer Alleged Perpetrators of Grave Breaches to the ICC?

The requirement that states handover suspected perpetrators to entities who will prosecute leads to the question of whether handover of a suspect to an international criminal tribunal (ICT), and the ICC in particular,

[6] See E. La Haye, "Article 49: Penal Sanctions," in International Committee of the Red Cross, *Commentary on the First Geneva Convention: Convention (I) for the Amelioration of the Conditions of the Wounded and Sick in Armed Forces in the Field* (Cambridge: Cambridge University Press, 2016), 2860.

[7] See *ibid.*, 2882.

[8] Geneva I, *supra* note 4, Art. 49; Geneva II, *supra* note 4, Art. 50; Geneva III, *supra* note 4, Art. 129; Geneva IV, *supra* note 4, Art. 146.

could satisfy grave breaches obligations. Can an ICC prosecution act as a substitute for prosecution in a domestic court and satisfy grave breaches obligations?

State practice in the application of the Geneva Conventions indicates that prosecution before the ICC satisfies the Geneva Conventions' requirements of handover "for trial." Specific statements by governments about the enforcement of the grave breaches provisions demonstrate this interpretation.[9] Federal executive officials from France, Germany, Argentina, Côte d'Ivoire, the then-Yugoslavia, Denmark, Finland, Iceland, Norway, Sweden, Ireland, and Switzerland have all made public statements indicating that ICTs play a vital role in fulfilling grave breaches obligations.[10] The Swiss Federal Department of Foreign Affairs' 2009 ABCs of International Humanitarian Law succinctly describes the role played by the ICC in the grave breaches regime: "States are obliged to [...] either themselves prosecute persons responsible for grave breaches, in particular of war crimes, or extradite such persons. If a State is either unwilling or unable to undertake prosecutions then, as appropriate, the responsibility passes to the International Criminal Court in The Hague."[11]

As individual statements of only a small fraction of the state parties to the Geneva Conventions, these statements cannot determine on their own the one authoritative interpretation, but their clarity and the fact that they emanate from official statements of government officials give them substantial interpretive value.

The case of *Kwoyelo v. Uganda* in the Ugandan Constitutional Court demonstrates one way the ICC can practically play a role in the fulfillment of a state's obligations under the grave breaches provisions of the Geneva Conventions.[12] Thomas Kwoyelo, a former commander in the Lord's Resistance Army, was charged with offenses constituting grave breaches of

[9] International Committee of the Red Cross, *Customary International Humanitarian Law Database: Practice Relating to Rule 158—Prosecution of War Crimes*, available at https://ihl-databases.icrc.org/en/customary-ihl/v2/rule158 (last visited 14 October 2024).

[10] *Ibid.*

[11] Switzerland, Federal Department of Foreign Affairs, "ABC of International Humanitarian Law" (2009) 40, in International Committee of the Red Cross, *Customary International Humanitarian Law Database: Practice relating to Rule 158—Prosecution of War Crimes*, available at https://ihl-databases.icrc.org/en/customary-ihl/v2/rule158 (last visited 14 October 2024).

[12] Judgment, *Prosecutor v Kwoyelo Thomas alias Latoni* (HCT-00-ICD-Case No. 02/10), UGCC 10, 22 September 2011 (hereafter *Uganda*).

the Geneva Conventions.[13] He argued that this prosecution was a violation of his rights because he should be covered by a domestic amnesty for all former combatants in the civil war.[14] One of several arguments made by the prosecution was that the amnesty violated Uganda's obligations under the grave breaches provisions of the Geneva Conventions and should be declared void.[15] The Court held that the amnesty was valid and that Uganda was continuing to live up to its international obligations because perpetrators of grave breaches were being prosecuted before the ICC.[16] According to the Court, the ICC's prosecution of Ugandans "shows that Uganda is aware of its international obligations."[17] Although Uganda had instituted a domestic amnesty that prevented it from prosecuting perpetrators of grave breaches domestically, the ICC's prosecution of such perpetrators ensured that they did not go unpunished and Uganda continued to live up to its Geneva Conventions obligations.

International Committee of the Red Cross (ICRC) practice also supports this interpretation. With the exception of the brief 1960 commentary on Geneva II that does not mention international courts at all, all of the ICRC commentaries on the grave breaches provisions of the Conventions explicitly support the option of a transfer to an ICT to fulfill grave breaches obligations.[18] The first commentary, written just nine years

[13] *Ibid.* There is some confusion in this case as the armed conflict involved appears to be a NIAC (non-international armed conflict), but Ugandan prosecutors and the Ugandan Constitutional Court consistently define the charges as alleged grave breaches of the Geneva Conventions. Uganda may interpret the grave breaches provisions as creating obligations in NIACs.

[14] *Ibid.*

[15] *Ibid.*

[16] *Ibid.*

[17] *Ibid.*

[18] J. S. Pictet, "Article 49: Penal Sanctions," in J. S. Pictet (ed.), *The Geneva Conventions of 12 August 1949: Commentary: I Geneva Conventions for the Amelioration of the Condition of the Wounded and Sick in Armed Forces in the Field* (Geneva: International Committee of the Red Cross, 1952) 362, at 366; J. S. Pictet, "Article 146: Penal Sanctions," in J. S. Pictet (ed.), *The Geneva Conventions of 12 August 1949: Commentary: IV Geneva Convention Relative to the Protection of Civilian Persons in Time of War* (Geneva: International Committee of the Red Cross, 1958),) 583, at 591; J. S. Pictet, "Article 50: Penal Sanctions," in J. S. Pictet (ed.), *The Geneva Conventions of 12 August 1949: Commentary: II Geneva Convention for the Amelioration of the Condition of the Wounded, Sick and Shipwrecked Members of Armed Forces at Sea* (Geneva: International Committee of the Red Cross, 1960) at 263; J. S. Pictet, "Article 129: Penal Sanctions," in J. S. Pictet (ed.), *The Geneva Conventions of 12 August 1949: Commentary: III Relative to the Treatment of Prisoners of*

after the adoption of the final text of the Conventions by Jean Pictet who had played a vital role in drafting the Conventions, states that "the grave breaches provision does not exclude handing over the accused to an international criminal court whose competence has been recognized by the Contracting Parties."[19] This exact phrase was also included in the 1958 commentary on Geneva IV and the 1960 commentary on Geneva III.[20] By the 2016 commentary on Geneva I, the ICRC removed the requirement of recognition of the jurisdiction of the tribunal, indicating that it has seen an evolution in the interpretation of the Conventions.[21] This commentary simply says that the grave breaches provision "does not exclude the possibility of a State Party handing over an accused person to an international criminal court or tribunal."[22] The 2017 and 2020 commentaries repeat the 2016 commentary's wording verbatim.[23]

All commentaries based their interpretations on indications in the drafting history that there was no intent to exclude the jurisdiction of ICTs.[24] The ICRC interprets the Conventions' drafting history as indicating that the drafters did not want to limit the development and codification of international criminal law by making explicit reference to it in the Conventions. Instead, the ICRC argues, they decided not to include any reference to an international criminal court or tribunal.[25]

War (Geneva: International Committee of the Red Cross, 1960) 617, at 624; Haye (Commentary, 2016), *supra* note 6, at 2887; E. La Haye, "Article 50: Penal Sanctions," in K. Dörmann at al. (ed.), *Commentary on the Second Geneva Convention: Convention (II) for the Amelioration of the Condition of the Wounded, Sick and Shipwrecked Members of Armed Forces at Sea* (Cambridge: Cambridge University Press, 2017), para. 2997; E. La Haye, "Article 129: Penal Sanctions," in International Committee of the Red Cross, *Commentary on the Third Geneva Convention: Convention (III) relative to the Treatment of Prisoners of War* (Cambridge: Cambridge University Press, 2020) para. 5153.

[19] Pictet (Commentary, 1952), *supra* note 18, at 366.

[20] Pictet (Commentary, 1958), *supra* note 18, at 591; Pictet (Commentary, 1960), *supra* note 18.

[21] Haye (Commentary, 2016), *supra* note 6, at 2887.

[22] *Ibid.*

[23] Haye (Commentary, 2017), *supra* note 18; Haye (Commentary, 2020), *supra* note 18.

[24] Pictet (Commentary, 1952), *supra* note 18, 366; Pictet (Commentary, 1958), *supra* note 18, at 591; Pictet (Commentary, 1960), *supra* note 18; Pictet (Commentary III, 1960), *supra* note 18, at 624; Haye (Commentary, 2016), *supra* note 6, 2887; Haye (Commentary, 2016), *supra* note 18; Haye (Commentary, 2020), *supra* note 18.

[25] Pictet (Commentary, 1952), *supra* note 18, at 366; Pictet (Commentary, 1958), *supra* note 18, at 591; Pictet (Commentary, 1960), *supra* note 18; Pictet (Commentary III, 1960), *supra* note 18, at 624; Haye (Commentary, 2016), *supra* note 6, 2887; Haye (Commentary, 2016), *supra* note 18; Haye (Commentary, 2020), *supra* note 18.

A deeper analysis of the drafting history partially supports this conclusion. The first draft of the grave breaches provisions was partially based on the Genocide Convention, which expressly contemplated the handover of suspected violators to an ICT.[26] The first draft explicitly allowed punishment "by any international jurisdiction, the competence of which has been recognized by [the Contracting Parties]."[27] In its commentary on this draft, the experts tasked by the ICRC to draft these articles argued that "an international tribunal would doubtless be the instrument best qualified to judge [grave] breaches."[28] However, they hesitated to rely solely on an ICT because such a tribunal did not exist at the time.[29]

This very pro-ICT picture changed, however, when the draft articles were negotiated by states at the 1949 Diplomatic Conference in Geneva.[30] All reference to an international tribunal was removed before the draft was presented at the Conference.[31] This occurred during backchannel negotiations so it is difficult to determine why.[32] The first ICRC commentary on the grave breaches provisions that was written by experts who were intimately involved in the drafting process indicates that the reference to an ICT was removed because drafters were not international criminal lawyers and did not want to take any action that would hinder the future development of that area of law.[33] An implied prohibition on handing over war crimes suspects to an ICT would go against that intention. The debate at the conference itself on the grave breaches provisions is less illuminating on this question because it did not directly discuss the possibility of handing over individuals to an ICT.[34]

[26] Final Record of the Diplomatic Conference of Geneva of 1949, Vol. II-B, at 115. See M. Lewis, "Revising the Geneva Conventions, 1946–1949: Synthesizing the Old and New Justice," in *The Birth of the New Justice: The Internationalization of Crime and Punishment 1919–1950* (2014) 229, at 266.

[27] International Committee of the Red Cross, *Revised and New Draft Conventions for the Protection of War Victims: Remarks and Proposals Submitted by the International Committee of the Red Cross* (1949), available at https://www.loc.gov/collections/military-legal-resources/?q= (last visited 14 October 2024).

[28] *Ibid.*, at 21.

[29] *Ibid.*

[30] Final Record Vol. II-B, *supra* note 26, at 115.

[31] *Ibid.* See Lewis, *supra* note 26, at 262–269.

[32] See Lewis, *supra* note 26, at 262–269.

[33] J. S. Pictet (Commentary, 1952), *supra* note 18, at 366.

[34] Final Record Vol. II-B, *supra* note 26. See Lewis, *supra* note 26, at 262–269.

Aspects of the final agreed wording indicate that the Conference did not intend to prohibit handover to an ICT.[35] The very use of the phrase "handover" as opposed to extradite indicates that the states intended as broad as possible a definition that did not necessarily mean extradition between two states.[36] In fact, the term "handover" was drawn from its use by the UN War Crimes Commission,[37] an international body tasked with investigating international crimes committed during World War II and supplying evidence to both international and domestic tribunals.[38] Drafters likely had the transfer to an international tribunal in mind when they deliberately chose a relatively novel phrase that had been used to refer to international tribunals, instead of more commonly used words such as extradite or surrender. The requirement that the receiving entity make out a *prima facie* case was also drawn from the UN War Crimes Commission and indicated a similar connection to international prosecutions.[39] Although this phrase was familiar to most common law jurisdictions, civil law jurisdictions would have only connected it with the UN War Crimes Commission's referrals to international tribunals.[40]

Overall, the indications from the drafting history on the possibility of a transfer to an ICT are mixed. A counter-argument can be made that the deletion of the reference to ICTs in the ICRC's original draft indicates that the states intended to exclude the possibility of a transfer to an ICT.[41] This counter-argument is not fully supported by the drafting history because the actual discussion on the removal of the provision is not publicly available and the wording finally arrived at contains some indications that the drafters contemplated a transfer to an ICT. The drafting history does not give a clear indication either way, but the state practice discussed

[35] See Geneva I, *supra* note 4, Art. 49; Geneva II, *supra* note 4, Art. 50; Geneva III, *supra* note 4, Art. 129; Geneva IV, *supra* note 4, Art. 146.

[36] *Ibid.*

[37] Final Record Vol. II-B, *supra* note 26.

[38] See D. Plesch, et al., "The Relevance of the United Nations War Crimes Commission to the Prosecution of Sexual and Gender-Based Crimes Today," 25 *Criminal Law Forum* (2014) 349, at 350.

[39] Final Record Vol. II-B, *supra* note 26) at 117.

[40] *Ibid.*

[41] See G. I. A. D. Draper, "The Implementation and Enforcement of the Geneva Conventions of 1949 and of the Two Additional Protocols of 1978," 164 *Collected Courses of the Hague Academy of International Law* (1979) 5, at 38.

above indicates an interpretation that allows for the transfer of a suspect to an ICT to satisfy grave breaches obligations.[42]

The three major pieces of scholarship to tackle this question are as mixed as the drafting history.[43] Writing in 1979, Draper argues that the grave breaches provisions exclude handover of suspects to an ICT.[44] He interprets the provisions as granting exclusive jurisdiction to the state with custody over the suspect, except in the specific circumstance where it decides to hand the suspect over to another state.[45] Gaeta argues that transfer to an ICT only satisfies grave breaches obligations if the individual to be transferred is a national of a state that has also recognized the jurisdiction of the tribunal.[46] She argues that the Geneva Conventions cannot extend jurisdiction of an ICT to a state that has not recognized its jurisdiction.[47] Kreß argues that the transfer of a suspect to an ICT always satisfies grave breaches obligations.[48] He bases his argument on the ICC-related subsequent state practice discussed above.[49]

The argument that transfer to an ICT is only allowed when the suspect's state of nationality is a member of the tribunal is initially plausible. However, it ignores the fact that the consent of the state of nationality is not required to exercise criminal jurisdiction over an individual.[50] It is uncontroversial that a state may exercise criminal jurisdiction over any individual, regardless of nationality, who commits a crime on their territory.[51] Quirks of nationality do not prevent states from exercising their sov-

[42] See Haye (Commentary, 2016), *supra* note 6, at 2887; C. Kreß, "Reflections on the Iudicare Limb of the Grave Breaches Regime," 7 *Journal of International Criminal Justice* (2009) 789, at 799.

[43] Draper, *supra* note 41; P. Gaeta, "Grave Breaches of the Geneva Conventions," in A. Clapham, M. Sassòli, and P. Gaeta (eds.), *The 1949 Geneva Conventions: A Commentary* (Oxford: Oxford University Press, 2015) 615; Kreß, *supra* note 42.

[44] Draper, *supra* note 41, at 38.

[45] *Ibid.*

[46] Gaeta, *supra* note 43, at 637.

[47] *Ibid.*

[48] Kreß, *supra* note 42, at 799.

[49] *Ibid.*

[50] See W. Schabas, "Article 12: Preconditions to the Exercise of Jurisdiction," in *The International Criminal Court: A Commentary on the Rome Statute* (2nd edn., Oxford: Oxford University Press, 2016) 345, at 354; D. Akande, "The Jurisdiction of the International Criminal Court over Nationals of Non-Parties: Legal Basis and Limits," 1 *Journal of International Criminal Justice* (2003) 618.

[51] See Schabas, *supra* note 50, at 354; Akande, *supra* note 50. The situation is different if there is potential immunity under international law.

ereign territorial jurisdiction. This does not change just because a state has decided to prosecute the individual before an ICT instead of a domestic tribunal.[52] It is unclear how the inclusion of obligations under the grave breaches provisions changes this fact. Assuming that the ICC already has valid jurisdiction over the individual, that individual may be transferred to the ICC regardless of their nationality. States that have grave breaches obligations to ensure the prosecution of that individual may hand the individual over to the ICC to satisfy those obligations.

2.2 *Must States Transfer Certain Alleged Perpetrators of Grave Breaches to the ICC?*

The ordinary meaning of the grave breaches provisions implies that states are obligated to hand over a suspected perpetrator of grave breaches to the ICC if not doing so would result in impunity for the suspect. State parties are obligated to either prosecute suspected perpetrators of grave breaches domestically or to hand them over to an entity that has made out a *prima facie* case against the suspect.[53] The state cannot allow a suspect to remain on its territory unprosecuted or hand over that suspect to an entity that has not made out a *prima facie* case against the suspect. Therefore, it must hand that suspect over to the ICC if the ICC is looking to prosecute the suspect for grave breaches, the state cannot or will not prosecute itself, and no other state or entity will or can prosecute.

Other treaty interpretation sources beyond this ordinary meaning are inconclusive on this question. The drafting history simply contains no public record of debates on this aspect of the grave breaches provisions.[54] As laid out below, subsequent state practice on this question is inconclusive because most international(ized) criminal tribunals have not prosecuted individuals for grave breaches committed in IACs and, when they have, they have had other sources to rely on for cooperation obligations.

State practice in relation to the ICC is limited by the fact that the ICC's only public arrest warrants for war crimes committed in an IAC (International Armed Conflict) have been in the Ukraine situation.[55] The

[52] See Schabas, *supra* note 50, at 354; Akande, *supra* note 50.

[53] See Geneva I, *supra* note 4, Art. 49; Geneva II, *supra* note 4, Art. 50; Geneva III, *supra* note 4, Art. 129; Geneva IV, *supra* note 4, Art. 146.

[54] Final Record Vol. II-B, *supra* note 26. See Lewis, *supra* note 26, at 262–269.

[55] International Criminal Court, *Defendants*, available at https://www.icc-cpi.int/defendants (last visited 14 October 2024).

Ukraine situation may prove particularly relevant given that the arrest warrants were issued against citizens and the leader of a non-state party, Russia. Russia is not a state party to the Rome Statute but is a party to all four Geneva Conventions and AP I.[56] These arrest warrants have generated reference to the Geneva Conventions in the international law blogosphere. A month after they were issued, Andrew Clapham wrote a blog post arguing that all state parties to the Geneva Conventions are obligated to assist the ICC in the arrest of the indicted Russians.[57] It is unclear whether this discussion has made its way to the ICC or states themselves and whether it will make any impact on the fulfillment of the still-outstanding warrants. Russia has clearly shown its lack of willingness to cooperate with the ICC by indicting several ICC officials in its own domestic system for "preparing to attack a representative of a foreign country enjoying international protection."[58]

Additionally, future cooperation issues in the situation in Georgia may prove instructive. The ICC's Pre-Trial Chamber I has preliminarily classified the armed conflict in Georgia as an IAC.[59] Georgia is a state party to the ICC with all of the accompanying cooperation obligations and so its obligations will be generally determined by those state party obligations.[60] In fact, in July 2017, the Georgian government signed a cooperation

[56] United Nations Treaty Collection, *Chapter 18: Penal Matters—Section 10: Rome Statute of the International Criminal Court* (1998), available at https://treaties.un.org/pages/ViewDetails.aspx?src=TREATY&mtdsg_no=XVIII-10&chapter=18&clang=_en (last visited 14 October 2024).

[57] A. Clapham, "We Need to Talk About Grave Breaches of the Geneva Conventions," Opinio Juris, 25 April 2023, available at https://opiniojuris.org/2023/04/25/we-need-to-talk-about-grave-breaches-of-the-geneva-conventions/ (last visited 14 October 2024).

[58] Associated Press, "Russia indicts ICC prosecutor, judge who issued war crimes warrant for Putin," 21 May 2023, available at https://apnews.com/article/russia-indictment-icc-prosecutor-judge-putin-260100f9ba533e15ebee3084dba74ff4 (last visited 14 October 2024).

[59] Decision Authorizing an Investigation, *Situation in Georgia* (ICC-01/15-12), Pre-Trial Chamber I, 27 January 2016, § 27.

[60] See N. Gogolashvili and N. Tsagareishvili, "Getting Full Cooperation from the Georgian Side Will Be One of the Challenges for ICC," Coalition for the International Criminal Court, 2 May 2017, available at https://www.coalitionfortheicc.org/news/20170502/getting-full-cooperation-georgian-side-will-be-one-challenges-icc (last visited 14 October 2024); "ICC Signs Cooperation Agreement with Government of Georgia," International Criminal Court, 27 July 2017, available at https://www.icc-cpi.int/news/icc-signs-cooperation-agreement-government-georgia (last visited 14 October 2024).

agreement with the ICC that explicitly spells out its cooperation obligations and how they will be fulfilled.[61]

However, the situation being investigated in Georgia is also likely to include investigations into Russian citizens and Russian military personnel for which the ICC could greatly benefit from Russia's cooperation.[62] Russia's cooperation with the ICC in this situation thus far has been mixed.[63] Before the authorization of the investigation, Russia assisted the Office of the Prosecutor's Preliminary Examination by handing it volumes of evidence.[64] Since the investigation authorization, Russia has categorically stated that it will not cooperate with the ICC.[65] Russia's potential Geneva Conventions obligations have not yet publicly factored into discussions on its cooperation so it is unclear if this cooperation has been altered by Russia's interpretation of these obligations.[66]

State practice in relation to other ICTs is also difficult to draw one distinct interpretation from. This state practice could potentially indicate whether states interpret the grave breaches provisions as obligating cooperation with ICTs in general. The relevance of this practice is, unfortunately, limited both by the fact that few of these tribunals have prosecuted war crimes committed in IACs and that the Geneva Conventions have never been brought up specifically in public discussions of cooperation obligations. The ICTR (International Criminal Tribunal for Rwanda) and the SCSL (Special Court for Sierra Leone) dealt with conflicts that they categorized as NIACs.[67] Additionally, the Special Panels for Serious Crimes in East Timor had jurisdiction over war crimes in an IAC but did not

[61] "ICC Signs Cooperation Agreement with Government of Georgia," International Criminal Court, 27 July 2017 available at https://www.icc-cpi.int/news/icc-signs-cooperation-agreement-government-georgia (last visited 14 October 2024).

[62] *Situation in Georgia* (Decision Authorizing an Investigation), *supra* note 59, § 6; Corrected Version of "Request for authorization of an investigation pursuant to article 15," 16 October 2015, ICC-01/15-4-Corr, *Situation in Georgia* (ICC-01/15-4-Corr2), Office of the Prosecutor, 17 November 2015, §§ 10–11.

[63] See K. Heller, "Russia's Short-Sighted Approach to the Georgia Investigation," Opinio Juris, 13 February 2016, available at http://opiniojuris.org/2016/02/13/russias-short-sighted-approach-to-the-icc/ (last visited 14 October 2024).

[64] *Situation in Georgia* (Decision Authorizing an Investigation), *supra* note 59, §§ 10–11; See *ibid*.

[65] See Heller, *supra* note 63.

[66] See *Ibid*; N. Gogolashvili and N. Tsagareishvili, *supra* note 60.

[67] S.C. Res. 1315 (2002), at Art. 3; S.C. Res. 955 (1994), at Art. 4.

indict anyone for war crimes and instead focused solely on its mandate to prosecute crimes against humanity.[68]

Although the International Criminal Tribunal for the former Yugoslavia (ICTY) and the ECCC (Extraordinary Chambers in the Courts of Cambodia) both prosecuted war crimes committed in an IAC, the Geneva Conventions were not raised in discussions of cooperation obligations.[69] The ICTY was created by a resolution of the UNSC that included binding cooperation obligations on all UN Member States.[70] The tribunals and domestic courts have relied solely on these UN Charter obligations to justify legal obligations to cooperate with the ICTY.[71] All persons indicted by the ECCC were Cambodian citizens and residents and were accused of crimes committed in Cambodia so the question of cooperation by other states has not arisen.[72]

This practice does not contradict the interpretation based on the ordinary meaning. The permissible act of surrendering an individual suspected of committing grave breaches of the Geneva Conventions to the ICC becomes an obligation when the state with custody over the suspect is unable or unwilling to prosecute the suspect in its own courts and no state has made out a *prima facie* case against the individual so that the custodial state could hand the suspect to another state. It is a breach of the grave breaches obligations under the Geneva Conventions to allow a suspect to either stay in a state party's jurisdiction without being prosecuted or to transfer that suspect to a jurisdiction that will not prosecute the suspect.[73] Therefore, when the ICC is looking to prosecute a suspect who is on the territory of a state party to the Geneva Conventions, that state party will

[68] Office of the General Prosecutor of the Republic of Timor-Leste—Serious Crimes Unit, *SCU-All Indictees*, available at https://www.ocf.berkeley.edu/~changmin/Serious%20Crimes%20Unit%20Files/suspects/SuspectsByName.html (last visited 14 October 2024). See S. Linton, "Prosecuting Atrocities at the District Court of Dili," 2 *Melbourne Journal of International Law* (2001) 414, at 438–448.

[69] S.C. Res. 808 (1993), at Art. 2; Law on the Establishment of the Extraordinary Chambers Art. 6, NS/RKM/1004/006 (Oct. 27, 2004, Cambodia).

[70] S.C. Res. 808 (1993), at Art. 2. See D. Stroh, "State Cooperation with the International Criminal Tribunals for the Former Yugoslavia and for Rwanda," 5 *Max Plank United Nations Yearbook* (2001) 249, at 250.

[71] See Stroh, *supra* note 70.

[72] Extraordinary Chambers in the Courts of Cambodia, *Case Load*, available at https://www.eccc.gov.kh/en/case-load (last visited 14 October 2024).

[73] Geneva I, *supra* note 4, Art. 49; Geneva II, *supra* note 4 Art. 50; Geneva III, *supra* note 4, Art. 129; Geneva IV, *supra* note 4, Art. 146; AP I, *supra* note 4, Art. 85.

not prosecute the suspect domestically, and no other state will prosecute the suspect, the state party must surrender the suspect to the ICC.

This is a situation that is likely to occur when the ICC Prosecutor has launched an investigation into a situation because cases are only admissible before the ICC if no other state is investigating or prosecuting the case and the Prosecutor and Chambers take this into account in their decision to launch an investigation or authorize the launching of an investigation.[74] Therefore, every case before the ICC is likely to involve suspects who are not being actively prosecuted by any state. The state on whose territory a suspect is found who will not or cannot prosecute domestically would be left with the sole option of handing that suspect over to the ICC, and the failure to do so would not be in line with a good faith interpretation of the grave breaches provisions of the Conventions.

Now that it has been established that surrender of a suspect to the ICC is both a permissible means of fulfilling obligations under the grave breaches provisions and, under certain circumstances, an obligation under the grave breaches provisions, it is necessary to determine under which circumstances states have any obligations at all under the grave breaches provisions and what those obligations consist of.

2.3 *Requirements for the Existence of an Obligation Under the Grave Breaches Provisions*

One important precondition to the existence of an obligation under the four 1949 Geneva Conventions is the type of conflict in which the breach is alleged to have occurred. With the exception of Common Article 3 of the Conventions, the Conventions and AP I only create obligations in IACs.[75] This is made clear in Common Article 2 of the Conventions which states the scope of application of the Conventions as "all cases of declared war or of any other armed conflict which may arise between two or more of the High Contracting Parties" and "all cases of partial or total occupation of the territory of a High Contracting Party."[76] Although Common

[74] Rome Statute of the International Criminal Court (adopted 17 July 1998, entered into force 1 July 2002, 2187 UNTS 90 (hereafter Rome Statute), Art. 12(3).

[75] Geneva I, *supra* note 4, Art. 2; Geneva II, *supra* note 4, Art. 2; Geneva III, *supra* note 4, Art. 2; Geneva IV, *supra* note 4, Art. 2; AP I, *supra* note 4, Art. 2.

[76] Geneva I, *supra* note 4, Art. 2; Geneva II, *supra* note 4, Art. 2; Geneva III, *supra* note 4, Art. 2; Geneva IV, *supra* note 4, Art. 2; AP I, *supra* note 4, Art. 2. Note: AP II which covers NIACs does not contain any grave breaches provision. Protocol Additional to the Geneva Conventions of 12 August 1949, and Relating to the Protection of Victims of Non-

Article 3 provides basic protections in NIACs, the grave breaches provisions only apply under the circumstances outlined in Common Article 2, which excludes NIACs.[77]

This restriction to IACs limits the potential application of this obligation to the ICC. Although the ICC has jurisdiction over war crimes committed in IACs (and specifically defined in the Rome Statute as grave breaches of the Geneva Conventions),[78] the Court has yet to convict anyone for war crimes committed in an IAC.[79] It issued its first public arrest warrants for war crimes allegedly committed in an IAC in the Ukraine situation in March 2023.[80] In addition, the investigation in Georgia and the ICC's jurisdictional provisions allow for the potential that a prosecution before the ICC could directly invoke grave breaches provisions obligations.[81]

The next relevant question is the temporal scope of the obligation. When is the obligation triggered and when does it end? Logically, states cannot be expected to be constantly investing resources in searching for all persons suspected of grave breaches all around the world. Such an interpretation of the obligation would be absurd and unenforceable. The wording of the provision provides very little direct indication on this question, but a good faith interpretation allows for a logical conclusion. A state can only be expected to begin searching for a suspect when it is aware that the suspect is in its jurisdiction.[82] So, the obligation to search for a suspect begins when the state becomes aware that a suspect is within its jurisdiction.[83] Similarly, the obligation ends once the suspect has left the state's jurisdiction (through no fault of the state) or the individual has been taken into custody by the state and either tried or handed over to a competent jurisdiction.

International Armed Conflict (adopted 8 June 1977, entered into force 7 December 1978) 1125 UNTS 609 (hereafter AP II).

[77] See Haye (Commentary, 2016), *supra* note 6, at 2903–2905; M. Öberg, "The Absorption of Grave Breaches into War Crimes Law," 91 *International Review of the Red Cross* (2009)163, at 170.

[78] Rome Statute, *super* note 74, at Art. 8 (2)(a).

[79] International criminal court, *Defendants*, available at https://www.icc-cpi.int/Pages/defendants-wip.aspx (last visited 14 October 2024).

[80] *Ibid.*

[81] See C. Kreß and K. Prost, "Article 87: Requests for Cooperation—General Provisions," in O. Triffterer and K. Ambos (eds.), *The Rome Statue of the International Criminal Court: A Commentary* (3rd edn., Munchen: Beck, 2016) 2019, at 2028.

[82] See Gaeta, *supra* note 43, at 629.

[83] See *ibid.*; International J. S. Pictet (Commentary, 1952), *supra* note 18, at 365–366.

2.4 *Specifics of the Obligation in Relation to the ICC*

Having established the precondition to and temporal scope of the obligations under the grave breaches provisions, it is now possible to establish the full content of the obligation in the specific context of a transfer to the ICC. The text of the provisions contains a very specific obligation to search for suspects so there is no question of a state being able to wait until a suspect somehow falls into their hands.[84] When a state is made aware that an individual whom the ICC wants for grave breaches (i.e., a charge under Article 8(2)(a) of the Rome Statute) is within their jurisdiction, that state must search for that individual. In the context of the ICC, a state is likely to be made aware of the presence of a suspect by either the issuance of an arrest warrant if it is public knowledge that the individual is in its jurisdiction or a communication from the ICC under Rome Statute Article 87(5) requesting the state's assistance in surrendering a suspect whom the ICC has reason to believe is in the state's jurisdiction.[85]

Should the state's search for the individual be successful, the state is obligated to take the individual into custody in a manner that allows for subsequent domestic prosecution or surrender to another jurisdiction.[86] The grave breaches provisions do not specifically require arrest; however, they do require the state be able to prosecute the individual so, in many states, that would require an official arrest.[87] At this point, the state has the obligation to prosecute the individual domestically.[88] If the state is unable or unwilling to do so, it must surrender the individual to another competent jurisdiction.[89] If the ICC is seeking the surrender of a suspect, it is unlikely that any other states would be willing or able to prosecute the suspect because the ICC's principle of complementarity limits it to prosecutions where no other states are able or willing to prosecute.[90] Therefore, this hypothetical state with custody over an individual wanted by the ICC for grave breaches, which is unable or unwilling to prosecute this individ-

[84] Geneva I, *supra* note 4, Art. 2; Geneva II, *supra* note 4, Art. 2; Geneva III, *supra* note 4, Art. 2; Geneva IV, *supra* note 4, Art. 2; AP I, *supra* note 4, Art. 2.

[85] Rome statute, *supra* note 74, Art. 87(5).

[86] See Kreß, *supra* note 42, at 800-801.

[87] See *ibid*.

[88] Geneva I, *supra* note 4, Art. 2; Geneva II, *supra* note 4, Art. 2; Geneva III, *supra* note 4, Art. 2; Geneva IV, *supra* note 4, Art. 2; AP I, *supra* note 4, Art. 2. See Haye (Commentary, 2016), *supra* note 6, at 2880.

[89] *Ibid*.

[90] Rome statute, *supra* note 74, Art. 17

ual domestically, would be obligated to surrender the individual to the ICC. Once the individual arrives safely at the ICC, the state no longer has any obligations under the grave breaches provisions in relation to that individual.

A slightly thornier question is that of whether the state would have an additional, corollary obligation to collect or share any evidence with the ICC.[91] This question particularly comes up when a state has collected evidence in the process of taking a suspect into custody.[92] The destruction of or failure to turn over this evidence would arguably not be in good faith and would arguably violate the grave breaches obligations.[93] The purpose of the grave breaches provisions is to ensure that perpetrators of grave breaches are prosecuted.[94] Obstructing this purpose by deliberately hindering prosecution in the jurisdiction to which the suspect is surrendered violates the grave breaches obligations.[95] Refusing to hand over evidence collected during the process of taking the suspect into custody would fall in this category of prohibited acts if that evidence is necessary for a fair and effective prosecution.[96]

3 Obligations Under Common Article 1 of the Geneva Conventions and of Additional Protocol I

Common Article 1 of the Geneva Conventions and AP I appears most frequently in scholarly discussions of the Geneva Conventions creating obligations to cooperate with the ICC.[97] Under this common article, state parties "undertake to respect and to ensure respect" for all four Geneva

[91] See Kreß, *supra* note 42, at 801.
[92] See *ibid*.
[93] See *ibid*.
[94] See *ibid*.
[95] See *ibid*.
[96] See *ibid*.
[97] See Z. Wenqi, "On Co-Operation by States Not Party to the International Criminal Court," 88 *International Review of the Red Cross* (2006) 87; Kreß and Prost, *supra* note 81: C. Vale, "Can the Geneva Conventions Shield the ICC from Attacks?" Center for International Relations and Sustainable Development (CIRSD), 28 March 2022, available at https://www.cirsd.org/en/expert-analysis/can-the-geneva-conventions-shield-the-icc-from-attacks (last visited 14 October 2024).

Conventions and AP I.[98] Because this obligation is written in such simple and short terms, it requires some unpacking to apply it to the ICC.

3.1 Is There an Obligation to Ensure That Other State Parties Respect the Geneva Conventions?

The first relevant question is whether the obligation to "ensure respect" mandates states to ensure the respect only of its own entities or also those of other state parties. The ordinary meaning of the text is not immediately clear in this respect. The inclusion of both "respect" and "ensure respect" indicates that ensure respect must mean something more than simply the state pledging to fulfill its obligations.[99] The word ensure implies an obligation to impact the actions of another entity outside of the state itself.[100] In the context of the law of armed conflict, this does not necessarily imply a universal obligation to ensure that all state parties respect the Convention.[101]

Some scholars argue that the obligation is to ensure that all entities and individuals within the state's jurisdiction respect the Conventions—including non-state armed groups.[102] The argument is generally based on the lack of reference to an obligation to ensure other states' respect in the drafting history.[103] If states had intended the innovative step in 1949 of obligating states to interfere with another state's internal affairs, there

[98] Geneva I, *supra* note 4, Art. 1; Geneva II, *supra* note 4, Art. 1; Geneva III, *supra* note 4, Art. 1; Geneva IV, *supra* note 4, Art. 1; AP I, *supra* note 4, Art. 1.

[99] See R. Geiß, "The Obligation to Respect and to Ensure Respect for the Conventions," in A. Clapham M. Sassòli, and P. Gaeta (eds.), *The 1949 Geneva Conventions: A Commentary* (Oxford: Oxford University Press, 2015) 112, at 117–122; A. Devillard, "L'obligation de faire respecter le droit international humanitaire: l'article 1 commun aux Conventions de Genève et à leur premier Protocole additionnel, fondement d'un droit international humanitaire de coopération?" 20 *Revue Québécoise de Droit International* (2007) 75, at 80.

[100] See R. Geiß, "Common Article 1 of the Geneva Conventions: Scope and Content of the Obligation to 'Ensure Respect'—'Narrow but Deep' or 'Wide and Shallow'?" in H. Krieger (ed.), *Inducing Compliance with International Humanitarian Law: Lessons from the African Great Lakes Region* (Cambridge: Cambridge University Press, 2015) 417, at 417.

[101] See F. Kalshoven, "The Undertaking to Respect and Ensure Respect in All Circumstances: From Tiny Seed to Ripening Fruit," in F. Kalshoven, *Reflections on the Law of War: Collected Essays* (Leiden: Martinus Nijhoff, 2007) 665.

[102] See C. Focarelli, "Common Article 1 of the 1949 Geneva Conventions: A Soap Bubble?" 21 *European Journal of International Law* (2010) 125; Kalshoven, *supra* note 101.

[103] See Focarelli, *supra* note 102, at 129–133.

would likely have been extensive discussion of the concept.[104] The drafting history does not indicate that the idea was ever mentioned.[105]

Despite this lack of discussion in the drafting history, subsequent practice indicates that states now interpret the Common Article 1 obligation as requiring states to ensure other state parties' compliance.[106] This is demonstrated by a uniform and consistent practice of all state parties both in their individual capacities and as members of international organizations to condemn Geneva Conventions violations committed in conflicts with no connection to the condemning state.[107] These states often rely on their Common Article 1 obligations to justify their condemnation.[108] This includes sixteen UNGA Resolutions on Geneva Conventions state parties' obligations to ensure Israel's respect for the Conventions specifically based on obligations under Common Article 1.[109] UNSC Resolution 681 (1990) on this same question is of particular relevance and interpretive force because it directed all Geneva Conventions state parties to ensure Israel's

[104] *Ibid.*

[105] See *ibid.*; Kalshoven, *supra* note 101, at 668–692.

[106] International Committee of the Red Cross, *Customary International Humanitarian Law Database: Practice Relating to Rule 144—Ensuring Respect for International Humanitarian Law Erga Omnes*, available at https://ihldatabases.icrc.org/customary-ihl/eng/docs/v2_rul_rule144 (last visited 14 October 2024). See Geiß, *supra* note 100; Devillard, *supra* note 99; K. Dörmann and J. Serralvo, "Common Article 1 to the Geneva Conventions and the Obligation to Prevent International Humanitarian Law Violations," 96 *International Review of the Red Cross* (2014) 707; B. Kessler, "The Duty to Ensure Respect under Common Article 1 of the Geneva Conventions: Its Implications on International and Non-International Armed Conflicts," 44 *German Yearbook of International Law* (2001) 498.

[107] International Committee of the Red Cross, *Customary International Humanitarian Law Database: Practice Relating to Rule 144—Ensuring Respect for International Humanitarian Law Erga Omnes*, available at https://ihldatabases.icrc.org/customary-ihl/eng/docs/v2_rul_rule144 (last visited 14 October 2024); see Geiß, *supra* note 100; Devillard, *supra* note 99; Dörmann and Serralvo, *supra* note 106.

[108] International Committee of the Red Cross, *Customary International Humanitarian Law Database: Practice Relating to Rule 144—Ensuring Respect for International Humanitarian Law Erga Omnes*, available at https://ihldatabases.icrc.org/en/customary-ihl/v2/rule144 (last visited 14 October 2024).

[109] G.A. Res. 58/97, 9 December 2003; G.A. Res. 59/122, 10 December 2004 ; G.A. Res. 60/105, 8 December 2005; G.A. Res. 61/117 14 December 2006; G.A. Res. 62/107, 17 December 2007; G.A. Res. 63/96, 5 December 2008); G.A. Res. 64/92, 10 December 2009; G.A. Res. 65/103, 10 December 2010; G.A. Res. 66/77, 9 December 2011; G.A. Res. 67/119, 18 December 2012; G.A. Res. 68/81, 11 December 2013; G.A. Res. 69/91, 5 December 2014; G.A. Res. 70/88, 9 December 2015; G.A. Res. 71/96, 6 December 2016; G.A. Res. 72/85, 7 December 2017; G.A. Res. 73/97, 7 December 2018.

respect of Geneva IV "in accordance with Article 1" of that Convention.[110] Both the binding nature of this resolution and its unequivocal reliance on Common Article 1 obligations allows it to establish a clear and nearly unanimous subsequent interpretation by the state parties.[111] This resolution indicates that Geneva Conventions state parties interpret Common Article 1 as obligating state parties to ensure other state parties' compliance.[112]

However, since the ICRC's 2016 Commentary on Geneva I that is discussed below, some states have expressed their disagreements with this interpretation.[113] One potential example of this is changes to UNGA Resolutions on the application of the Geneva Conventions to the Palestinian territory. As stated above, the UNGA explicitly relied on Common Article 1 to support obligations to ensure Israel's respect for the Conventions in sixteen resolutions from 2003 to 2018.[114] Beginning in

[110] S.C. Res. 681 (1990) at 5.

[111] See G. Nolte, *First report on subsequent agreements and subsequent practice in relation to the interpretation of treaties* (2013), U.N. Doc. A/CN.4/660, para. 141 available at https://legal.un.org/ilc/documentation/english/a_cn4_660.pdf (last visited 14 October 2024).

[112] See International Committee of the Red Cross, *Customary International Humanitarian Law Database: Practice Relating to Rule 144—Ensuring Respect for International Humanitarian Law Erga Omnes*, available at https://ihldatabases.icrc.org/en/customary-ihl/v2/rule144 (last visited 14 October 2024); Geiß, *supra* note 100; Devillard, *supra* note 99; Dörmann and Serralvo, *supra* note 106.

[113] See B. Egan (Legal Advisor, US Dept. of State), "Address at the American Society of International Law Annual Meeting: International Law, Legal Diplomacy, and the Counter-ISIL Campaign," U.S. Department of State, 1 April 2016, available at https://2009-2017.state.gov/s/l/releases/remarks/255493.htm (last visited 14 October 2024); J. Reid (Head, Office of International Law, Commonwealth Attorney-General's Department, Australia), "Ensuring Respect: The Role of State Practice in Interpreting the Geneva Conventions," International Law Association Reporter, 11 September 2016, available at https://ilareporter.org.au/2016/11/ensuring-respect-the-role-of-state-practice-in-interpreting-the-geneva-conventions-john-reid/ (last visited 14 October 2024); Haye (Commentary, 2020), *supra* note 18; V. Robson, "The Common Approach to Article 1: The Scope of Each State's Obligation to Ensure Respect for the Geneva Conventions," 25 *Journal of Conflict and Security Law* (2020) 101, at 108–109.

[114] G.A. Res. 58/97, 9 December 2003; G.A. Res. 59/122, 10 December 2004 ; G.A. Res. 60/105, 8 December 2005; G.A. Res. 61/117 14 December 2006; G.A. Res. 62/107, 17 December 2007; G.A. Res. 63/96, 5 December 2008); G.A. Res. 64/92, 10 December 2009; G.A. Res. 65/103, 10 December 2010; G.A. Res. 66/77, 9 December 2011; G.A. Res. 67/119, 18 December 2012; G.A. Res. 68/81, 11 December 2013; G.A. Res. 69/91, 5 December 2014; G.A. Res. 70/88, 9 December 2015; G.A. Res. 71/96, 6 December 2016; G.A. Res. 72/85, 7 December 2017; G.A. Res. 73/97, 7 December 2018.

2019, resolutions on this topic lost their specific reference to Common Article 1.[115] Instead, they refer to the grave breaches provisions and to statements made at the 2001 and 2014 Conference of High Contracting Parties to the Geneva Conventions on the need to ensure respect for the Geneva Conventions in the Palestinian territories.[116] This failure to explicitly cite Common Article 1 obligations might indicate a change in states' interpretation of the provision or it may simply indicate states' fatigue at constantly asking states to fulfill an obligation that they consistently fail to adequately fulfill. Additionally, the US made clear in a 2016 speech by its State Department's legal advisor that it interprets Common Article 1 as not requiring states to ensure the other states' respect.[117] These responses potentially indicate a change in the state practice that could alter the interpretation. It is, however, too early to tell if this trend will be followed by other countries.[118] The whole of the current state practice continues to support the interpretation that states are obligated to ensure other state parties' respect.

ICRC commentaries confirm this interpretation. In its twentieth-century commentaries, the ICRC defined the obligation to ensure respect by other states in a less robust manner than in its twenty-first-century commentaries.[119] In its early commentaries, it interprets Common Article

[115] G.A. Res. 74/89, 13 December 2019; G.A. Res. 75/98, 10 December 2020.

[116] G.A. Res. 74/89, 13 December 2019; G.A. Res. 75/98, 10 December 2020.

[117] See Egan, *supra* note 113.

[118] See Robson, *supra* note 113, at 108–109 (arguing for a limited interpretation but only citing potential practice from four states, some of which is less than clear on the interpretation); M. Schmitt and S. Watts, "Common Article 1 and the Duty to 'Ensure Respect,'" 96 *International Law Studies* (2020) 674 (arguing for a limited interpretation but only finding the practice of three states).

[119] Compare J. S. Pictet, "Article 1: Respect for the Convention," in J. S. Pictet (ed.), *The Geneva Conventions of 12 August 1949: Commentary: (I) Geneva Conventions for the Amelioration of the Condition of the Wounded and Sick in Armed Forces in the Field* (Geneva: International Committee of the Red Cross, 1952) 24, at 26; J. S. Pictet, "Article 1: Respect for the Convention," in J. S. Pictet, The Geneva Conventions of 12 August 1949: Commentary: IV Geneva Convention Relative to the Protection of Civilian Persons in Time of War (Geneva: International Committee of the Red Cross, 1958) 15, at 16; J. S. Pictet, "Article 1: Respect for the Convention" in J. S. Pictet (ed.), *The Geneva Conventions of 12 August 1949: Commentary: II Geneva Convention for the Amelioration of the Condition of the Wounded, Sick and Shipwrecked Members of Armed Forces at Sea* (Geneva: International Committee of the Red Cross, 1960) at 25–26; J. S Pictet, "Article 1: Respect for the Convention," in J. S. Pictet (ed.), *The Geneva Conventions of 12 August 1949: Commentary: III Relative to the Treatment of Prisoners of War* (Geneva: International Committee of the

1 as meaning that "in the event of a [state party] failing to fulfil its obligations, the other Contracting Parties (neutral, allied or enemy) may, and should, endeavour to bring it back to an attitude of respect for the Convention."[120] In its twenty-first-century commentaries, the ICRC more boldly states that "States, whether neutral, allied or enemy, must do everything reasonably in their power to ensure respect for the Conventions by others that are Party to a conflict."[121] This is a stronger and clearer obligation than the obligation to vaguely bring other state parties "back to an attitude of respect." The ICRC justifies this stronger obligation by citing the subsequent practice that is referenced above.[122]

In addition, the ICJ has found that Common Article 1 includes an obligation to ensure other state parties' respect in the *Nicaragua v. US* Judgment and the Wall Advisory Opinion.[123] In the *Nicaragua* case, the ICJ found that the US was obligated to ensure that rebel groups in Nicaragua respected the Geneva Conventions by not encouraging them to commit violations.[124] This is a fairly narrow negative obligation applied to a non-state actor's compliance but the ICJ expanded upon it in the Wall opinion. In that opinion, the ICJ found that Common Article 1 obligated

Red Cross, 1960) 17, at 18 with J. M. Henckaerts, "Article 1—Respect for the Convention," in International Committee of the Red Cross, *Commentary on the First Geneva Convention: Convention (I) for the Amelioration of the Condition of the Wounded and Sick in Armed Forces in the Field* (Cambridge: Cambridge University Press, 2016) 153; J. M. Henckaerts, "Article 1: Respect for the Convention," in K. Dörmann at al. (ed.), *Commentary on the Second Geneva Convention: Convention (II) for the Amelioration of the Condition of the Wounded, Sick and Shipwrecked Members of Armed Forces at Sea* (Cambridge: Cambridge University Press, 2017) para. 175; J. M. Henckaerts, "Article 1: Respect for the Convention," in International Committee of the Red Cross, *Commentary on the Third Geneva Convention: Convention (III) relative to the Treatment of Prisoners of War* (Cambridge: Cambridge University Press, 2020) para. 186.

120 Pictet (Commentary, 1952), *supra* note 119, at 26; Pictet (Commentary, 1958), *supra* note 119, at 16; Pictet (Commentary, 1960), *supra* note 119, at 25–26; Pictet (Commentary III, 1960), *supra* note 119, at 18.

121 Henckaerts (Commentary, 2016), *supra* note 119; Henckaerts (Commentary, 2017), *supra* note 119; Henckaerts (Commentary, 2020), *supra* note 119.

122 *Ibid.*

123 Judgment, *Military and Paramilitary Activities in and Against Nicaragua (Nicaragua. v. U.S.)*, 27 June 1986, at 219–220, 255; Advisory Opinion, *Legal Consequences of the Construction of a Wall in the Occupied Palestinian Territory*, 9 July 2004, at 159. See Dörmann and Serralvo, *supra* note 106, at 717.

124 Judgment, *Military and Paramilitary Activities in and Against Nicaragua (Nicaragua. v. U.S.)*, 27 June 1986, at 219–220, 255.

all state parties to ensure Israel's compliance.[125] This opinion expanded the obligation to a positive obligation and explicitly applied it to another state's conduct.

State, ICRC, and ICJ practice indicate that states interpret Common Article 1 to create an obligation to ensure that other state parties to the Geneva Conventions fulfill their obligations.

3.2 *Does the Obligation Apply in NIACs?*

The next relevant question on the scope of application of Common Article 1 is whether, and to what extent, it applies in NIACs as well as IACs. The ordinary meaning of the provision indicates that it applies in a limited way to NIACs. Because Common Article 1 obligates state parties to ensure respect "for the present Convention," it also obligates state parties to ensure respect for Common Article 3's minimum protections in NIACs.[126] Common Article 3 does not contain any obligation to prosecute violators so the ICC is unlikely to play a role in ensuring respect for Common Article 3.[127] Because the obligation in NIACs is unlikely to create any obligations in relation to the ICC, this section will focus on the obligation in IACs.

3.3 *Nature of the Obligation in Relation to the ICC*

In an IAC, as established in the previous section, a state party is obligated to ensure the prosecution of suspected war criminals within their jurisdiction—as is specifically provided for in the grave breaches provisions.[128] Common Article 1 adds to this obligation a duty to assist in the prosecution of all persons suspected of grave breaches who are within any state

[125] Advisory Opinion, *Legal Consequences of the Construction of a Wall in the Occupied Palestinian Territory*, 9 July 2004, at 159.

[126] Geneva I, *supra* note 4, Art. 1; Geneva II, *supra* note 4, Art. 1; Geneva III, *supra* note 4 Art. 1; Geneva IV, *supra* note 4 Art. 1; AP I, *supra* note 4, Art. 1. See L . Boisson de Chazournes and L. Condorelli, "Common Article 1 of the Geneva Conventions Revisited: Protecting Collective Interests," 82 *International Review of the Red Cross* (2000) 67; Geiß, *supra* note 99, at 115–116; Kessler, *supra* note 106, at 507–509.

[127] Geneva I, *supra* note 4, Art. 3; Geneva II, *supra* note 4, Art. 3; Geneva III, *supra* note 4, Art. 3; Geneva IV, *supra* note 4 Art. 3.

[128] Geneva I, *supra* note 4, Art. 49; Geneva II, *supra* note 4, Art. 50; Geneva III, *supra* note 4, Art. 129; Geneva IV, *supra* note 4, Art. 146; AP I, *supra* note 4, Art. 85. See *supra* Sect. 2.1.

party's jurisdiction. This obligation derives from the Common Article 1 obligation to ensure that every state party respect the Conventions, which includes fulfillment of the obligation to prosecute those suspected of grave breaches.[129] Therefore, state parties to the Geneva Conventions are obligated to assist other state parties in prosecuting persons suspected of grave breaches.[130]

This obligation to assist with prosecutions is a due diligence obligation.[131] Logically, every state party cannot be expected to materially alter the behavior of every other state party and so cannot be held responsible for another state party's failure to fulfill their obligations.[132] So the obligation must be one of conduct and not of result—a due diligence obligation.[133] The due diligence nature of this obligation can also be derived from an analogy with other international legal obligations that require a state to affect the actions of another entity, such as human rights law and the duty to prevent genocide.[134] In such situations, states are obligated, in the words of the ICJ in the *Bosnia Genocide* case, "to employ all means reasonably available to them."[135]

In the context of ensuring that state parties to the Geneva Conventions fulfill their grave breaches obligations, this leaves various means open to state parties that are relevant to cooperation with the ICC.[136] One general means to fulfill the obligation is to assist the prosecuting jurisdiction with investigation and prosecution.[137] Specifically, a state is obligated to hand

[129] See Henckaerts (Commentary, 2016), *supra* note 119, at 153; Geiß, *supra* note 99, at 438.

[130] See Kessler, *supra* note 106, at 510 (finding that one means to fulfill the ensure respect obligation is to offer other states assistance).

[131] See Geiß, *supra* note 99; Dörmann and Serralvo, *supra* note 106, at 723–725.

[132] *Ibid.*

[133] *Ibid.*

[134] *Ibid.*

[135] Judgment, *Application of the Convention on the Prevention and Punishment of the Crime of Genocide (Bosnia and Herzegovina v. Serbia and Montenegro)* (ICJ Rep 1996), International Court of Justice, 26 February 2007, 430.

[136] See Dörmann and Serralvo, *supra* note 106, at 725–726; Official Journal of the European Union, *Updated European Union Guidelines on Promoting Compliance with International Humanitarian Law (IHL) (2009/C 303/06)* (2009), available at https://eur-lex.europa.eu/legal-content/EN/TXT/PDF/?uri=CELEX:52009XG1215(01) (last visited 14 October 2024); Devillard, *supra* note 99; Wenqi, *supra* note 97, at 93–94; Kessler, *supra* note 106, at 506–507.

[137] See Updated European Union Guidelines on Promoting Compliance with International Humanitarian Law, 2009 O.J. (C 303/06); Kessler, *supra* note 106, at 506–507.

any relevant evidence that is in its possession to the prosecuting jurisdiction. This follows from the due diligence nature of the obligation because it is a means that is reasonably available to a state and one that is likely to ensure that the prosecuting state fulfills its grave breaches obligations. Another means of assisting with the investigation and prosecution would be to protect and provide witnesses that are within a state's jurisdiction. Again, this is a means that is reasonably available to a state and one that is likely to ensure that the prosecuting state fulfills its Geneva Conventions obligations.

When the grave breaches prosecution is occurring at the ICC, these obligations to assist the prosecuting state become obligations to assist the ICC.[138] As argued in the previous section, prosecution by the ICC can constitute an adequate substitute for domestic prosecution to fulfill grave breaches obligations.[139] In the frequent circumstance where the ICC is the only available prosecution venue, Geneva Conventions State Parties must ensure that the ICC's prosecution is as fair and effective as they can or they will be failing to ensure the fulfillment of grave breaches obligations.[140] If the ICC is unable to prosecute, the perpetrator will enjoy impunity and Geneva Conventions State Parties who were in a position to assist will have failed to fulfill their obligations to ensure the prosecution of that suspect. They had the very clear and reasonably available means of assisting a tribunal prosecuting a suspect and have failed to do so—violating their due diligence obligation. Geneva Conventions State Parties who were in a position to provide evidence or other means of assistance to the ICC could, therefore, be held internationally responsible for their failure to cooperate with the ICC as a breach of their obligations under Common Article 1 of the Geneva Conventions.[141]

4 Conclusion

State parties to the Geneva Conventions and AP I are obligated by both the Convention's grave breaches provisions and Common Article 1 to cooperate with the ICC under certain circumstances and in certain ways. The grave breaches provisions obligate states to surrender suspects to the

[138] See Wenqi, *supra* note 97, at 92–94; Kreß and Prost, *supra* note 81, at 2028.
[139] See *supra* Sect. 2.1.
[140] See Wenqi, *supra* note 97, at 92–94; Kreß and Prost, *supra* note 81, at 2028.
[141] See Kreß and Prost, *supra* note 81, at 2028.

ICC if the suspect is on the state's territory, the state is unwilling or unable to prosecute, no other state has made out a *prima facie* case for prosecution of the suspect, and the ICC is seeking the suspect's arrest for acts that amount to grave breaches of the Conventions. Common Article 1 obligates states to provide evidence to the ICC or protect and provide witnesses to the ICC when such acts are a clear and reasonably available means for the state to ensure the prosecution of an individual charged with grave breaches of the Conventions.

CHAPTER 9

Conclusions

Ondřej Svaček

The author of all contributions presented their arguments for conclusions they reached in respective chapters. A. Sánchez Frías hails the Appeals Chamber's (ACH) endorsement of the scope of the authorized investigation in the context of the situation in Afghanistan and requirement of the war nexus to include not only war crimes committed in detention facilities in Afghanistan, but also in the black site facilities run by the US in Poland, Lithuania, and Romania. O. Svaček concludes that contrary to the opinion presented in the ACH's seminal decision in the *Al-Bashir* case, customary international law's path for the removal of personal immunities of sitting heads of the third states is not yet established, and proposes two options for how to overcome this obstacle through dynamic formation of customary international law, or application of self-defence as a circumstance precluding wrongfulness. M. Lipovský concludes that given the fact that war crimes are the most prevalent category of crime under international law, and unfortunately also given the number of suspected war crimes being committed in the world, correct and proper functioning of

O. Svaček (✉)
Centre for International Humanitarian and Operational Law, Faculty of Law, Palacký University, Olomouc, Czechia
e-mail: ondrej.svacek@upol.cz

O. Svaček, M. Faix (eds.), *Prosecution of War Crimes before the ICC*, Global Issues, https://doi.org/10.1007/978-3-031-84216-0_9

complementarity is necessary both for the states and for the ICC in order for it not to be over-burdened and thus pushed to choosing how to allocate its limited resources. Such correct functioning may only be possible when the detailed interpretation and application of the principle is conducted in an expected and predictable manner. Y. Naggan proposes the adoption of a more nuanced approach when contemplating cumulative charges for war crimes and crimes against humanity that involves an in-depth examination of the "nexus to an armed conflict" requirement of war crimes. In her contribution on digital evidence K. Gavrysh—based on analysis of a sparse practice of the ICC—opines that the ICC is more confident to consider the digital evidence only if corroborated by other types of evidence relevant to the facts of the case. She points out that this type of evidence has not yet had a real opportunity to enhance the prosecution of war crimes before the ICC. L. Morgan proposes strengthening of the assistance mandate of the Trust Fund for Victims (TFV), which might overcome difficulties of the reparation regime that is available only for the benefit of victims who suffered harm as a result of crimes within the jurisdiction of the ICC when the person standing trial for his or her participation in those crimes has been found guilty. Finally, E. Brandon proves that the Geneva Conventions might serve as a source of obligation to cooperate with the ICC in relation to the third states, non-state parties to the Rome Statute.

To address the opening question formulated in the introductory part of this book and consider whether the selected procedural aspects enhance or hinder prosecution of war crimes in proceedings before the ICC, the following additional comments are presented.

First, the jurisdictional decision in the situation of Afghanistan positively impacts the prosecution of war crimes by expanding the interpretative boundaries of jurisdiction, promoting accountability, and aligning legal principles with the realities of modern armed conflicts. It provides a framework for prosecuting individuals involved in war crimes committed outside the immediate theater of war (e.g. in Poland, Lithuania, and Romania), thus enhancing the scope of the ICC's mission to uphold international justice. The rejection of the restrictive approach taken in this situation by the Pre-Trial Chamber should be considered as a welcome achievement supported both by historical interpretation of Common Article 3 and relevant practice of the ICC's predecessors, which confirmed that the requirement that the acts of the accused must be closely related to the armed conflict would not be negated if the crimes were temporally and geographically remote from the actual fighting.

Second, at first glance, extension of the jurisdiction, or more precisely denial of personal immunity of a sitting head (and correspondingly prime minister and minister of foreign affairs), of the third states in proceedings before the ICC might be also categorized as an achievement since it removes a legal obstacle for prosecution of an important category of war criminal. Unfortunately, the interpretative approach of the ICC is built on shaky foundations, which might eventually threaten its institutional legitimacy. Once again, the co-editors of this book suggest that a preferable option would be to adopt a dynamic rather than a deductive approach to the formation of customary international law that would better reflect the practice of states, as a legal ingredient of customary international law.

Third, more than 20 years of the ICC's practice has shed some light on basic concepts of complementarity, which is certainly positive; nevertheless, it did not escape some critics pointing to the fact that adopting a strict interpretation of Article 17 of the Rome Statute makes it difficult for states to meet its requirements. In that respect, S. Nouwen speaks about precarious exercise of prediction and, referring to the Lubanga case, argues that

> Even if the domestic proceedings focus on conduct that constitutes the basis of charges of genocide or crimes against humanity, the ICC's case will be admissible as long as it involves only one type of conduct not covered by the domestic proceedings (in Lubanga's case, the charges of war crimes related to child soldiers), including where the ICC's charges are less serious.[1]

In his contribution, M. Lipovský rightly stresses another challenge and mentions the in-built contradiction between the need to embarrass a state (as the ICC is supposed to decide that a state did not sufficiently fulfil its obligations under international law to investigate and prosecute crimes under international law) and at the same time total dependency of the ICC on their cooperation in areas such as providing evidence, which may cause significant difficulties and obviously produces tensions between the ICC and states.

[1] S. Nouwen, *Complementarity in the Line of Fire: The Catalysing Effect of the International Criminal Court in Uganda and Sudan* (Cambridge: Cambridge University Press, 2013), at 52.

Fourth, the issue of cumulative charges and convictions for war crimes and crimes against humanity on the basis of the same underlying conduct has still not been fully elucidated in ICC jurisprudence from the perspective of promoting the unique goals that the war crimes regime was intended to fulfil. While war crimes charges and convictions are regularly brought forth, considerations of historical records, fair labelling, and concerns over avoiding the perception of a hierarchy of crimes and misguided interpretations of international humanitarian law (IHL) rules and standards are not fully addressed when employing the current jurisprudential test for cumulative charges across categories of crimes. Therefore, one may conclude that the cumulative charging remains a challenge rather than an achievement for the ICC.

Fifth, the same conclusion might be formulated with respect to the usage of digital evidence in proceedings before the ICC, which is still waiting for its test case here. K. Gavrysh believes that such a case can eventually turn up in the context of the Ukrainian situation where a large amount of digital evidence is expected to be processed by the ICC's Office of the Prosecutor. One may ask what role AI will have in the process of assessment of such evidence and whether the Court will use digital evidence only if corroborated by other types of material.

Sixth, the potential catalyzing effect in the prosecution of war crimes before the ICC might be brought about also by the participation of victims in the criminal proceedings, which is—without any doubt—a great achievement in itself. The participation of victims incorporates into international criminal proceedings before the ICC a new quality that transgresses the traditional dichotomy and perception of a proceeding as a clash between the defense and the prosecutor in international criminal proceedings before the ICC. Nevertheless, there are still some important challenges that limit the overall impact of this development. The regime of victim participation provided in the Rome Statute and related regulations grants access to reparations to only a limited number of victims as it excludes those victims harmed by the atrocity crimes falling—for various reasons—outside of the jurisdictional framework of the Court. L. Morgan thus rightly points out that this approach produces an unintended outcome, the hierarchization of victims, and therefore recommends shifting the focus of the TFV from criminals to victims, meaning that instead of emphasizing the connection between victims and perpetrators of (war) crimes, the TFV should prioritize the connection between victims and (war) crimes generally.

Seventh, the conclusions drawn by E. Brandon in her chapter on the possibility for the Geneva Conventions to create standalone obligations to cooperate with the ICC have the potential to improve the ICC's ability to ensure respect for IHL and therefore to enhance prosecution of war crimes. However, the ICC (and, specifically, its Assembly of State Parties that has the most relevant role) have yet to use this tool to assist it in obtaining cooperation from states that is of vital importance for its effective functioning, encompassing also the prosecution of war criminals.

To sum up, previous considerations confirm that every single issue analyzed by the contributors to this volume must be assessed as comprehensively as possible. It seems that the proposed categorization of achievement on the one hand and challenges on the other is only an ideal conception that does not exist in isolation. Like in a real life, there are two sides to every coin, meaning that even if a particular institute might be qualified as a positive outcome contributing to the effective prosecution of war crimes (e.g. removal of personal immunity), it definitively does not preclude the possibility that it produces some shortcomings and difficulties at the same (e.g. lack of state practice for formation of the rule of customary international law on inapplicability of personal immunity before international courts and tribunals). On the other hand, achievements are accomplished only through overcoming of obstacles and challenges (e.g. lack of the ICC's practice concerning usage of digital evidence). Be this as it may, it remains to be seen how responsive the ICC will be to all these challenges and any new development related to the prosecution of war crimes at international level.

Literature and Sources

Books

K. Ambos, *Treatise on International Criminal Law, Vol. I: Foundations and General Part* ((1st edn., Oxford: Oxford University Press, 2013) 520 pp.; Vol. II: *The Crimes and Sentencing* (Oxford: Oxford University Press, 2014) 384 pp.

M. Cherif Bassiouni, *Crimes Against Humanity in International Criminal Law* (2nd edn., Kluwer, 1999), 652 pp.

M. Ch. Bassiouni, *Crimes Against Humanity: Historical Evolution and Contemporary Application* (: Cambridge University Press, 2011) 884 pp.

B. Bonafé, *The Relationship between State and Individual Responsibility for International Crimes* (: Brill, 2009) 281 pp.

E. Casey, *Digital Evidence and Computer Crime* (: Academic Press, 2011) 840 pp.

A. Cassese, P. Gaeta et al. *Cassese's International Criminal Law* (3rd edn., : Oxford University Press, 2013) 472 pp.

N. Combs, *Fact-Finding Without Facts. The Uncertain Evidentiary Foundations of International Criminal Convictions* (Cambridge: Cambridge University Press, 2010) 430 pp.

O. Corten, Olivier, V. Koutroulis, *Tribunal for the crime of aggression against Ukraine – a legal assessment* (Brussels, EU, 2022) 52 pp.

R. Cryer et al., *An Introduction to International Criminal Law and Procedure* (3rd edn., : Cambridge University Press, 2014) 706 pp.

P. de Grieff (ed.), *The Handbook of Reparations* (Oxford: Oxford University Press, 2006) 1054 pp.

O. Svaček, M. Faix (eds.), *Prosecution of War Crimes before the ICC*, Global Issues, https://doi.org/10.1007/978-3-031-84216-0

T. Dias, *Beyond Imperfect Justice: Legality and Fair Labelling in International Criminal Law* (: Martinus Nijhoff, 2022) 314 pp.
M. Faix, O. Svaček (eds.), *ICC Jurisprudence and the Development of International Humanitarian Law* (Cham: Palgrave Macmillan, 2024) 273 pp.
International Committee of the Red Cross. (2016). *Commentary on the First Geneva Convention: Convention (I) for the Amelioration of the Conditions of the Wounded and Sick in Armed Forces in the Field.* Cambridge University Press.
International Committee of the Red Cross. (2017). *Commentary on the Second Geneva Convention: Convention (II) for the Amelioration of the Condition of the Wounded, Sick and Shipwrecked Members of Armed Forces at Sea.* Cambridge University Press.
International Committee of the Red Cross. (2020). *Commentary on the Third Geneva Convention: Convention (III) relative to the Treatment of Prisoners of War.* Cambridge University Press.
International Institute of Humanitarian Law, *The Manual on the Law of Non-International Armed Conflict* (San Remo, 2006) 75 pp.
M. Klamberg, *Commentary on the Law of the International Criminal Court* (: Torkel Opsahl Academic EPublisher, 2017) 818 pp.
N. Melzer, *Targeted Killing in International Law* (: Oxford University Press, 2008) 528 pp.
G. Mettraux, *International Crimes and the ad hoc Tribunals* (: Oxford University Press, 2005) 442 pp.
G. Mettraux, *International Crimes: Law and Practice: Volume II: Crimes Against Humanity* (: Oxford University Press, 2020) 952 pp.
L. Moir, *The Law of Internal Armed Conflict* (: Cambridge University Press, 2002) 306 pp.
S. Nouwen, *Complementarity in the Line of Fire: The Catalysing Effect of the International Criminal Court in Uganda and Sudan* (: Cambridge University Press, 2013) 525 pp.
A. Novak, *The International Criminal Court. An Introduction* (Heidelberg: Springer, 2015) 133 pp.
K. Novotná, *Head of state Immunity in International Law: The Charles Taylor Case before the Special Court for Sierra Leone* (: Masaryk University 2013) 172 pp.
R. O'Keefe, *International Criminal Law* (: Oxford University Press, 2015) 678 pp.
O. Olusanya, *Double Jeopardy Without Parameters: Re-characterisation in International Criminal Law* (: Intersentia, 2004) 278 pp.
J. S. Pictet (ed.), *The Geneva Conventions of 12 August 1949: Commentary: I Geneva Conventions for the Amelioration of the Condition of the Wounded and Sick in Armed Forces in the Field* (: International Committee of the Red Cross, 1952).

J. S. Pictet (ed.), *The Geneva Conventions of 12 August 1949: Commentary: IV Geneva Convention Relative to the Protection of Civilian Persons in Time of War* (: International Committee of the Red Cross, 1958).

J. S. Pictet (ed.), *The Geneva Conventions of 12 August 1949: Commentary: II Geneva Convention for the Amelioration of the Condition of the Wounded, Sick and Shipwrecked Members of Armed Forces at Sea* (: International Committee of the Red Cross, 1960a).

J. S. Pictet (ed.), *The Geneva Conventions of 12 August 1949: Commentary: III Relative to the Treatment of Prisoners of War* (: International Committee of the Red Cross, 1960b).

A. Quintin, *The Nature of International Humanitarian Law: a Permissive or Restrictive Regime?* (: Edward Elgar, 2020) 384 pp.

W. Schabas, *The International Criminal Court: A Commentary on the Rome Statute* (1st edn., : Oxford University Press, 2010) 1258 pp.

W. Schabas, *The International Criminal Court: A Commentary on the Rome Statute* (2nd edn., : Oxford University Press, 2016) 1589 pp.

W. Schabas, *The UN International Criminal Tribunals. The Former Yugoslavia, Rwanda and Sierra Leone* (Cambridge: Cambridge University Press, 2006) 711 pp.

A.P. Simester, *Fundamentals of Criminal Law: Responsibility, Culpability and Wrongdoing* (: Oxford University Press, 2021) 536 pp.

S. Sivakumaran, *The Law of Non-International Armed Conflict* (: Oxford University Press, 2012) 657 pp.

O. Svaček, *Mezinárodní trestní soud (2005–2017)* [International Criminal Court (2005–2017)] (: C. H. Beck, 2017a) 292 pp.

K. Šmigová, *Princíp komplementarity v medzinárodnom trestnom práve* [Principle of complementarity in international criminal law] ((Passau/Berlin/Prague/ Waldkirchen: rw&w Science & New Media, 2019) 131 pp.

O. Triffterer and K. Ambos (eds), *The Rome Statute of the International Criminal Court - A Commentary* (3rd edn., : C. H. Beck, 2016) pp. 2392.

E. van Sliedregt, *Individual Criminal Responsibility in International Law* (: Oxford University Press, 2012) 370 pp.

G. Werle and F. Jeβberger, *Principles of International Criminal Law* (4th edn., : Oxford University Press 2020) 720 pp.

L. Zegveld, *The Accountability of Armed Opposition Groups in International Law* (: Cambridge University Press, 2002) 260 pp.

Chapters in the Books/Edited Collections

M. Ch. Bassiouni, 'Crimes against Humanity' in M. Ch. Bassiouni (ed.), *International Criminal Law, Volume I: Sources, Subjects and Contents* (3rd edn., : Martinus Nijhoff, 2008) pp. 437–492.

O. Bekou and D. Birkett, 'Introduction', in O. Bekou and D. Birkett (eds.) *Cooperation and the International Criminal Court: Perspectives from Theory and Practice* (: Martinus Nijhoff, 2016) pp. 1–6.

M. Bergsmo and P. Webb, 'International Criminal Courts and Tribunals, Complementarity and Jurisdiction', in R. Wolfrum (ed.), *The Max Planck Encyclopedia of Public International Law. Vol. V* (: Oxford University Press, 2012) pp. 688–691.

M. Bothe, 'War Crimes', in A. Cassese, P. Gaeta and J. R. W. D. Jones (eds), *The Rome statute of the International Criminal Court: A Commentary Vol. I* (Oxford: Oxford University Press, 2002).

H. Brady, 'The System of Evidence in the Statute of the International Criminal Court', F. Lattanzi and W. A. Schabas (eds.), *Essays on the Rome Statute of the International Criminal Court* (1st edn., : Il Sirente, 1999) pp. 279–302.

E. Cannizzaro, 'Customary International Law on the Use of Force: Inductive Approach v. Value-Oriented Approach', in: E. Cannizzaro, P. Palchetti, *Customary International Law on the Use of Force: Methodological Approach* (Brill: Leiden, 2005) pp. 245–268.

L. Condorelli, S. Villalpando, 'Can the Security Council Extend the ICC's Jurisdiction?', in A. Cassese et al. (eds.), *The Rome Statute of the International Criminal Court: A Commentary* (: Oxford University Press, 2002) pp. 571–582.

M. Cottier and J. Grignon, 'Article 8(2)(b)(xxvi)', in O. Triffterer and K. Ambos (eds), *The Rome Statute of the International Criminal Court—A Commentary* (3rd edn., : C. H. Beck, 2016) pp. 519–528.

R. Cryer, 'War Crimes', in B. Saul and D. Akande (eds), *The Oxford Guide to International Humanitarian Law* (: Oxford University Press, 2020) pp. 339–358.

Y. Dinstein, 'Concluding Remarks on Non-International Armed Conflicts', in K. Watkin and A.J. Norris (eds.), *Non-International Armed Conflict in the Twenty-first Century* (Naval War College, 2012) pp. 399–421.

G. I. A. D. Draper, 'The Implementation and Enforcement of the Geneva Conventions of 1949 and of the Two Additional Protocols of 1978', 164 *Collected Courses of the Hague Academy of International Law* (1979) pp. 1–54.

P. Gaeta, 'Grave Breaches of the Geneva Conventions', in A. Clapham, M. Sassòli, and P. Gaeta (eds), *The 1949 Geneva Conventions: A Commentary* (: Oxford University Press, 2015) pp. 615–646.

R. Gallmetzer, 'The Trial Chamber's Discretionary Power to Devise the Proceedings Before It and Its Exercise in the Trial of Thomas Lubanga Dyilo', in C. Stahn and G. Sluiter (eds), *The Emerging Practice of the International Criminal Court* (: Martinus Nijhoff, 2009) pp. 501–524.

R. Geiß, 'Common Article 1 of the Geneva Conventions: Scope and Content of the Obligation to 'Ensure Respect' – 'Narrow but Deep' or 'Wide and Shallow'?', in H. Krieger (ed.), *Inducing Compliance with International*

Humanitarian Law: Lessons from the African Great Lakes Region (: Cambridge University Press, 2015a) pp. 417–440.

R. Geiß, 'The Obligation to Respect and to Ensure Respect for the Conventions', in A. Clapham et al (eds), *The 1949 Geneva Conventions: A Commentary* (: OUP, 2015b) pp. 111–134.

J. T. Holmes, 'Complementarity: National Courts versus the ICC', in A. Cassese, P. Gaeta and J.R.W.D. Jones (eds), *The Rome Statute of the International Criminal Court: A Commentary Vol. I* (Oxford: Oxford University Press, 2002) pp. 667–687.

B. B. Jia, 'The Differing Concepts of War Crimes and Crimes against Humanity in International Criminal Law' in G. S. Goodwin-Gill and Stefan Talmon (eds), *The Reality of International Law: Essays in Honour of Ian Brownlie* (Oxford: Oxford University Press, 1999) pp. 243–272.

F. Kalshoven, 'The Undertaking to Respect and Ensure Respect in all Circumstances: From Tiny Seed to Ripening Fruit', in *Reflections on the Law of War: Collected Essays* (: Martinus Nijhoff, 2007) pp. 665–727.

C. Kreß and K. Prost, 'Article 87: Requests for Cooperation - General Provisions', in O. Triffterer and K. Ambos (eds), *The Rome Statue of the International Criminal Court: A Commentary* (3rd edn., : Beck, 2016) pp. 1517–1549.

C. Kress, 'International Criminal Law', in R. Wolfrum (ed.) *The Max Planck Encyclopedia of Public International Law.* Vol. V (Oxford: Oxford University Press, 2012) pp.

M. Lewis, 'Revising the Geneva Conventions, 1946–1949: Synthesizing the Old and New Justice', in *The Birth of the New Justice: The Internationalization of Crime and Punishment* (: Oxford University Press, 2014) pp. 229–273.

M. Lipovský, 'Podněstří – de facto stát? [Transnistria - A de facto state?]', in P. Šturma (ed.), *Mezinárodní právo a státní území* [International law and state territory] (: Charles University, 2015) pp. 166–178.

M. Lipovský, 'Universal Jurisdiction and the Crime of Genocide', in P. Šturma and M. Lipovský (eds), *The Crime of Genocide: Then and Now. Evolution of a Crime* (Leiden/Boston: Martinus Nijhoff, 2022) pp. 270–295.

Y. McDermott, 'Strengthening the Evaluation of Evidence in International Criminal Trials', in J. Nicholson, *Strengthening the Validity of International Criminal Tribunals* (Leiden/Boston: Martinus Nijhoff, 2018) pp. 179–200.

M. Milanovic and V. Hadzi-Vidanovic, 'A taxonomy of armed conflict', in N. D. White and C. Henderson (eds.), *Research Handbook on International Conflict and Security Law* (: Edward Elgar, 2013) pp. 256–314.

M. Nerenberg and W. Timmermann, 'Documentary Evidence', in K.A.A. Kham, C. Buisman and C. Gosnell (eds), *Principles of Evidence in International Criminal Justice* (: Oxford University Press, 2010) pp. 443–498.

V. Petrović, 'A Crack in the Wall of Denial: The Scorpions Video in and out of the Courtroom', in D. Zarkov, M. Glasius (eds), *Narratives of Justice In and Out of the Courtroom* (: Springer, 2014) pp. 89–109.

F. Pocar, 'The criminalization of the violations of international humanitarian law from Nuremberg to the Rome Statute', in Pocar et al. (eds), *War Crimes and the Conduct of Hostilities: Challenges to Adjudication and Investigation* (Cheltenham: Edward Elgar, 2013) pp. 3–19.

S. SáCouto and K. C. Thompson, 'Investigative Management, Strategies, and Techniques of the ICC's OTP', in C. Stahn (ed.), *The Law and Practice of the International Criminal Court* (: Oxford Academic, 2015) pp. 328–349.

Y. Sandoz, 'Penal Aspects of International Humanitarian Law', in M. Ch. Bassiouni (ed.), *International Criminal Law, Volume I: Sources, Subjects and Contents* (3rd edn., : Martinus Nijhoff, 2008) pp. 293–322.

M. Sassòli, 'Humanitarian Law and International Criminal Law', in A. Cassese (ed.), *The Oxford Companion to International Criminal Justice* (: Oxford University Press, 2009) pp. 111–120.

W. Schabas and M. El Zeidy, 'Art. 17. Issues of admissibility', in K. Ambos (ed.), *Rome Statute of the International Criminal Court. Article-by-Article Commentary* (Munich/Oxford/Baden-Baden: Beck/Hart/Nomos, 2022) pp. 945–1009.

C. Stuckenberg, 'Cumulative Charges and Cumulative Convictions' in C. Stahn (ed.), *The Law and Practice of the International Criminal Court* (Oxford: Oxford University Press, 2015), pp. 840–858.

O. Svaček, 'Al-Bashir and the ICC – Tag, Hide-and-Seek … or Rather Blind Man's Bluff?', in P. Šturma (ed.), *The Rome Statute of the ICC at its Twentieth Anniversary (Achievements and Perspectives)* (Leiden: Brill, 2019) pp. 177–190.

K. Urbanová, 'The International Criminal Court Principle of Complementarity in Practice and the Situation in Colombia', in O. de Frouville and P. Šturma (eds), *Vers la Pénalisationx du Droit International des Droits de l'Homme?* (: Editions A. Pedone, 2022) pp. 27–42.

P. Wrange, 'The crime of aggression, domestic prosecutions and complementarity', in C. Kreß and S. Barriga (eds), *The Crime of aggression: A commentary. Vol. 1* (: Cambridge University Press, 2017) pp. 704–751.

Articles

D. Akande, 'The Jurisdiction of the International Criminal Court over Nationals of Non-Parties: Legal Basis and Limits', 1 *Journal of International Criminal Justice* (2003) pp. 618–650.

D. Akande, 'The Legal Nature of Security Council Referrals to the ICC and its Impact on Al Bashir's Immunities', 2 *Journal of International Criminal Justice* (2009) pp. 333–352.

P. Akhavan, 'Reconciling Crimes Against Humanity with the Laws of War: Human Rights, Armed Conflict, and the Limits of Progressive Jurisprudence', 6 *Journal of International Criminal Justice* (2008) pp. 21–37.

K. Ambos, 'Remarks on the General Part of International Criminal Law', 4 *Journal of International Criminal Justice* (2006) pp. 660–673.

R. Bartels, 'Dealing with the Principle of Proportionality in Armed Conflict in Retrospect: The Application of the Principle in International Criminal Trials', 46 *Israel Law Review* (2013) pp. 271–315.

R. Bartels, 'Timelines, borderlines and conflicts: The historical evolution of the legal divide between international and non-international armed conflicts', 91 *International Review of the Red Cross* (2009) pp. 35–67.

L. R. Blank, 'Defining the Battlefield in Contemporary Conflict and Counterterrorism: Understanding the Parameters of the Zone of Combat', 39(1) *Georgia Journal of International and Comparative Law* (2010) pp. 1–38.

G. Blum and P. Heymann, 'Law and Policy of Targeted Killing', 1 *Harvard National Security Journal* (2019) pp. 145–170.

A. Bogdan, 'Cumulative Charges, Convictions and Sentencing at the Ad Hoc International Tribunals for the Former Yugoslavia and Rwanda', *3 Melbourne Journal of International Law* (2002) pp. 1–32.

L. Boisson de Chazournes & L. Condorelli, 'Common Article 1 of the Geneva Conventions Revisited: Protecting Collective Interests', 837 *International Review of the Red Cross* (2000) pp. 67–87.

M. M. Bradley, 'Expanding the Borders of Common Article 3 in Non-International Armed Conflicts: Amending Its Geographical Application Through Subsequent Practice?', 64 *Netherlands International Law Review* (2017) pp. 375–406.

F. Capone, 'The Wave of Russian Attacks on Ukraine's Power Infrastructures: An Opportunity to Infuse Meaningfulness into the Notion of 'Dual-use Objects'?', 8 *European Papers* (2023) pp. 741–754.

A. Cassese, 'On the Current Trends towards Criminal Prosecution and Punishment of Breaches of International Humanitarian Law' 9 *European Journal of International Law* (1998) pp. 2–17.

A. Cassese, 'The Nexus Requirement for War Crimes', 10 *Journal of International Criminal Justice* (2012) pp. 1395–1417.

A. Cassese, 'The Statute of the International Criminal Court: Some Preliminary Reflections', 10 *European Journal of International Law* (1999) pp. 144–171.

J. Chalmers and F. Leverick, 'Fair Labelling in Criminal Law', 71 *The Modern Law Review* (2008) pp. 217–246.

N. Combs, 'Evidentiary Deficiencies in International Criminal Law: Tracing the Trajectory from Ignored to Integral to Irrelevant', 22 *International Criminal Law Review* (2022) pp. 835–843.

M. Cormier, 'Testing the boundaries of the ICC's territorial jurisdiction in the Afghanistan situation', 78 *Question of International Law* (2021) pp. 43–56.

R. B. da Silva, 'Updating the Authentication of Digital Evidence in the International Criminal Court', 22 *International Criminal Law Review* (2021) pp. 941–962.
M. de Arcos Tejerizo, 'Digital evidence and fair trial rights at the International Criminal Court', 36 *Leiden Journal of International Law* (2023) pp. 749–769.
T. De Souza Dias, 'Interests of justice: Defining the scope of Prosecutorial discretion in Article 53(1)(c) and (2)(c) of the Rome Statute of the International Criminal Court', *Leiden Journal of International Law* (2017) pp. 731–751.
T. de Souza Dias, 'Recharacterisation of Crimes and the Principle of Fair Labelling in International Criminal Law', 18 *International Criminal Law Review* (2018) pp. 788–821.
A. Devillard, 'L'obligation de faire respecter le droit international humanitaire : l'article 1 commun aux Conventions de Genève et à leur premier Protocole additionnel, fondement d'un droit international humanitaire de coopération?', 20 *Revue Québécoise de Droit International* (2007) pp. 75–129.
C. M. De Vos, 'Investigating from Afar: The ICC's Evidence Problem', 26 *Leiden Journal of International Law* (2013) pp. 1009–1024.
K. Dörmann & J. Serralvo, 'Common Article 1 to the Geneva Conventions and the Obligation to Prevent International Humanitarian Law Violations', 96 *International Review of the Red Cross* (2015) pp. 707–736.
C.F. Estrada, 'The International Criminal Court and the Čelebići Test: Convictions Based on the Same Set of Facts from a Comparative Perspective', 15 *Journal of International Criminal Justice* (2017) pp. 689–712.
W. J. Fenrick, 'Should Crimes Against Humanity Replace War Crimes?', 37 *Columbia Journal of Transnational Law* (1999) pp. 767–785.
C. Focarelli, 'Common Article 1 of the 1949 Geneva Conventions: A Soap Bubble?', 21 *European Journal of International Law* (2010) pp. 125–171.
L. Freeman, 'Digitally Disappeared: The Struggle to Preserve Social Media Evidence of Mass Atrocities', 23 *Georgetown Journal of International Affairs* (2022) pp. 105–113.
L. Freeman, 'Digital Evidence and War Crimes Prosecutions: The Impact of Digital Technologies on International Criminal Investigations and Trials' 41 *Fordham International Law Journal* (2018) pp. 283–336.
L. Freeman, 'Hacked and Leaked: Legal Issues Arising from the Use of Unlawfully Obtained Digital Evidence in International Criminal Cases', 25 *UCLA Journal of International Law and Foreign Affairs* (2021) pp. 45–92.
M. Frulli, 'Are Crimes against Humanity More Serious than War Crimes?', 12 *European Journal of International Law* (2001) pp. 329–350.
K. Gavrysh, 'La circolazione probatoria nella giustizia penale internazionale (judicial notice)', 107 *Rivista di diritto internazionale* (2024) pp. 31–75.
A. Giannini, 'Theories of Evaluation of Evidence and the International Criminal Court Practice', *SSRN Electronic Journal* (2017) pp. 1–16.

J. A. Green, 'The ratione temporis elements of self-defense' 1, *Journal on the Use of Force and International Law* (2015) pp. 97–118.

C. Greenwood, 'The Development of International Humanitarian Law by the International Criminal Tribunal for the Former Yugoslavia', 2 *Yearbook of United Nations Law* (1998) pp. 97–140.

D. Guilfoyle, 'Responsibility for Collective Atrocities: Fair Labelling and Approaches to Commission in International Criminal Law', 64 *Current Legal Problems* (2011) pp. 255–286.

R. J. Hamilton, 'Social Media Platforms in International Criminal Investigations', 52 *Case Western Reserve Journal of International Law* (2020) pp. 213–223.

R. J. Hamilton, 'User-Generated Evidence', 57 *Columbia Journal of Transnational Law* (2018) pp. 1–61.

K. J. Heller, 'A Sentence-Based Theory of Complementarity', 53 *Harvard International Law Journal* (2012) pp. 85–133.

K. Hellwig, 'The Potential and the Challenges of Digital Evidence in International Criminal Proceedings', 22 *International Criminal Law Review* (2022) pp. 965–988.

L. Hill-Cawthorne, 'Rights under International Humanitarian Law', 28(4) *European Journal of International Law* (2018) pp. 1187–1215.

L. Hiromoto and L.F. Sparr, 'Ongwen and Mental Health Defenses at the International Criminal Court', 51 *Journal of the American Academy of Psychiatry and the Law* (2023) pp. 61–71.

N.N. Jurdi, 'The Complementarity Regime of the International Criminal Court in Practice: Is It Truly Serving its Purpose? Some Lessons from Libya', 30 *Leiden Journal of International Law* (2017) pp. 199–220.

C. Kenny and Y. McDermott, 'The Expanding Protection of Members of a Party's Own Armed Forces under International Criminal Law', 68 *International and Comparative Law Quarterly* (2019) pp. 943–976.

B. Kessler, 'The Duty to Ensure Respect under Common Article 1 of the Geneva Conventions: Its Implications on International and Non-International Armed Conflicts', 44 *German Yearbook of International Law* (2001) pp. 498–516.

T. R. Kirabira, 'Technology as a Key Tool for the Prosecution of International Crimes: Lessons from Uganda', 22 *International Criminal Law Review* (2022) pp. 1143–1167.

A. Koenig, 'From 'Capture to Courtroom' Collaboration and the Digital Documentation of International Crimes in Ukraine', 20 *Journal of International Criminal Justice* (2022) pp. 829–842.

C. Kreß, 'Reflections on the Iudicare Limb of the Grave Breaches Regime', 7 *Journal of International Criminal Justice* (2009) pp. 789–809.

C. Kreß, 'Some Reflections on the International Legal Framework Governing Transnational Armed Conflicts', 15 (2) *Journal of Conflict and Security Law* (2010) pp. 245–274.

B. Krzan, 'Admissibility of Evidence and International Criminal Justice', 7 *Revista brasileira de direito processual penal* (2021) pp. 161–188.

H. Lauterpacht, 'The Law of Nations and the Punishment of War Crimes', 21 *British Yearbook of International Law* (1944) pp. 58–95.

S. Linton, 'Prosecuting Atrocities at the District Court of Dili', 2 *Melbourne Journal of International Law* (2001) pp. 414–458.

D. Luban, 'A Theory of Crimes against Humanity', 29 *Yale Journal of International Law* (2004) pp. 85–167.

N. Lubell and N. Derejko, 'A Global Battlefield? Drones and the Geographical Scope of Armed Conflict', 11 *Journal of International Criminal Justice* (2013) pp. 65–88.

S. R. Lüder, 'The legal nature of the International Criminal Court and the emergence of supranational elements in international criminal justice' 845, *International Review of the Red Cross* (2002) pp. 79–92.

D. Marchesi, 'Intercepted Communications in the Ongwen Case: Lessons to Learn on Documentary Evidence at the ICC', 22 *International Criminal Law Review* (2021) pp. 920–940.

S.S. Mera, 'Fighters, Not Victims: On Victimhood Recognition and Gender Representations in the Enslavement Charges in the Ongwen Case', 23 *International Criminal Law Review* (2023) pp. 1–22.

P. Murphy, 'Excluding Justice or Facilitating Justice? International Criminal Law Would Benefit from Rules of Evidence', 12 *The International Journal of Evidence and Proof* (2008).

P. Murphy, 'No Free Lunch, No Free Proof: The Indiscriminate Admission of Evidence is a Serious Flaw in International Criminal Trials', *8 Journal of International Criminal Justice* (2010) pp. 539–573.

W. Nortje and N. Quénivet, 'Fertile or Futile Grounds for Excluding Criminal Responsibility? A Critical Analysis of the Ongwen Judgment in Relation to the Claim of Coercive Environment', 23 *International Criminal Law Review* (2023) pp. 675–704.

M. Öberg, 'The Absorption of Grave Breaches into War Crimes Law', 91 *International Review of the Red Cross* (2009) pp. 163–183.

E. Orihuela Calatayud, 'La autorización para investigar los crímenes cometidos en Afganistán. Luces y sombras de la sentencia, de 5 de marzo de 2020, de la Sala de Apelaciones de la Corte Penal Internacional', 39 *Revista electrónica de estudios internacionales* (2020) pp. 1–19.

F. M. Palombino, 'Should Genocide Subsume Crimes Against Humanity? Some Remarks in the Light of the Krstić Appeal Judgement', 3 *Journal of International Criminal Justice* (2005) pp. 778–789.

J. Pejic, 'The protective scope of Common Article 3: more than meets the eye', 93 *International Review of the Red Cross* (2011) pp. 1–37.

J. P. Perez-Leon Acevedo, 'Realising the Right to Health for Victims of International Crimes. The Case of Medical Rehabilitation Reparations Ordered by International Courts: Challenges, Possibilities and Ways of Improvement', 3 *Groningen Journal of International Law* (2015) pp. 17–48.

M. Plachta, 'European Union Steps Up Effort to Bring Russia for Accountability for Aggression Against Ukraine', 39 *International Enforcement Law Reporter* (2023).

D. Plesch, et al., 'The Relevance of the United Nations War Crimes Commission to the Prosecution of Sexual and Gender-Based Crimes Today', 25 Criminal Law Forum (2014) pp. 349–381.

L. Poltronieri Rossetti, 'The Pre-Trial Chamber's Afghanistan Decision: A Step Too Far in the Judicial Review of Prosecutorial Discretion?', 17(3) *Journal of International Criminal Justice* (2019) pp. 585–608.

S. Radin, 'Global Armed Conflict? The Threshold of Extraterritorial Non-International Armed Conflicts', 89 *International Law Studies* (2013) pp. 696–743.

V. Robson, 'The Common Approach to Article 1: The Scope of Each State's Obligation to Ensure Respect for the Geneva Conventions', 25 *Journal of Conflict and Security Law* (2020) pp. 101–115.

N. Roht-Arriaza, 'Reparations Decisions and Dilemmas', 27 *Hastings Int'l & Comp. L. Rev.* (2004) pp. 157–219.

L. N. Sadat, 'Crimes Against Humanity in the Modern Age', 107 *American Journal of International Law* (2013) pp. 334–377.

L. N. Sadat, 'Putting Peacetime First: Crimes Against Humanity and the Civilian Population Requirement', 31 *Emory International Law Review* (2017) pp. 198–269.

B. Sander, 'History on Trial: Historical Narrative Pluralism Within and beyond International Criminal Courts', 67 *International and Comparative Law Quarterly* (2018) pp. 547–576.

M. Sassòli, 'Transnational Armed Groups and International Humanitarian Law', 6 *HPCR Occasional Paper Series* (2006) pp. 1–46.

W. Schabas, 'Complementarity in Practice: Some Uncomplimentary Thoughts', 19 *Criminal Law Forum* (2008) pp. 5–33.

D. Schindler, 'International Humanitarian Law and internationalized internal armed conflicts', 22 *International Review of the Red Cross* (1982) pp. 255–264.

M. N. Schmitt, 'Charting the Legal Geography of Non-International Armed Conflict', 90 *International Law Studies* (2014) pp. 1–19.

M. N. Schmitt and S. Watts, 'Common Article 1 and the Duty to "Ensure Respect"', 96 *International Law Studies* (2020) pp. 674–706.

C. Schuon, 'The Appeals Decision in the ICC's Case on the Trial on the Appeals Decision Jean-Pierre Bemba Gombo Chamber's 'Decision Admission into

Evidence of Materials Contained in the Prosecution's List of Evidence', 25 *Leiden Journal of International Law* (2012) pp. 511–520.

R.V. Segate, 'Cognitive Bias, Privacy Rights, and Digital Evidence in International Criminal Proceedings: Demystifying the Double-Edged AI Revolution', 21 *International Criminal Law Review* (2021) pp. 242–279.

K'S. O. Smith 'Prosecutor v. Lubanga: How the International Criminal Court Failed the Women and Girls of the Congo', 54 *Howard Law Journal* (2011) pp. 467–500.

D. F. Sorvatzioti, 'Free Evaluation of Evidence: Does the ICC Need a Law of Evidence?', 22 *International Criminal Law Review* (2021) pp. 895–919.

Y. Tan and S. Yang, 'The Joint Investigation Team in Ukraine: An Opportunity for the International Criminal Court?', 22 *Chinese Journal of International Law* (2023) pp. 103–119.

O. Svaček, 'Brothers and Sisters in Arms As Victims of War Crimes: Ntaganda Case Before the ICC', 8 *Czech Yearbook of Public and Private International Law* (2017b) pp. 346–357.

'The United States Promotes Individual Criminal Accountability for Aggression and Atrocity Crimes Committed by Russians in Ukraine', 117 *American Journal of International Law* (2023) pp. 516–521.

R. van Alebeek et al., 'Prosecuting Russian Officials for the Crime of Aggression: What About Immunities?' 4, *European Convention on Human Rights Law Review* (2022) pp. 115–132.

L. van den Herik, 'A Quest for Jurisdiction and an Appropriate Definition of Crime—Mpambara before the Dutch Courts', 7 *Journal of International Criminal Justice* (2009) pp. 1117–1131.

H. van der Wilt, 'War Crimes and the Requirement of a Nexus with an Armed Conflict', 10 *Journal of International Criminal Justice* (2012) pp. 1113–1128.

B. Van Schaack, 'Introductory Note To Executive Order 13928 On Blocking Property Of Certain Persons Associated With The International Criminal Court', 60 *International Legal Materials* (2020) pp. 18–23.

C. Stahn, 'Reparative Justice after the *Lubanga* Appeal Judgment: New Prospects for Expressivism and Participatory Justice or 'Juridified Victimhood' by Other Means?', 13 *Journal of International Criminal Justice* (2015) pp. 801–813.

D. Strob, 'State Cooperation with the International Criminal Tribunals for the Former Yugoslavia and for Rwanda', 5 *Max Plank United Nations Yearbook* (2001) pp. 249–283.

O. Svaček, 'Crime of Aggression before Domestic Courts: Some Contemporary Challenges', 2, *International and Comparative Law Review* (2023) pp. 111–128.

S. Vité, 'Typology of armed conflicts in international humanitarian law: legal concepts and actual situations', 91 *International Review of the Red Cross* (2009) pp. 69–94.

Z. Wenqi, 'On Co-Operation by States Not Party to the International Criminal Court', 88 *International Review of the Red Cross* (2006) pp. 87–110.
B. Zagaris, 'International Center for the Prosecution of the Crime of Aggression against Ukraine Opens', 39 *International Enforcement Law Reporter* (2023).

On-line Sources

S. Aalto-Setälä and M. F. Jaramillo Gomez, 'ICC Investigations in Ukraine: How Digitally Derived Evidence Can Make a Difference', *leidenlawblog*, 19 May 2022. Available at: https://www.leidenlawblog.nl/articles/icc-investigations-in-ukraine-how-digitally-derived-evidence-can-make-a-difference
K. Ambos, 'The return of "positive complementarity"', *EJIL: Talk!*, 3 November 2021. Available at: https://www.ejiltalk.org/the-return-of-positive-complementarity/
Amnesty International, 'Afghanistan: ICC authorizes historic investigation', 5 March 2020. Available at: https://www.amnesty.org/en/latest/news/2020/03/afghanistan-icc-authorizes-historic-investigation/.
Associated Press, 'Russia indicts ICC prosecutor, judge who issued war crimes warrant for Putin', 21 May 2023. Available at: https://apnews.com/article/russia-indictment-icc-prosecutor-judge-putin-260100f9ba533e15ebee3084dba74ff4
S. Baldo and L. Magarrell, 'Reparation and the Darfur Peace Progress: Ensuring Victims' Rights' (2007), *International Center for Transitional Justice*. Available at: https://www.ictj.org/sites/default/files/ICTJ-Sudan-Darfur-Reparations-2007-English_0.pdf
R. Barrantes Segura, 'Reparations and Displacement in Peru' (2012), *International Center for Transitional Justice*. Available at: https://www.ictj.org/sites/default/files/ICTJ-Brookings-Displacement-Reparations-Peru-CaseStudy-2012-English.pdf
V. Bergengruen, 'How Ukraine Is Crowdsourcing Digital Evidence of War Crimes', *Time*, 18 April 2022. Available at: https://time.com/6166781/ukraine-crowdsourcing-war-crimes/
R. Carranza and C. Correa, E. Naughton, 'More Than Words: Apologies as a Form of Reparation' (2015), *International Center for Transitional Justice*. Available at: https://www.ictj.org/sites/default/files/ICTJ-Report-Apologies-2015.pdf
L. Carrée, 'The Role of Technology in the Exposition of War Crimes in Ukraine: How the Use of Cutting-Edge Technologies and Open-Sources Investigations Can Expose Human Rights Violations', *LSE Human Rights*, 2 February 2023. Available at: https://blogs.lse.ac.uk/humanrights/2023/02/02/the-role-of-technology-in-the-exposition-of-war-crimes-in-ukraine-how-the-use-of-cutting-edge-technologies-and-open-sources-investigations-can-expose-

human-rights-violations/#:~:text=With%20the%20development%20of%20new,alleged%20perpetrators%20and%20victims%2Fsurvivors

A. Clapham, 'We Need to Talk About Grave Breaches of the Geneva Conventions', *Opinio Juris*, 25 April 2023. Available at: https://opiniojuris.org/2023/04/25/we-need-to-talk-about-grave-breaches-of-the-geneva-conventions/

T. de Sousa Diaz, 'The 'Security Council Route' to the Derogation from Personal Head of State Immunity in the Al-Bashir Case: How Explicit must Security Council Resolutions be?', *EJIL: Talk!*, 19 September 2018. Available at: https://www.ejiltalk.org/the-discussion-of-the-security-council-roots-to-the-derogation-from-personal-immunities-in-the-al-bashir-case-how-explicit-must-security-council-resolutions-be/

'Documenting International Crimes and Human Rights Violations for Accountability Purposes: Guidelines for Civil Society Organisations', *Eurojust*, 21 September 2022. Available at: https://www.eurojust.europa.eu/publication/documenting-international-crimes-and-human-rights-violations

B. Egan (Legal Advisor, U.S. Dept of State), 'Address at the American Society of International Law Annual Meeting: International Law, Legal Diplomacy, and the Europol, SIRIUS EU Digital Evidence Situation Report—2nd Annual Report (2020). Available at: https://www.europol.europa.eu/cms/sites/default/files/documents/sirius_desr_2020.pdf

'Counter-ISIL Campaign', *U.S. Department of State*, 1 April 2016. Available at: https://2009-2017.state.gov/s/l/releases/remarks/255493.htm

N. Gogolashvili and N. Tsagareishvili, 'Getting Full Cooperation from the Georgian Side Will Be One of the Challenges for ICC', *Coalition for the International Criminal Court*, 2 May 2017. Available at: https://www.coalitionfortheicc.org/news/20170502/getting-full-cooperation-georgian-side-will-be-one-challenges-icc

K. J. Heller, 'ICC Appeals Chamber Says a War Crime Does not have to Violate IHL', *Opinio Juris*, 15 June 2017. Available at: http://opiniojuris.org/2017/06/15/icc-appeals-chamber-holds-a-war-crime-does-not-have-to-violate-ihl/

K. Heller, 'Russia's Short-Sighted Approach to the Georgia Investigation', *Opinio Juris*, 13 February 2016. Available at: http://opiniojuris.org/2016/02/13/russias-short-sighted-approach-to-the-icc/

J. Hendrix, 'Ukraine May Mark a Turning Point in Documenting War Crimes', *Just security*, 28 March 2022. Available at: https://www.justsecurity.org/80871/ukraine-may-mark-a-turning-point-in-documenting-war-crimes/

International Centre for Transitional Justice, 'Reparations'. Available at: https://www.ictj.org/our-work/transitional-justice-issues/reparations

International Committee of the Red Cross, 'Customary International Humanitarian Law Database: Practice Relating to Rule 144 - Ensuring Respect for

International Humanitarian Law Erga Omnes'. Available at: https://ihl-databases.icrc.org/customary-ihl/eng/docs/v2_rul_rule144
International Committee of the Red Cross, 'Customary International Humanitarian Law Database: Practice Relating to Rule 158 - Prosecution of War Crimes'. Available at: https://ihl-databases.icrc.org/en/customary-ihl/v2/rule158
International Committee of the Red Cross, 'How is the Term "Armed Conflict" Defined in International Humanitarian Law? ', Opinion Paper, March 2008. Available at: https://www.icrc.org/en/doc/assets/files/other/opinion-paper-armed-conflict.pdf
International Committee of the Red Cross, 'Official working document of the 31st International Conference of the Red Cross and Red Crescent', 31IC/11/5.1.2, 28 November to 1 December 2011, at 22. Available at: https://www.icrc.org/en/doc/assets/files/red-cross-crescent-movement/31st-international-conference/31-int-conference-ihl-challenges-report-11-5-1-2-en.pdf
International Committee of the Red Cross, 'Revised and New Draft Conventions for the Protection of War Victims: Remarks and Proposals Submitted by the International Committee of the Red Cross' (Feb. 1949). Available at: https://www.loc.gov/rr/frd/Military_Law/pdf/RC_Remarks-proposals.pdf.
International Criminal Court, 'Following Mr Bemba's acquittal, Trust Fund for Victims at the ICC decides to accelerate launch of assistance programme in Central African Republic', 13 June 2018a. Available at: https://www.icc-cpi.int/news/following-mr-bembas-acquittal-trust-fund-victims-icc-decides-accelerate-launch-assistance
International Criminal Court, 'ICC Prosecutor Karim A.A. Khan KC announces launch of advanced evidence submission platform: OTPLink', 24 May 2023a. Available at: https://www.icc-cpi.int/news/icc-prosecutor-karim-aa-khan-kc-announces-launch-advanced-evidence-submission-platform-otplink
International Criminal Court, 'ICC Signs Cooperation Agreement with Government of Georgia', International Criminal Court, 27 July 2017. Available at:https://www.icc-cpi.int/news/icc-signs-cooperation-agreement-government-georgia
International Criminal Court, Independent Expert Review of the International Criminal Court and the Rome Statute System: Final Report (2020). Available at: https://asp.icc-cpi.int/sites/asp/files/asp_docs/ASP19/IER-Final-Report-ENG.pdf
International Criminal Court, The Office of the Prosecutor, 'Policy Paper on Sexual and Gender-Based Crimes (2014)'. Available at: https://www.icc-cpi.int/sites/default/files/iccdocs/otp/OTP-Policy-Paper-on-Sexual-and-Gender-Based-Crimes%2D%2DJune-2014.pdf
International Criminal Court, 'Situation in Ukraine: ICC judges issue arrest warrants against Sergei Ivanovich Kobylash and Viktor Nikolayevich Sokolov', 5

March 2024. Available at: https://www.icc-cpi.int/news/situation-ukraine-icc-judges-issue-arrest-warrants-against-sergei-ivanovich-kobylash-and.

International Criminal Court, 'Situation in Ukraine: ICC judges issue arrest warrants against Vladimir Vladimirovich Putin and Maria Alekseyevna Lvova-Belova', 17 March 2023b. Available at: https://www.icc-cpi.int/news/situation-ukraine-icc-judges-issue-arrest-warrants-against-vladimir-vladimirovich-putin-and

International Criminal Court, 'Statement by Prosecutor Karim A. A. Khan KC on the issuance of arrest warrants against President Vladimir Putin and Ms. Maria Lvova-Belova', 17 March 2023c. Available at: https://www.icc-cpi.int/news/statement-prosecutor-karim-khan-kc-issuance-arrest-warrants-against-president-vladimir-putin.

International Justice Monitor, 'Lubanga Trial: Victims Recount UPC Brutality, Seek Reparations', 15 January 2010. Available at: https://www.ijmonitor.org/2010/01/lubanga-trial-victims-recount-upc-brutality-seek-reparations/

Joint Committee, 'Seventh Report drawn up by the Special Committee of the Joint Committee', 16 July 1949, Final Record of the Diplomatic Conference of Geneva, Vol. II, Section B., at 120. Available at: https://www.loc.gov/rr/frd/Military_Law/pdf/Dipl-Conf-1949-Final_Vol-2-B.pdf

Kalshoven-Gieskes Forum, Leiden University, Leiden Guidelines on the Use of Digitally Derived Evidence in International Criminal Courts and Tribunals (2021). Available at: https://leiden-guidelines.com/assets/Leiden%20Guidelines%20on%20the%20Use%20of%20DDE%20in%20ICCTs_20220404.pdf.

M. Kersten, 'The moral and legal correctness of Dominic Ongwen's conviction', *Justice in Conflict*, 10 February 2021. Available at: https://justiceinconflict.org/2021/02/10/the-moral-and-legal-correctness-of-dominic-ongwens-conviction/

P. Labuda, 'The Special Criminal Court in the Central African Republic', *ASIL Insights*, 22 January 2018. Available at: https://www.asil.org/insights/volume/22/issue/2/special-criminal-court-central-african-republic

T. Mimran and L. Weinstein, 'Digitalize It: Digital Evidence at the ICC', *Lieber Institute*, 14 August 2023. Available at https://lieber.westpoint.edu/digitalize-it-digital-evidence-icc/

A. Jachec-Neale, 'The Unintended Consequences of International Court Decisions', *Lieber Institute*, 19 November 2020. Available at: https://lieber.westpoint.edu/unintended-consequences-international-courts-decisions/

Nuba Reports, '75 Trips to 22 Countries in 7 Years: An Indicted War Criminal's Travels', 7 March 2016. Available at: https://nubareports.org/bashir-travels/

Open Society Justice Initiative. Fact Sheet: ICC Katanga Reparations. *Open Society Foundation*.. Available at: https://www.justiceinitiative.org/uploads/d473c39a-26c6-44dd-b47d-a29b0058355c/Katanga%20Reparations%20Factsheet%20-%20032317_0.pdf

Office of the General Prosecutor of the Republic of Timor-Leste – Serious Crimes Unit, SCU-All Indictees. Available at: https://www.ocf.berkeley.edu/~changmin/Serious%20Crimes%20Unit%20Files/suspects/SuspectsByName.html

O. Pomson, ‘Ntaganda Appeals Chamber Judgment Divided on Meaning of “Attack”’, *Lieber Institute*, 12 May 2021. Available at: https://lieber.westpoint.edu/ntaganda-appeals-chamber-judgment-divided-meaning-attack/

E. Pothelet, ‘War crimes in Afghanistan and Beyond: Will the ICC Weigh in on the “Global Battlefield” Debate?’, EJIL! Talk, 9 November 2017. Available at: https://www.ejiltalk.org/war-crimes-in-afghanistan-and-beyond-will-the-icc-weigh-in-on-the-global-battlefield-debate/

Radio Canal Révélation, ‘Reactions from the local population to collective reparations in the Katanga case’, *Coalition for the International Criminal Court*, 20 July 2017. Available at: https://www.coalitionfortheicc.org/news/20170720/reactions-local-population-collective-reparations-katanga-case

J. Reid (Head, Office of International Law, Commonwealth Attorney-General’s Department, Australia), ‘Ensuring Respect: The Role of State Practice in Interpreting the Geneva Conventions’, *International Law Association Reporter*, 11 September 2016. Available at: https://ilareporter.org.au/2016/11/ensuring-respect-the-role-of-state-practice-in-interpreting-the-geneva-conventions-john-reid/

‘Removing Myanmar Military Officials from Facebook’, *Meta*, 28 August 2018. Available at: https://about.fb.com/news/2018/08/removing-myanmar-officials/.

D. Suarez Vargas and L. Moffett, ‘Reparations in Colombia: Redressing Civilian Harm in the Midst of Armed Conflict’, *Lieber Institute*, 5 September 2024. Available at: https://lieber.westpoint.edu/reparations-colombia-redressing-civilian-harm-midst-armed-conflict/

P. P. Singh, ‘In Afghanistan, the ICC Abandons the Field’, Human Rights Watch, 23 April 2019. Available at: https://www.hrw.org/news/2019/04/23/afghanistan-icc-abandons-field

Switzerland, Federal Department of Foreign Affairs, ABCs of International Humanitarian Law 40 (2009). Available at https://ihl-databases.icrc.org/customary-ihl/eng/docs/v2_rul_rule158.

J. Trahan, ‘The Significance of the ICC Appeals Chamber’s Ruling in the Afghanistan Situation’, *Opinio Juris*, 10 March 2020. Available at: http://opiniojuris.org/2020/03/10/the-significance-of-the-icc-appeals-chambers-ruling-in-the-afghanistan-situation/

United Nations, Report of the Human Rights Council, 42nd session (2019). Available at: https://digitallibrary.un.org/record/3900742/files/A_74_53_Add.1-EN.pdf?ln=en.

C. Vale, 'Can the Geneva Conventions Shield the ICC from Attacks?', *Center for International Relations and Sustainable Development (CIRSD)*, 28 March 2022. Available at https://www.cirsd.org/en/expert-analysis/can-the-geneva-conventions-shield-the-icc-from-attacks

S. van Campen, 'A Legal First in International Criminal Justice: A Conviction for Forced Pregnancy in the Ongwen Case', *IntLawGrrls*, 18 May 2021. Available at: https://ilg2.org/2021/05/18/a-legal-first-in-international-criminal-justice-a-conviction-for-forced-pregnancy-in-the-ongwen-case/

S. Vasilev, 'Not just another 'cri11/24/2022sis': Could the blocking of the Afghanistan investigation spell the end of the ICC? (Part I)', *EJIL: Talk!*, 19 April 2019. Available at: https://www.ejiltalk.org/not-just-another-crisis-could-the-blocking-of-the-afghanistan-investigation-spell-the-end-of-the-icc-part-i/

K. Vlamis, 'Satellite images show the destruction of a Mariupol theatre that had 'CHILDREN' written outside—before and after it was bombed by Russia', *Insider*, 20 March 2022. Available at: https://www.businessinsider.com/satellite-images-show-destruction-of-mariupol-theater-bombed-by-russia-2022-3

W. Wakabi, 'Bemba's Acquittal Raises Concerns on Reparations to Victims in the Central African Republic', *International Justice Monitor*, 18 July 2018a. Available at: https://www.ijmonitor.org/2018/07/bembas-acquittal-raises-concerns-on-reparations-to-victims-in-the-central-african-republic/

W. Wakabi, 'Judges Close Reparations Proceedings in Bemba's War Crimes Trial', *International Justice Monitor*, 15 August 2018b. Available at: https://www.ijmonitor.org/2018/08/judges-close-reparations-proceedings-in-bembas-war-crimes-trial/

W. Wakabi, 'Lubanga's Financial Liability for Reparations Set at US$ 10 Million', *International Justice Monitor*, 15 December 2017a. Available at: https://www.ijmonitor.org/2017/12/lubangas-financial-liability-for-reparations-set-at-us-10-million/

W. Wakabi, 'Trust Fund Unveils Reparations Plan for Katanga Victims', *International Justice Monitor*, 6 September 2017b. Available at: https://www.ijmonitor.org/2017/09/trust-fund-unveils-reparations-plan-for-katanga-victims/

Case Law of ICJ

Judgment, *Application of the Convention on the Prevention and Punishment of the Crime of Genocide (Bosnia and Herzegovina* v. *Serbia and Montenegro)*, I.C.J. Reports 2007a.

Judgment, *Arrest Warrant of 11 April 2000 (Democratic Republic of the Congo v. Belgium)*, I.C.J. Reports 2002a.

Judgment, *Delimitation of the Maritime Boundary in the Gulf of Maine Area*, I.C.J. Reports 1984.

Advisory Opinion, *Legal Consequences of the Construction of a Wall in the Occupied Palestinian Territory*, I.C.J. Reports 2004.

Advisory Opinion, *Legality of the Use by a State of Nuclear Weapons in Armed Conflict*, I.C.J. Reports 1996.

Judgment, *Military and Paramilitary Activities in and against Nicaragua (Nicaragua v. United States of America)*, I.C.J. Reports 1986.

Judgment, *North Sea Continental Shelf*, I.C.J. Reports 1969.

Judgment, *Nuclear Tests (Australia v. France; New Zealand v. France)*, I.C.J. Reports 1974.

Case Law and Practice of ICC

Decision on the Confirmation of Charges, *Prosecutor v. Bahr Idriss Abu Garda* (ICC-02/05- 02/09-243-Red), PTCH I, 8 February 2010.

Decision, *The Prosecutor v. Omar Hassan Ahmad Al Bashir*, ICC-02/05-01/09-3, PTCH I, 4 March 2009.

Decision, *The Prosecutor v. Omar Hassan Ahmad Al Bashir*, ICC-02/05-01/09-139, PTCH I, 12 December 2011a.

Decision, *The Prosecutor v. Omar Hassan Ahmad Al Bashir*, ICC-02/05-01/09-140, PTCH I, 13 December 2011b.

Decision, *The Prosecutor v. Omar Hassan Ahmad Al Bashir*, ICC-02/05-01/09-195, PTCH II, 9 April 2014.

Decision, *The Prosecutor v. Omar Hassan Ahmad Al Bashir*, ICC-02/05-01/09-302, 6 July 2017.

Judgment in the Jordan Referral re Al-Bashir Appeal, *The Prosecutor v. Omar Hassan Ahmad Al Bashir*, ICC-02/05-01/09-397, ACH, 6 May 2019.

Joint Concurring Opinion of Judge Eboe-Osuji, Morrison, Hofmański and Bossa, *The Prosecutor v. Omar Hassan Ahmad Al Bashir*, ICC-02/05-01/09-397-Anx1, 6 May 2019.

Judgment and Sentence, *The Prosecutor v. Ahmad Al Faqi Al Mahdi* (ICC-01/12-01/15), TCH VIII, 27 September 2016.

Reparations Order, *Prosecutor v. Ahmad Al Faqi Mahdi* (ICC-01/12-01/15), TCH VIII, 17 August 2017.

Decision on admissibility of the case against Saif Al-Islam Gaddafi, *Prosecutor v. Saif Al-Islam Gaddafi and Abdullah Al-Senussi* (ICC-01/11-01/11-344-Red), PTCH I, 31 May 2013.

Decision on the admissibility of the case against Abdullah Al-Senussi, *Prosecutor v. Saif Al-Islam Gaddafi and Abdullah Al-Senussi* (ICC-01/11-01/11-466-Red), PTCH I, 11 October 2013.

Judgment on the appeal of Libya against the decision of Pre-Trial Chamber I of 31 May 2013 entitled "Decision on the admissibility of the case against Saif Al-Islam Gaddafi", *Prosecutor v. Sail Al-Islam Gaddafi and Abdullah Al-Senussi* (ICC-01/11-01/11-547-Red), ACH, 21 May 2014.

Judgment on the appeal of Mr Abdullah Al-Senussi against the decision of Pre-Trial Chamber I of 11 October 2013 entitled "Decision on the admissibility of the case against Abdullah Al-Senussi", *Prosecutor v. Saif Al-Islam Gaddafi and Abdullah Al-Senussi* (ICC-01/11-01/11-565), ACH, 24 July 2014.

Decision on the 'Admissibility Challenge by Dr. Saif Al-Islam Gadafi pursuant to Articles 17(1)(c), 19 and 20(3) of the Rome Statute', *Prosecutor v. Saif Al-Islam Gaddafi* (ICC-01/11-01/11-662), PTCH I, 5 April 2019.

Public Warrant of Arrest, *Prosecutor v. Mahmoud Mustafa Busayf Al-Werfalli* (ICC-01/11-01/17), PTCH I, 15 August 2017.

Second Warrant of Arrest, *Prosecutor v. Mahmoud Mustafa Busayf Al-Werfalli* (ICC-01/11- 01/17), PTCH I, 4 July 2018.

Decision on the Prosecutor's Application for a Warrant of Arrest against Jean-Pierre Bemba Gombo, *Prosecutor v Jean-Pierre Bemba Gombo* (ICC-01/05-01/08- 14-tENG), PTCH III, 10 June 2008.

Decision on the Evidence Disclosure System and Setting a Timetable for Disclosure between the Parties, *Prosecutor v. Jean-Pierre Bemba Gombo* (ICC-01/05-01/08-55), PTCH III, 31 July 2008.

Decision Pursuant to Article 61(7)(a) and (b) of the Rome Statute, *Prosecutor v Jean-Pierre Bemba Gombo* (ICC-01/05-01/08-424), PTCH III, 15 June 2009.

Decision on the Admissibility and Abuse of Process Challenges, *Prosecutor v. Jean-Pierre Bemba Gombo* (ICC-01/05-01/08-802), TCH III, 24 June 2010.

Judgment on the appeal of Mr. Jean-Pierre Bemba Gombo against the decision of Trial Chamber III of 24 June 2010 entitled "Decision on the Admissibility and Abuse of Process Challenges", *Prosecutor v. Jean-Pierre Bemba Gombo* (ICC-01/05-01/08-962), ACH, 19 October 2010.

Decision on the admission into evidence of materials contained in the prosecution's list of evidence, *Prosecutor v. Jean-Pierre Bemba Gombo* (ICC-01/05-01/08-1022), TCH III, 19 November 2010.

Judgment on the appeals of Mr. Jean-Pierre Bemba Gombo and the Prosecutor against the decision of Trial Chamber III entitled 'Decision on the admission into evidence of materials contained in the prosecution's list of evidence', *Prosecutor v. Jean-Pierre Bemba Gombo* (ICC-01/05-01/08-1386), ACH, 3 May 2011.

Decision on the Prosecution's Application for Admission of Materials into Evidence Pursuant to Article 64(9) of the Rome Statute of 6 September 2012, *Prosecutor v. Jean-Pierre Bemba Gombo* (ICC-01/05-01/08), TCH III, 8 October 2012.

Defence Response to Prosecution's Third Request for the Admission of Evidence from the Bar Table, *Prosecutor v. Jean-Pierre Bemba Gombo et al.* (ICC-01/05-01/13), TCH VII, 9 October 2015.

Judgment pursuant to Article 74 of the Statute, *Prosecutor v. Jean-Pierre Bemba Gombo* (ICC-01/05-01/08- 3343), TCH III, 21 March 2016.

Judgment on the appeals of Mr Jean-Pierre Bemba Gombo, Mr Aimé Kilolo Musamba, Mr Jean-Jacques Mangenda Kabongo, Mr Fidèle Babala and Mr Narcisse Arido against the Decision of Trial Chamber VII entitled "Judgment pursuant to Article 74 of the Statute", *Prosecutor v Jean-Pierre Bemba Gombo et al.* (ICC-01/05-01/13-2275-Red), ACH, 8 March 2018.

Judgment pursuant to Article 74 of the Statute, *Prosecutor v. Mathieu Ngudjolo Chui* (ICC-01/04-02/12-3-t), TCH II, 26 December 2012.

Judgment on the Prosecutor's appeal against the decision of Trial Chamber II entitled 'Judgment pursuant to Article 74 of the Statute', *Prosecutor v. Mathieu Ngudjolo Chui* (ICC-01/04-02/12-271-Corr), ACH, 7 April 2015.

Judgment on the appeal of Côte d'Ivoire against the decision of Pre-Trial Chamber I of 11 December 2014 entitled "Decision on Côte d'Ivoire's challenge to the admissibility of the case against Simone Gbagbo", *Prosecutor v. Simone Gbagbo* (ICC-02/11-01/12-75-Red), ACH, 27 May 2015.

Corrigendum to the Decision on Evidentiary Scope of the Confirmation Hearing, Preventive Relocation and Disclosure under Article 67(2) of the Statute and Rule 77 of the Rules, *Prosecutor v. Germain Katanga Mathieu Ngudjolo Chui* (ICC-01/04-01/07-428-Corr), PTCH I, 25 April 2008.

Decision on the Set of Procedural Rights Attached to Procedural Status of Victim at the Pre-Trial Stage of the Case, *Prosecutor v. Germain Katanga and Mathieu Ngudjolo Chui* (ICC-01/04-01/07-474), PTCH I, 13 May 2008.

Decision on the Confirmation of Charges, *Prosecutor v. Germain Katanga and Mathieu Ngudjolo Chui* (ICC-01/04-01/07), PTCH I, 30 September 2008.

Judgment on the Appeal of Mr. Germain Katanga against the Oral Decision of Trial Chamber II of 12 June 2009 on the Admissibility of the Case, *Prosecutor v. German Katanga and Mathieu Ngudjolo Chui* (ICC-01/04-01/07-1497), ACH, 25 September 2009.

Decision on the Bar Table Motion of the Defence of Germain Katanga, *Prosecutor v. Germain Katanga and Mathieu Ngudjolo Chui* (ICC-01/04–01/07-3184), TCH II, 21 October 2011.

Judgment pursuant to Article 74 of the Statute, *Prosecutor v. Germain Katanga* (ICC-01/04-01/07), TCH II, 7 March 2014.

Draft implementation plan relevant to Trial Chamber II's order for reparations of 24 March 2017 (ICC-01/04-01/07-3728), *Prosecutor v. Germain Katanga* (ICC-01/04-01/07-3751-Red), TCH II, 25 July 2017.

Decision on Confirmation of Charges, *Prosecutor v. Thomas Lubanga Dyilo* (ICC-01/04-01/06-803-tEN), PTCH I, 29 January 2007.

Decision on the Prosecution's and Defence's applications for leave to appeal the Decision on the confirmation of charges, *Prosecutor v. Thomas Lubanga Dyilo* (ICC-01/04-01/06), PTCH I, 24 May 2007.
Decision on the admissibility of four documents, *The Prosecutor v. Thomas Lubanga Dyilo* (ICC-01/04-01/06), TCH I, 13 June 2008.
Decision on the Prosecution's Application for Admission of four documents from the bar table pursuant to Article 64(9), *Prosecutor v. Thomas Lubanga Dyilo* (ICC-01/04–01/06), TCH I, 20 January 2011.
Corrigendum to Decision on the admissibility of four documents, *Prosecutor v. Thomas Lubanga Dyilo* (ICC-01/04-01/06-1399-Corr), TCH I, 21 January 2011.
Judgement, *Prosecutor v. Thomas Lubanga Dyilo* (ICC-01/04-01/06), TCH I, 14 March 2012a.
Decision on the Confirmation of Charges, *Prosecutor v. Callixte Mbarushimana* (ICC-01/04-01/10-465-Red), PTCH I, 16 December 2011.
Judgment on the appeal of the Republic of Kenya against the decision of Pre-Trial Chamber II of 30 May 2011 entitled "Decision on the Application by the Government of Kenya Challenging the Admissibility of the Case Pursuant to Article 19(2)(b) of the Statute", *Prosecutor v. Francis Kirimi Muthaura, Uhuru Muigai Kenyatta and Mohammed Hussein Ali* (ICC-01/09-02/11-274), ACH, 30 August 2011a.
Decision on the Confirmation of Charges Pursuant to Article 61(7)(a) and (b) of the Rome Statute, *Prosecutor v. Francis Kirimi Muthaura et al.* (ICC-01/09-02/11-382-Red), PTCH II, 23 January 2012a.
Judgment, *The Prosecutor v. Bosco Ntaganda* (ICC-01/04-02/06-1962), 15 June 2017.
Judgment Pursuant to Article 74 of the Statute, *Prosecutor v Bosco Ntaganda* (ICC-01/04-02/06-2359), TCH VI, 8 July 2019.
Order inviting expressions of interest as amici curiae in judicial proceedings, *Prosecutor v Bosco Ntaganda* (ICC-01/04-02/06-2554), ACH, 24 July 2020.
Judgment on the appeals of Mr Bosco Ntaganda and the Prosecutor against the decision of Trial Chamber VI of 8 July 2019 entitled 'Judgment', *Prosecutor v Bosco Ntaganda* (ICC01/04-02/06-2666-Anx5-Corr), ACH, 30 March 2021.
Judgment, *Prosecutor v. Dominic Ongwen* (ICC-02/04-01/15), TCH IX, 4 February 2021.
Sentence, *Prosecutor v Dominic Ongwen* (ICC02/04-01/15-1819-Red), TCH IX, 6 May 2021.
Order inviting expressions of interest as amici curiae in judicial proceedings (pursuant to rule 103 of the Rules of Procedure and Evidence), *Prosecutor v Dominic Ongwen* (ICC-02/04-01/15-1884), ACH, 25 October 2021.

Judgment on the appeal of Mr Ongwen against the decision of Trial Chamber IX of 4 February 2021 entitled "Trial Judgment", *Prosecutor v Dominic Ongwen* (ICC-02/04-01/15-A), ACH, 15 December 2022.

Corrected Version of 'Request for authorization of an investigation pursuant to article 15', *Situation in Georgia* (ICC-01/15-12), Office of the Prosecutor, 17 November 2015.

Decision Authorizing an Investigation, *Situation in Georgia* (ICC-01/15-12), PTCH I, 27 January 2016.

Separate opinion of Judge Péter Kovács to Decision on the Prosecutor's request for authorization of an investigation, *Situation in Georgia* (ICC-01/15-12-Anx-Corr), PTCH I, 27 January 2016.

Dissenting Opinion of Judge Hans-Peter Kaul, *Situation in Kenya*, ICC-01/09-19, 31 March 2010.

Request for authorisation of an investigation pursuant to Article 15, *Situation in the Islamic Republic of Afghanistan* (ICC-02/17), Office of the Prosecutor, 20 November 2017.

Decision Pursuant to Article 15 of the Rome Statute on the Authorisation of an Investigation, *Situation in the Islamic Republic of Afghanistan* (ICC-02/17), 12 April 2019.

Judgment on the appeal against the decision on the authorisation of an investigation, *Situation in the Islamic Republic of Afghanistan* (ICC-02/17 OA4), 5 March 2020.

International Criminal Court, *Report to the Assembly of States Parties on the projects and the activities of the Board of Directors of the Trust Fund for Victims for the period 1 July 2017 to 30 June 2018* (ICC-ASP/17/14), Assembly of States Parties, 23 July 2018b.

Judgment on the appeal of the Republic of Kenya against the decision of Pre-Trial Chamber II of 30 May 2011 entitled "Decision on the Application by the Government of Kenya Challenging the Admissibility of the Case Pursuant to Article 19(2)(b) of the Statute", *Prosecutor v. William Samoei Ruto, Henry Kiprono Kosgey and Joshua Arap Sang* (ICC-01/09-01/11-307), ACH, 30 August 2011b.

Decision on the Confirmation of Charges Pursuant to Article 61(7)(a) and (b) of the Rome Statute, *Prosecutor v. William Samoei Ruto et al.* (ICC-01/09-01/11-373), PTCH II, 23 January 2012b.

Judgment on Mr Yekatom's appeal against Trial Chamber V's "Decision on the Yekatom Defence's Admissibility Challenge", *Prosecutor v. Alfred Yekatom and Patrice-Edouard Ngaissona* (ICC-01/14-01/18-678-Red), ACH, 11 February 2021.

Case Law of Other International Courts and Tribunals

Judgment, *Prosecutor v Jean-Paul Akayesu* (ICTR-96-4-T), TCH, ICTR, 2 September 1995.

Judgment, ECHR, *Al-Jedda v. the United Kingdom*, appl. no. 27021/08, Grand Chamber, 7 July 2011.

Judgement, *Prosecutor v. Vidoje Blagojević and Dragan Jokić* (IT-02-60-T), TCH I, ICTY, 17 January 2005.

Judgement, *Prosecutor v. Boškoski et al.* (IT-04-82), TCH II, ICTY, 10 July 2008.

Judgment, *Prosecutor v Alex Tamba Brima et al.* (SCSL-2004-16-A), ACH, SCSL, 22 February 2008.

Judgment, *Prosecutor v Kaig Guek Eav 'Duch'* (001/18-07-2007-ECCC/SC), Supreme Court Chamber ECCC, 3 February 2012.

Judgement, *Prosecutor v. Sefer Halilović* (IT-01-48), ACH, ICTY, 16 October 2007.

Partial Dissenting Opinion of Judge Shahabuddeen, *Prosecutor v Goran Jelisić* (IT-95-10-A), ACH, ICTY, 5 July 2001.

Judgement, *Prosecutor v. Radislav Krstić* (IT-98-33-T), TCH, ICTY, 2 August 2001.

Judgment, *Prosecutor v. Dragoljub Kunarać, Radomir Kovać Zoran Vuković* (IT-96-23 & IT-96-23/1-A), ICTY, 12 June 2002b.

Judgment, *Prosecutor v Zoran Kupreškić et al.* (IT-95-16-T), TCH, ICTY, 14 January 2000.

Decision on Zoran Zigic's Motion for Rescinding Confidentiality of Schedules Attached to the Indictment Decision on Exhibits, *Prosecutor v. Miroslav Kvočka et al.* (IT-98-30/1-T), TCH, ICTY, 19 July 2001.

Judgement, *Prosecutor v. Milutinović et al.* (IT-05-87-T), TCH, ICTY, 26 February 2009.

Judgment, *Prosecutor v Zdravko Mucić et al.* (IT-96-21-A), ACH, ICTY, 20 February 2001.

Judgment and Sentence, *The Prosecutor v. Ferdisand Nahimana et al.* (ICTR-99-52-T), TCH I, ICTR, 3 December 2003.

Judgment, *Prosecutor v Ferdinand Nahimana et al.* (ICTR-99-52-A), ACH, ICTR, 28 November 2007b.

Judgement, *Prosecutor v. Andre Ntagerura et al.* (ICTR-99-46-A), ACH, ICTR, 7 July 2006.

Judgement, *Prosecutor v. Vujadin Popović et al.* (IT-05-88-T), TCH II, ICTY, 10 June 2010.

Separate and Dissenting Opinion of Judge Pavel Dolenc, Judgement, *Prosecutor v Laurent Semanza* (ICTR-97-20-T), TCH III, ICTR, 15 May 2003.

Judgment, *Prosecutor v Milomir Stakić* (IT-97-24-A), ACH, ICTY, 22 March 2006a.

Judgment, *Prosecutor v. Dusko Tadić* (IT-94-1-A), ACH, ICTY, 15 July 1999.
Decision in the defence motion for interlocutory appeal on jurisdiction, *Prosecutor v. Dusko Tadić* (IT-94-1-I), ICTY, 2 October 1995.
Judgement, *Prosecutor v. Zdravko Tolimir* (IT-05-88/2-T), TCH II, ICTY, 12 December 2012b.
Judgment, IACtHR, *Velasquez-Rodriguez v. Honduras*, (ser. C) No. 4, 29 July 1988.
Decision, *Charles Ghankay Taylor*, SCSL-2003-01-I, ACH, 31 May 2004.

International Treaties

Additional Protocol I to the Geneva Conventions.
Additional Protocol II to the Geneva Conventions.
Agreement between the State of Israel and the Federal Republic of Germany (1952).
American Convention on Human Rights (1969).
Charter of the International Military Tribunal (1945).
Geneva Convention I on Wounded and Sick in Armed Forces in the Field.
Geneva Convention II on Wounded, Sick and Shipwrecked of Armed Forces at Sea.
Geneva Convention III on Prisoners of War.
Geneva Convention IV relative to the Protection of Civilian Persons in Time of War.
International Covenant of Civil and Political Rights.
Protocol No. 7 to the European Convention on Human Rights and Fundamental Freedoms (1984).
Rome Statute of the International Criminal Court.

UN Documents

G.A. Res. 58/97, 9 December 2003.
G.A. Res. 59/122, 10 December 2004.
G.A. Res. 60/105, 8 December 2005.
G.A. Res. 61/117 14 December 2006.
G.A. Res. 62/107, 17 December 2007.
G.A. Res. 63/96, 5 December 2008).
G.A. Res. 64/92, 10 December 2009.
G.A. Res. 65/103, 10 December 2010.
G.A. Res. 66/77, 9 December 2011.
G.A. Res. 67/119, 18 December 2012.
G.A. Res. 68/81, 11 December 2013.
G.A. Res. 69/91, 5 December 2014.
G.A. Res. 70/88, 9 December 2015.
G.A. Res. 71/96, 6 December 2016.

G.A. Res. 72/85, 7 December 2017.
G.A. Res. 73/97, 7 December 2018.
G.A. Res. 74/89, 13 December 2019.
G.A. Res. 75/98, 10 December 2020.
S.C. Res. 681 (1990).
S.C. Res. 808 (1993).
S.C. Res. 955 (1994).
S.C. Res. 1315 (2002).
S.C. Res. 1593 (2005).

Other Sources (ILC, Domestic Cases, Domestic Law, Other Sources)

Trial Judgement, *US v Josef Altstoetter et al. (Justice Case)*, Military Tribunal III, 4 December 1947.

Amicus curiae observations on issues raised in the Appeals Chamber Order of 25 October 2021 inviting expressions of interest as amici curiae in judicial proceedings (pursuant to Rule 103 of the Rules of Procedure and Evidence), *Prosecutor v Dominic Ongwen* (ICC-02/04-01/15- 1943), ACH, 23 December 2021.

Amici Curiae Observations on Sexual- and Gender-Based Crimes, Particularly Sexual Slavery, and on Cumulative Convictions Pursuant to Rule 103 of the Rules of Procedure and Evidence, *Prosecutor v Dominic Ongwen* (ICC-02/04-01/15- 1934), ACH, 23 December 2021.

J. Biden, 'Executive Order on the Termination of Emergency With Respect to the International Criminal Court', 1 April 2021.

Blockburger v US, 284 U.S. 299, 304 (1932).

Final Record of the Diplomatic Conference of Geneva of 1949 n.d. (Vol.2, sec. b).

First Rep. of Mr. Georg Nolte, International Law Commission Special Rapporteur on Subsequent Agreements and Subsequent Practice in Relation to the Interpretation of Treaties, U.N. Doc. A/CN.4/660, 19 March 2013.

Judgment, *Salim Ahmed Hamdan v. Donald H. Rumsfeld et al*; 548 U.S. 557 (2006b).

International Criminal Court, Rules of Procedure and Evidence (2002).

International Law Commission, Draft Articles on Immunity of State Officials from Foreign Criminal Jurisdiction with commentaries, 2022.

International Law Commission, Draft Articles on the Responsibility of States for Internationally Wrongful Acts with commentaries, 2001.

International Law Commission, Draft Conclusions on Identification of Customary International Law with commentaries, 2018.

International Law Commission, Fourth report on crimes against humanity, UN Doc. A. CN.4/725, 18 February 2019.
International Law Commission, Report of the Commission to the General Assembly on the Work of its 58th Session, A/CN.LASER.AJzoo6/Add.1 (Part 2).
International Law Commission, Report of the ILC, 68th session, A/71/10.
Kwoyelo v. Uganda [2011] U.G.C.C. 10 (*Uganda*).
Law on the Establishment of the Extraordinary Chambers art. 6, NS/RKM/1004/006 (Oct. 27, 2004, Cambodia).
Observations of the Association of Defence Counsel Practising Before the International Courts and Tribunals (ADC-ICT) As Amicus Curiae Regarding Questions Posed by the Appeals Chamber in Prosecutor v. Ongwen, *Prosecutor v Dominic Ongwen* (ICC-02/04-01/15-1937), ACH, 23 December 2021.
G. Rona, 'Observations on the Pre-Trial Chamber's Conclusion that Events Beyond the Territory of Afghanistan Lack Sufficient Nexus to the Armed Conflict There for Purposes of Application of Rome Statute War Crimes' (ICC-02/17-111), 14 November 2019.
Report of the Special Rapporteur on extrajudicial, summary or arbitrary executions, Christof Heyns, UN Doc. A/HRC/26/36, 1 April 2014.
Report of the Special Rapporteur on extrajudicial, summary or arbitrary executions, Agnès Callamard, UN Doc. A/HRC/44/38, 15 August 2020.
Updated European Union Guidelines on Promoting Compliance with International Humanitarian Law, 2009 O.J. (C 303/06).

Index

O. Svaček, M. Faix (eds.), *Prosecution of War Crimes before the ICC*, Global Issues, https://doi.org/10.1007/978-3-031-84216-0

Kolibri 360 GmbH
Ferdinand-Jühlke-Straße 7
99095 Erfurt, Deutschland
produktsicherheit@kolibri360.de